DRAGON COUNTRY

By TENNESSEE WILLIAMS

DRAGON COUNTRY

A Book of Plays

by TENNESSEE WILLIAMS

A NEW DIRECTIONS BOOK

A PERFECT ANALYSIS GIVEN BY A PARROT and I CAN'T IMAGINE TOMORROW were first published in ESQUIRE Magazine.

Manufactured in the United States of America

New Directions Books are printed on acid-free paper.

First published as New Directions Paperbook 287, 1970.

Published simultaneously in Canada by
Penguin Books Canada Limited.

New Directions Books are published for James Laughlin
by New Directions Publishing Corporation,
80 Eighth Avenue, New York 10011.

TENTH PRINTING

Contents

IN THE BAR OF A TOKYO HOTEL

In the Bar of a Tokyo Hotel was presented at the Eastside Playhouse in New York on May 11, 1969, by Richard Lee Marks and Henry Jaffe. It was directed by Herbert Machiz; the stage setting and lighting by Neil Peter Jampolis; costumes by Stanley Simmons; musical effects by Hayward Morris. The cast was as follows:

BARMAN	Jon Lee
MIRIAM	Anne Meacham
MARK	Donald Madden
HAWAIIAN LADY	Elsa Raven
LEONARD	Lester Rawlins

The time is spring; the place, Tokyo. A smartly and exotically dressed American woman is seated at a small round table in a small area of intense light. She is glossily handsome. She wears a hat crowned with blue-black cock feathers. The Barman, behind a bar of polished bamboo, is in a pin-spot of light. He is young and his appearance suggests an Oriental idol. He raises a metal shaker, a few moments after the rise of the curtain, as if to signal the start of the scene.

MIRIAM: I like this room.

BARMAN: Thank you.

MIRIAM: There is an atmosphere of such vitality in Tokyo.

BARMAN: Thank you.

MIRIAM: You understand and speak English remarkably well.

BARMAN: Thank you.

MIRIAM: You have a very impressive suicide rate.

BARMAN: Thank you.

MIRIAM: I don't think you understood what I said.

BARMAN: I was.

MIRIAM: I said that you have a very impressive rate of suicide in—

BARMAN: In America there is no suicide rate?

MIRIAM: In America what we have is an explosion of vitality which is world-wide.

BARMAN: Many cowboys exported?

MIRIAM: Ha-ha, yes, it could be put that way. "Many cowboys exported!" Yes, but speaking for myself, I don't really need an atmosphere of vitality around me.

BARMAN: You have enough in yourself?

MIRIAM: Let's say that I have enough and a little more than enough.

BARMAN: —I am not astonished.

MIRIAM: Hmmm. How many hours of sleep do you need a night?

BARMAN: Thank you for being interested, but why are you interested?

MIRIAM: I'm always interested. For me, only four hours of sleep are necessary.

BARMAN: You waken in the dark?

MIRIAM: Not usually. You see, I go to bed late.

BARMAN: You make excursions at night?

MIRIAM: Yes, I'm restless at night. What's your name?

BARMAN: I am the Barman.

MIRIAM: Yes, I've noticed you are. Why don't you look for an occupation that's not so confining?

BARMAN: Thank you.

MIRIAM: You're welcome. See what I'm doing? I'm taking out of my handbag a mirror. [*She removes a large mirror from her bag.*]

BARMAN: Why are you staring at me?

MIRIAM: I like to see what is going on about me in the circle of light.

BARMAN: Excuse me while I. [*He carries a tray of drinks offstage.*]

4

MIRIAM: Yes. The best idea. Cable to Leonard. Place in his hands. [*The Barman returns with the tray. She observes him in the mirror.*] Hmmm. Your activity with the shaker is very distracting.

BARMAN: Pardon me. I am the Barman.

MIRIAM: "Inner resources of serenity." Some professor mentioned them to me once. Hog-wash, wash a hog in it, don't turn it on me. "Inner resources of serenity" is a polite way of describing a lack of vital energy. There may be exceptions but.

BARMAN: The light from the mirror is in my eyes.

MIRIAM: For light in your eyes be grateful. I am happy to lower the focus of the. Don't stand behind the bar.

BARMAN: My instruction is.

MIRIAM: Your employer wouldn't object if you stood in front of the bar.

[*After a moment, the Barman moves in front of the bar.*]

BARMAN: —The light from the mirror burns through my clothes.

MIRIAM: Are you sure it isn't my observation of you?

BARMAN: I am.

MIRIAM: You are. So am I. Will you please bring me some ice for my drink?

BARMAN: With pleasure and precaution and a little delay. [*Miriam takes a small pipe from her handbag and fills it from a pouch.*]

MIRIAM: Hmmm.

BARMAN: There is a party of diplomats in the restaurant, excuse me please.

MIRIAM: I will excuse you if you don't stay long. [*He leaves with a tray of drinks.*] Hmm. Difficult, yes, but unobtainable, no. —A little Panama Red. [*After she has taken a few puffs of the little pipe, the Barman returns.*] Hmmm. Diplomats. Young?

BARMAN: Venerable.

MIRIAM: I haven't heard that word in a long long time.

BARMAN: Perhaps there are a number of words in English, not idiomatic, that it would not be useless for you to.

MIRIAM: I like the idioms of my native country.

BARMAN: You are smoking a pipe of marijuana.

MIRIAM: A pipe of Panama Red.

BARMAN: The pleasure of a guest is usually my pleasure, but will you do for me the kindness?

MIRIAM: I will put it out for you. Put it out means extinguish.

BARMAN: Thank you.

MIRIAM: Panama Red is not essential to my.

BARMAN: Vitality. Natural to your nature.

MIRIAM: Hmmmm. No. I don't say it doesn't augment it, but it.

BARMAN: Thank you.

MIRIAM: I will teach you the idioms of English. Some of them centuries old. Venerable. The important idioms can be learned very.

BARMAN: Not necessary, but thank you.

MIRIAM: Are you married?

BARMAN: I am engaged. And faithful.

MIRIAM: A terrible mistake. For marriage, some preliminary instruction is necessary.

BARMAN: Thank you. I have had the necessary instruction.

MIRIAM: There are fairly good instructors and there are brilliant instructors.

BARMAN: It is kind of you to be interested in my instruction.

[*He carries out another tray of drinks. From time to time a wind sweeps through the bar. Ornamented glass pendants—suspended from the arch of a door leading offstage—chatter musically when the wind blows through. This is used as a way of underlining or punctuating. Each time the pendants sound, Miriam touches the feathers on her hat and makes her humming sound, then rearranges the bracelets on her arms and moves her head from side to side more noticeably. Now the Barman returns.*]

MIRIAM: I have noticed a lot of very stout women in the hotel, their doors open on the corridors. They sit on the edge of their beds, doing nothing at all.

BARMAN: Ladies from Hawaii.

MIRIAM: Just sitting. No energy in them to get up and be on the go?

BARMAN: The ladies are a party of.

MIRIAM: Not enough vitality for an argument, or even a conversation.

BARMAN: Nice ladies from Hawaii.

MIRIAM: I didn't say they weren't nice. Being nice or not nice is. What I said about the Hawaiian ladies is that they should be up and about. They should be on the move. Did their husbands suggest this trip to Japan to them?

sentences not completed

BARMAN: I think their husbands are satisfied with the.

MIRIAM: Perhaps in Hawaii a very fat wife is what we call, in America, a status symbol.

BARMAN: That is nothing I know.

[*A Hawaiian Lady enters. She wears a dress printed with large flowers. She crosses to the arch and goes out.*]

MIRIAM: My God, one of them off her bed, it must have collapsed so she had to get on the move. Probably has no idea of where she's headed. Where I'm headed is something I always know.

BARMAN: Japan has other places.

MIRIAM: I've been told that I shouldn't miss Kyoto. The person, the acquaintance, the man that mentioned Kyoto to me said that Kyoto is a place of lovely old pagodas and flowering trees in flower at this time of.

BARMAN: Yes, go to Kyoto.

MIRIAM: Yes, I'll go to Kyoto on an evening train. I love the clackety-clack of the wheels and the cool wind through the windows. I hope there's a train leaving at.

BARMAN: The concierge can give you the schedules.

MIRIAM: I'll go this evening.

BARMAN: It is possible to go more early.

MIRIAM: I prefer an evening train. Kyoto. To absorb Kyoto wouldn't take me long. A woman of my vitality absorbs a place quickly. I could absorb a pagoda in a minute. Well, if I walked around it, a few minutes more. That sounds as if I meant superficial absorption, but.

BARMAN: Some of the pagodas are five or six hundred years old.

8

MIRIAM: Venerable, but I'd absorb them, well, at the most in five minutes. I look. I absorb. I go on.

BARMAN: Your method of absorption is not a reverent absorption.

MIRIAM: An adequate absorption.

BARMAN: You may think so, but.

MIRIAM: Reverence is a thing I am happy to leave in the hands of the reverent.

BARMAN: Will your husband go with you?

MIRIAM: No. It would take him an hour to absorb a pagoda.

BARMAN: Some that go to Kyoto sit before a pagoda all day and then all night. Reverence.

MIRIAM: Or pretension. —Has a woman ever held you with?

BARMAN: In our country the man prefers to hold our delicate ladies.

MIRIAM: Delicate ladies like dolls.

BARMAN: Delicate ladies with delicate manners and gestures.

[*He comes from behind the bar with a tray of drinks.*]

MIRIAM: The venerable diplomats are going to fall under their tables.

BARMAN: Not unless there is a tremor, a quake of the earth caused by an explosion of vitality which is world-wide. [*He goes out.*]

MIRIAM: Ha! That boy moves well, yes, he knows how to move. I'm sorry he has a position that ties him down. Otherwise, I'd not be going to Kyoto alone. Oh, well. I'll not be lonely. I know the word for hello. [*She addresses the audience.*] At a country club dance on Long Island—oh, I'm popular on Long

9

Island! —I was dancing with this attractive but inexperienced-looking young man—and I whispered in his ear: "Do you mind if I manipulate your genitals?" —Scared him out of. He said "Here?" as if he was in church. I said, "I'll step out for some air and you follow me out." Did he? —Hmmm. —You bet he did! —And I manipulated his genitals all right. —HMMM. —Yaisses! —Between a Cadillac and a—hmm—Cadillac. —Sure, we got into one. —Burrghh. —Recollections are insufficient. I like present action.

[*The Barman returns with an empty tray. He crosses to behind the bar.*]

Barman. You, Barman!

[*He continues filling a tray of drinks behind the bar. She takes out of her handbag a little silver whistle and blows it shrilly.*]

I use this to catch the attention of a cab when I'm in New York.

BARMAN: What is? Did you say—?

MIRIAM: Cab. A public conveyance.

BARMAN: I am not a public convenience. I do not respond to whistles.

MIRIAM: I would like you to get me a cablegram blank from the concierge with the unfortunate face.

BARMAN: I will get you a cablegram and place it on the green table. [*He goes out through the arch at right. She goes to the arch. The Barman returns.*] Pardon me. you are instructing my way.

MIRIAM: Do you mean obstructing?

BARMAN: Thank you. I mean obstructing. To deliver the cablegrams to you, I must request that you return to your table.

10

MIRIAM: If I return to my table, will you bring the cablegram to me?

BARMAN: I will place it in reach of.

MIRIAM: You must place it on my table.

BARMAN: I will place the cablegram where you can reach it —You are still obstructing my way. [*She lets him pass.*]

MIRIAM: He won that little encounter, but you can lose a lot of preliminary encounters and still wind up as. He's put a book of cablegrams on that other. Barman, I asked for a cablegram and you've brought me a whole book of them.

BARMAN: Is that enough, or do you want several books?

MIRIAM: You thought I was going to send cables all over the world? [*She laughs boisterously.*] —Oh. Could you give me a pencil?

BARMAN: Only one pencil?

MIRIAM: Only one pencil will do at the present moment. [*She speaks aloud as she writes.*] Mr. Leonard Frisbie. World Galleries. New York. Dear Leonard. I'm sorry to tell you that Mark has suffered a total collapse of the nervous system. Hmmm. Mental and physical, too. With most situations I am able to cope but not this one. I mean not alone. Mark is your most lucrative property. Please fly to Tokyo at once to protect it. Otherwise I will be forced to. Hmmm. Unless you arrive as quickly as. With love as ever and with desperate appeal. Miriam Conley. There, now. That should do it. Young man? Give the cablegram to the concierge. It has to go out at once.

BARMAN: I am instructed to stay in my position at the bar at this time of.

MIRIAM: Disregard your instructions. I will give you two hundred yen to take the cablegram to the concierge and tell him it has to go out immediately.

11

BARMAN: —Put the cablegram on another table and I will pick it up.

MIRIAM: You're afraid to come to my table?

BARMAN: When I come to your table you place your hand improperly on my body.

MIRIAM: Ha! Look. The two hundred yen.

BARMAN: Place the cablegram on another table and.

MIRIAM: The cablegram stays here.

BARMAN: Then you must take it to the concierge.

MIRIAM: A pagan idol with the propriety of. Another two hundred yen.

[The Barman comes from behind the bar and comes to a position that should be safely away from the table; he extends his arm to its full length.]

You have to remove that cablegram from the table or there's no deal.

BARMAN: Throw it at me, please, with the four hundred yen.

MIRIAM: I'll be damned if I will. You come to the table and take the cablegram off it and the four hundred yen.

[After some hesitation he comes to the table. She immediately places her hand on his crotch.]

Stay a while. You have no real objection.

BARMAN: —It's

MIRIAM: What?

BARMAN: In Tokyo women bathe us.

MIRIAM: An interesting, a very intriguing idea. When do you want a bath?

BARMAN: I have had my bath. Without indecency.

MIRIAM: But you stay by the table.

BARMAN: Four hundred yen is a large sum for delivering a cablegram to the concierge and your hand is.

MIRIAM: The hand of a woman who burns.

BARMAN: Yes.

MIRIAM [*She releases him, gives him the money and cablegram.*]: Here is the cablegram and the four hundred yen. Tense. Irritable nerve ends. Convex demanding concave.

[*He starts to the bar, then stops.*]

What's the matter?

BARMAN: I forgot the direction. [*He exits through the arch.*]

MIRIAM [*to the audience*]: I'm fully aware, of course, that there's no magical trick to defend me indefinitely from the hideous product of calendars, clocks, watches. However I've made a covenant with them. When, on the unexpected but always possible advent of incurable illness [*She removes a tiny pillbox from her bag.*] —A Regency snuff-box: innocent-looking. It contains one pill, just one, but the one is enough. When then. I will carry it into a grove of afternoon trees. Swallow the. And in a single, immeasurable moment—

[*The Barman returns.*]

Did you?

BARMAN: The cablegram is.

MIRIAM: Thank you. I hope the evening train leaves before the light fades away.

[*The wind chimes are heard. The woman's husband enters. He is her age but ravaged looking. There are vivid paint stains on his unpressed suit.*]

13

MARK: No chair for me at the table.

MIRIAM: You weren't expected.

[*He attempts to draw a chair to the table but stumbles to his knees, then staggers up with an apologetic laugh.*]

MARK: Too soon after work.

MIRIAM: Much.

MARK: I was afraid you'd.

MIRIAM: I wasn't waiting for you.

MARK: I'm glad I came down in time.

MIRIAM: Time for what?

MARK: To catch you.

MIRIAM: I can't be caught.

MARK: Barman, yes, please.

MIRIAM: Infantile dependence.

MARK: The work is.

MIRIAM: I'm not going to discuss it. You're leaning on the table for support, crouched over it.

MARK [*sitting down*]: It's always been exhausting to.

MIRIAM: The manager of the hotel has complained of the paint stains on the floor of your room.

MARK: I covered the floor with several sheets of newspaper before I.

MIRIAM: The paint from the spray guns obviously goes through them.

MARK: If there are stains, I scrub them out with turpentine.

14

MIRIAM: Not well enough, it seems.

MARK: If I damage the floor of the room, I'll pay for a new one.

MIRIAM: Why not rent a loft to work in?

MARK: Where?

MIRIAM: Somewhere. A loft that has a window.

MARK: The time getting to a loft.

MIRIAM: Yes?

MARK: Would probably be too long to hold an image.

MIRIAM: The image of your new work must be extremely.

MARK: No, not at all. They're so vivid they.

MIRIAM. You could hire a car with a chauffeur and a siren to.

MARK: Miriam, don't ridicule the—To doubt is necessary . . .

[*The Barman places a cocktail before Mark. His hand is too tremulous to lift the glass to his mouth. He laughs breathlessly.*]

MIRIAM: If you can't lift the glass, put the hand not holding it under the elbow of. Oh, too late, now, you've spilt it.

[*The Barman impassively wipes the table.*]

Mr. Conley is.

BARMAN: I see. I know.

MIRIAM: Mix another for him, I'll pour it down him. His hands are.

BARMAN: Nerveless a little.

MARK: I've always been excited by work. But this time the excitement and the tension are.

15

[*The Barman serves him another cocktail and returns to the bar, leaving the shaker on the table.*]

MIRIAM: Don't touch it. I'll lift it to your mouth. [*She does.*] Your teeth are *chattering*— More?

MARK: Yes, all of it, please.

MIRIAM: Don't bite the glass. Open your mouth wider. Now.

[*He chokes a little.*]

That's all of it.

MARK: Thanks. I'd better have another.

BARMAN: There is another in the shaker.

MIRIAM: I'd better lift this one, too. Now. Mouth open wide. I said wide. If you're not the man in the side show that swallows glass. This is.

MARK: Ridiculous of me.

BARMAN: Nerveless.

MARK: It's hard to come downstairs immediately after work.

MIRIAM: Yes. Apparently so.

MARK: Do you know how I. [*He laughs breathlessly.*] Move in my room?

MIRIAM: I think it's difficult for you to move anywhere.

MARK: I catch hold of a chair. I catch hold of the bureau. I catch hold of.

MIRIAM: How do you get to the elevator?

MARK: By. [*He laughs breathlessly.*] By leaning onto the wall. Stumbling along it.

MIRIAM: Would you go to a doctor if I found one for you?

MARK: All I could tell him is that the tension of my work.

MIRIAM: He might want to test your reflexes.

MARK: For the first time, nothing that sep, sep!

MIRIAM: Are you trying to say separates?

MARK: Yes, separates, holds at some dis!

MIRIAM: To translate your incoherence, holds at some distance, is that it?

MARK: You understand what I'm trying to say.

MIRIAM: Maybe that, yes, but not what you're doing. Don't touch me with those stained fingers. Don't crouch and lean forward, try to sit straight in the chair. When I looked in your room and saw you crawling naked over a huge nailed-down canvas, I thought, "My God, it's time for the."

MARK: I've understood the *intimacy* that should, that has to exist between the, the—painter and the—I! It! Now it turned to me, or I turned to it, no division between us at all any more! The one-ness, the!

MIRIAM: Are you hysterical? I'll get the bell captain to get you a tape recorder to preserve your delirious ravings. Play them back to yourself and you might be as shocked as I am by the.

MARK: Images in!

MIRIAM: Recorded.

MARK: There was always a sense of division till! Gone! Now absolute one-ness with!

MIRIAM: You're shaking the table so that I have to grip the other side of it to keep it from.

MARK [*He leans back.*]: If I said that I'm.

MIRIAM: What?

MARK: Actually *terrified* of. Would you believe me?

MIRIAM: I have no reason to doubt it.

MARK: Excited, yes, *wildly*, but *terrified* at the same time, I.

MIRIAM: Mark.

MARK: This work is hard to confine to.

MIRIAM: Wants to run out, does it?

MARK: Always before I felt controllable limits, I.

MIRIAM: Shaking, unbathed, unshaved, blotches of paint in your hair. Look at yourself in this mirror if you're not blind. [*She holds her large mirror but he stares above it at her.*] Yes. [*She puts the mirror on the table.*] Blind.

MIRIAM: Mark, fly back and.

MARK: Sometimes the interruption of work, especially in a new style, causes a, causes a—loss of momentum that's never recovered! If I, you'd fly back with me? Naturally you'd.

MIRIAM: No, Mark, I wouldn't.

MARK: You want me to?

MIRIAM: Deliver yourself to the loving care of your Aunt Grace who dotes on human catastrophes. I've never been around her more than two minutes before she says, "Oh, do you know that so-and-so passed away or has had his spinal column removed." And of course you'd have Leonard's un-limited understanding. They'd meet you at the airport. They'd see your condition. It's their problem from there. I won't let it be mine.

MARK: Miriam, you don't mean you want me to fly back alone.

MIRIAM: No, not alone, with a nurse, and under heavy sedation, an oxygen mask, the whole bit, you wouldn't even be conscious that you were.

MARK: I can't interrupt my work here before I've controlled it.

MIRIAM: Mark, to be honest with you, the canvasses that I was privileged to look at.

MARK: Prematurely.

MIRIAM: Were circus-colored mudpies.

MARK: That was in the beginning.

MIRIAM: Recently.

MARK: I feel as if I were crossing the frontier of a country I have no permission to enter, but I enter, this, this! I tell you, it *terrifies* me! Now! In the beginning.

MIRIAM: Let it rest. At least, don't inflict the. Mark, it's not too late for surroundings familiar to you. Fifteen acres of pacifying green meadows.

MARK: The drink was a mistake. Excuse me a moment.

MIRIAM: Indefinitely.

MARK: While I stick a finger down my throat. [*He leaves.*]

MIRIAM: Yes. Well. Gone. This Goddam flower disturbs me. I can't stand it on the table. —Young man? Barman?

BARMAN: What is it?

MIRIAM: This flower on the table, will you please remove it?

BARMAN: Why?

MIRIAM: I don't like objects that disguise their true nature, and there is nothing on earth that disguises its true nature more

19

cunningly than a flower, even when cut and stuck in a vase in a bar.

BARMAN: If I have understood you, what is the true nature of?

MIRIAM: Rapacious. You know that word?

BARMAN: I think you have taught me that word.

MIRIAM [*rising and crossing toward the bar*]: Maybe a stronger word is ravenous.

BARMAN: Do you mean you are a flower?

MIRIAM: You know what I am.

BARMAN: I have had—am I speaking correctly?

MIRIAM: Yes. Continue. Go on with.

BARMAN: On our island which is too small for its habitations?

MIRIAM: Inhabitants.

BARMAN: Thank you. We prefer flowers to.

MIRIAM [*Smiling, she crosses to her chair and sits.*]: You had an idiomatic expression in your mind.

BARMAN: I believe the word is ancient and universal.

MIRIAM [*She picks up flower and gives it to him.*]: Here. Not wanted.

BARMAN: Oh?

MIRIAM: No.

BARMAN: I have been instructed to be sure that a vase containing a flower is on each table. The purple flower on the red table is. [*He returns the vase and flower to her table.*]

MIRIAM: Not wanted by a hotel guest in the bar. [*She hands the Barman the vase and flower.*]

20

BARMAN: Before your trip to Kyoto, you might, may, would enjoy a long stroll about the garden of the hotel.

MIRIAM: There is something you "might, may, would" enjoy, too.

BARMAN: Thank you. No. Madam Flower. [*The Barman replaces the vase and flower on the table. He picks up the shaker and Mark's glass and returns to the bar.*]

MIRIAM: Crock.

[*Mark staggers back to the table. Miriam rises.*]

I'll get a bellboy to help you back to your room.

MARK: No, no, no. I'm afraid to go in it again.

MIRIAM: Then go in my room. Here's my key. Throw that fantastically decorated suit out the window, take a shower, have the bellboy bring you a clean suit, if you have one, and.

MARK: When I say that I'm terrified of the new canvasses, you think I'm exaggerating.

MIRIAM: Not at all in the least.

MARK: No separation between myself and.

MIRIAM: Don't keep repeating it to me. Saying a thing once to me is enough, you know. Sometimes a thing doesn't even have to be said to me. I'm able to guess it.

MARK: It's something that.

MIRIAM: I said, "Don't discuss it." Not outside the office of a.

MARK: In the beginning, a new style of work can be stronger than you, but you learn to control it. It has to be controlled. You learn to control it.

MIRIAM: Fly back immediately.

21

MARK: I always suspected that tigers were hiding in.

MIRIAM [*She sits in her chair.*]: It's not a question of whether you want to or not, it's something you've got to face as something that's.

MARK: Fly back?

MIRIAM: Yes. Imperative. At once. I've suggested to you, I've urged you to follow, the. More? I can't do more. Yes, I could do more. I could have you put in a sanitarium here. I could, and I will if you force me. I'm right. Barman, a.

MARK: Yes. One for me, too.

MIRIAM: Mr. Conley will have a Coca-cola. For God's sake, Mark, you must have noticed your loss of balance. Why, your stumbling into things is. And you admit how you move around in your room.

MARK: An artist has to lay his life on the line.

MIRIAM: Once I dreamed that the shy, gifted man that you were would lift me above the trivialities in my life. I took the initiative and didn't mind taking it. Mark, I said, why don't we go somewhere together, married or not married.

MARK: A friend of yours loaned you.

MIRIAM: His yacht. The shy, gifted man said the bunks are too narrow for two. I'll take the upper, good night. Hell. OK. I mounted the ladder to the upper bunk, and I lay on the body of a secret vendor of silk.

MARK: You were remarkably skilled in overcoming timidity.

MIRIAM: Had to be or no show.

MARK: Afterwards we went up on the deck and I pointed out to you.

22

MIRIAM: Stars and constellations. You could name them. Oh and the northern lights that night they made a crackling sound like giant white sheets being shaken out in the sky.

MARK: While I fondled your breasts, as I still desperately long to.

MIRIAM: Mark, your hands are.

MARK: I know, I know—I know.

MIRIAM: Your condition has to be diagnosed by a good neuropathologist, soon as. Immediately.

MARK: Miriam, I swear it's the intensity of. Why did you say a neuropathologist?

MIRIAM: I had an uncle that had a brain tumor and the symptoms were identical.

MARK: I'm not going to interrupt my.

MIRIAM: Well, take a loft with a window.

MARK: The images flash in my brain, and I have to get them on nailed-down canvas at once or they.

MIRIAM: Flash back out of your brain. A neuropathologist would be interested in that. I'm not a neuropathologist and I'm not concerned with a thing about this thing but flying you into the care of.

MARK: There's a feeling of, a sense of.

MIRIAM: You won't shut up about it.

MARK: Of, of.

MIRIAM: Stop it.

MARK: Adventuring into a jungle country with wild men crouching in bushes, in in, in—trees, with poison arrows to.

MIRIAM: Yes, to kill you, and they've nearly done it.

MARK: Color.

MIRIAM: That's right. Color. On your suit, your hands, even in your hair.

MARK: I didn't know it till now. Color, color, and light! Before us and after us, too. What I'm saying is—color isn't passive, it, it—has a fierce life in it!

MIRIAM: This sort of talk isn't suitable to a public room in a.

MARK: The possibilities of color and light, discovered all at once, can make a man fall on the street. I've heard that finally on earth there'll be nothing but gigantic insects but now I know the last things, the imperishable things, are color and light. Finished. No more about it. I won't fly back to New York with a nurse under heavy sedation.

MIRIAM: I could have you committed to a.

MARK: It wouldn't be the first time you've tried to put me away, without.

MIRIAM: Without what?

MARK: Without considering the.

MIRIAM: What?

MARK: The consequences. I never could stand confinement.

MIRIAM: When a person needs help.

MARK: Let's make a bargain, Miriam. You fly back with me. And we'll go to Long Island and I'll, I'll—I'll take the chance of the interruption.

MIRIAM: Oh, no, that's no acceptable bargain.

MARK: What was it, the work I've done, but a preparation for.

MIRIAM: If you take a shower, odious as a shower's become to you lately, you can sleep off your exhaustion in the twin bed by the door in my room.

BARMAN: Mr. Conley is nerveless.

MIRIAM: You keep saying nerveless for nervous.

BARMAN: Pardon, please.

MIRIAM [*speaking quietly to Mark, her head turned away from the Barman*]: While you were sticking a finger down your throat, there was a controversy between me and that impertinent Barman.

MARK: Over?

MIRIAM: Over the flower on the table. Do you think you could remove the flower and vase and explain to the Barman, who seems to understand you better than he does me, that I will not share a small table with that purple flower.

MARK: —Yes, of course, but I.

MIRIAM: You know how some objects, for no expana, explisa.

MARK: —Yes. I'll simply put it on the bar and say that my wife hates flowers.

MIRIAM: Say that *you* hate them too.

[*He crosses toward bar and falls to his knees before it.*]

BARMAN: Did you injure yourself, Mr. Conley?

MARK: I—hate flowers.

BARMAN: I don't think it is you. Let me help you to.

MARK: Thank you, yes, please.

BARMAN: A beautiful flower has to be on each table.

25

MARK: Please help me back to the table, and explain to my wife.

[*Mark moves slowly, but stops the Barman from helping him. He reaches Miriam, swings at her hat, misses. She rises and he takes her seat. The Barman places the vase and flower on the table.*]

MIRIAM [*Rising*]: Flower, you're cut and you'll die. The sentence of death is imposed on you, purple flower. [*She turns to Mark.*] Yesterday, on the Ginza, I ran into an old schoolmate from Silver Hall, Elaine. We're lunching together and she said strictly no husbands. I think she wants to discuss what's called a marital problem.

MARK: When? How much time is?

MIRIAM: I said that she said no husbands.

MARK: I could sit at a different table till the discussion of the marriage problem is.

MIRIAM: Even if I weren't having lunch with Elaine I wouldn't with you today.

MARK: I have an immaculately clean summer suit.

MIRIAM: It would do nothing for your disequilibrium on the.

MARK: After a quick, cold shower, I.

MIRIAM: You don't hear what I say. It's useless talking to you.

MARK: The loss of balance comes from the.

MIRIAM: I said that she said that.

MARK: I can't be left alone now. I have a clean summer suit and after a cold shower, I.

MIRIAM: For God's sake, can't I be allowed some freedom of?

MARK: Yes, of course. It's only that.

MIRIAM: Tyrannical dependence.

MARK: I'm sorry. It's all right. It's just that.

MIRIAM: If you need a hired companion. You're sitting on my coat. Barman, call me a cab.

MARK: I'll have a little lunch here. [*He rises.*] Or maybe I would be able to sleep awhile in your room.

MIRIAM: Visit the galleries of Tokyo. The concierge can engage an art student to guide you. [*She turns to the Barman.*] Did you call me a cab?

BARMAN: There are cabs waiting outside the door.

MARK: Your friend would understand, if.

MIRIAM: She said as I said strictly no husbands, meaning none in any condition. —What?

[*Wind chimes are heard.*]

MARK [*Slowly*]: I've always approached my work with a feeling of frightened timidity because the possibilities are.

MIRIAM: You are making an effort to explain a mystery that I.

MARK: The possibilities of a canvas that presents itself for.

MIRIAM: The assault of a madman. You're destroying.

MARK: I suppose I might say it's.

MIRIAM: Crock.

MARK: *Adventure.*

MARK: I'll.

MIRIAM: You'll stay here with your work.

MARK: —It could be a fantasy that I'm.

MIRIAM: Shattering a frontier?

MARK [*crossing to the arch*]: In my room is a suit I've never worn. A shower takes me two minutes. I'll be down in five.

MIRIAM: I won't be seen today with a man that.

MARK: I've always felt that. After the work, so little is left of me. To give to another person.

MIRIAM: Mark.

MARK: Miriam.

MIRIAM: Go back to the States. Enter a. Consult a. As your wife, I.

MARK: I can't interrupt the.

MIRIAM: I have clipped flowers outside your studio and heard you talk to your work as if you were talking to another person in the studio with you.

MARK: No. To myself.

MIRIAM: And I was clipping flowers. It's natural that I felt a little excluded, but I never spoke of it, did I?

MARK: The work of a painter is lonely.

MIRIAM: So is clipping flowers. I'm afraid that loneliness has become a worn-out thing to discuss.

MARK: When I heard you clipping flowers outside my studio, it would sometimes occur to me that you wished the flowers you were clipping were my.

MIRIAM: What's become of the man that?

MARK: What's become of the woman that?

MIRIAM: I'm usually tolerant of men that are unknown to me, but you've become one.

MARK: The constant unbearable of.

MIRIAM: *Mine!*

MARK: *Mine!* —Did you really think I was sleeping night after Goddam night when you slipped out of your bed and threw on a coat over you? Did you think I didn't hear you starting your car that you never put in the garage but left in front of the house? How many kinds of a fool do you take me for? Every? ALL? And near daybreak, did you think I didn't hear your coming back? Sometimes the hanger dropping in the closet? Your slipping demurely back into your bed, your, your satisfied sighs of?

MIRIAM: Assuming.

MARK: *Knowing!*

MIRIAM: Assuming—

MARK: I said knowing, and you know that I knew!

MIRIAM: You never—

MARK: Spoke of it to you? No!

MIRIAM: —Why?

MARK: I said to myself—

MIRIAM: What did you say to yourself? Something or nothing?

29

MARK: She offers the compliment to me of waiting until she thinks that I'm asleep.

[*The wind chimes are heard.*]

MIRIAM: —Are we two people, Mark, or are we—

MARK [*with the force of dread*]: Stop there! [*She lifts her hands to her face, but the words continue through it.*]

MIRIAM: Two sides of!

MARK: Stop!

MIRIAM: One! An artist inhabiting the body of a compulsive—

MARK: Bitch!

MIRIAM: Call me that, but remember that you're denouncing a side of yourself, denied by you! And remember this, too. You'd enter my bed at daybreak, and tired as I was, I never refused myself to you. The vendor of silk that was secret! I probably knew that he knew.

MARK [*cutting through her line above*]: Give me five minutes, all I need, to look proper for this occasion.

MIRIAM: None, not one.

MARK: Go on, you cunt, to this, this—lunch with a gentleman named Elaine. I'm sure you'll be on time. You won't keep him waiting, this gentleman named Elaine with his marital difficulties. You'll give him invaluable counsel. And I, as for me, the man that you married is still a living man with no broken bones, and if later on I feel hungry, I'll have lunch alone, but not in my room with canvasses demanding what I can't give them yet, no, but as for flying back, we'll fly back together, or.

[*He siezes her shoulders. She staggers to her knees; he lifts her and flings her through the arch, out of the bar.*]

BARMAN: —Mr. Conley, do you want to be assisted to your room?

MARK [*crossing to the center table and sitting in a chair*]: I think that I will stay here till my wife returns from.

[*The stage is dimmed out.*]

PART II

The Barman, jacket open, is washing glasses in a cloud of steam. Miriam enters through the arch.

BARMAN: The bar is not open.

MIRIAM: It's open when I come in.

[*The Hawaiian Lady enters through the arch and then exits.*]

The bed has been repaired! And I see you're putting the vase with the flower back on my table. OK. Hmm. Your jacket is open today. Becoming.

BARMAN: The bar is not open until twelve o'clock and I am washing glasses in hot water. The steam may paralyze you.

MIRIAM: There's no danger of that. I'll tell you something I've noticed about Japanese men. On their bodies, as a usual thing, they have almost no hair.

BARMAN: You have investigated?

MIRIAM: Yes, I've conducted some little investigations that aren't in a travel book. I don't like hairy men. I like men to have just the essential hair on their bodies. In their armpits and over their sexual organs. More than that? No. Permissible, sometimes, but essential never. I'll have a French 75 to celebrate the.

BARMAN: You'll have a what?

MIRIAM: I was just putting you on—

BARMAN: Putting me on what?

MIRIAM: I'll have a stinger.

BARMAN: The bar is closed until.

MIRIAM: You've been too busy to look at the clock. It says three minutes to twelve, and by the time you've mixed a stinger for me, if you know how to mix one, it will be twelve or after.

BARMAN: A stinger is made with gin and?

MIRIAM: I think I'd better mix it myself. [*She goes back of the bar and he goes in front of it with noticeable rapidity.*] You've got the ingredients, but you don't know the mix. And you sure did get out of here on the double quick when I got in with you.

BARMAN: You have delayed your trip to Kyoto.

MIRIAM: I have some little business matters to settle here before absorbing Kyoto.

BARMAN: You should absorb the Uzu Peninsula.

MIRIAM [*remaining behind the bar*]: Hmmm. What is there to absorb there?

BARMAN: Very beautiful sights of the sea, and the restful hot springs.

MIRIAM: Oh? So. I've mixed my stinger. Equal parts of brandy and creme de menthe. Green or white. Remember that and remember me as the lady that taught you that.

BARMAN: I doubt that this particular instruction is all that would prevent?

MIRIAM: Yes, prevent.

BARMAN: My remembering that you spent a little time here. Will you please to take your drink to your table now.

MIRIAM: You're supposed to take the drinks to the tables.

BARMAN: I know that I am, and I have told you that I am engaged and not faithless.

33

MIRIAM: Yes, you did tell me that. Hmm. I haven't forgotten that sad bit of information. But despite it. I've known very few men that I couldn't surprise a little.

BARMAN: Go to Kyoto. Go to Kyoto today.

MIRIAM: Oh, I'll go to Kyoto. [*She returns with the drink to her table.*] Lovely old pagodas with clear pools to reflect them and the flowering trees in flower. Perhaps after that I'll absorb the Uzu Peninsula with you.

BARMAN: I have steady employment.

MIRIAM: Never worry, never fear,
     Someday you'll meet a rich old queer.
A recent addition to the Mother Goose Book. Hmmm. Yes. Kon-nichi-Wa. That's the word for hello. Hong-Kong. Singapore. Bangkok—what a name for a city! Hmmm. I think I'll skip India where on the streets they drop dead of starvation. Misfortunes don't attract me.

[*The buzzer sounds.*]

BARMAN: Pardon me. I am called to the restaurant. [*He walks out through the arch.*]

[*Leonard, a middle-aged man who looks younger, enters the circle of light.*]

LEONARD: I like your costume.

MIRIAM: Do you think I cabled you that it was desperately urgent for you to fly from New York to Tokyo in order for you to make a comment on what I'm wearing?

LEONARD: I spent an hour with him. A painter with Mark's talent and originality is a restless creature that lives in his private jungle.

MIRIAM: Crock.

34

LEONARD: He doesn't work for the purpose of having a price tag in four figures on his paintings.

MIRIAM: More crock. Is that all I'm going to get from you?

LEONARD: Of course I'm stalling. If I said that I've never seen so much torment expressed in canvasses before, your response would be "crock," I suppose.

MIRIAM [*hurling the flower vase at the bar*]: There. That's my response.

LEONARD: Violence isn't an element missing from your nature. Let's consider a little.

MIRIAM: I've considered all I'm going to consider, but how did you like his room?

LEONARD: His room, when he let me in it, well, it. I understood the urgency of your cable, yes, I. But, Miriam, it's the physical thing, his physical condition that mainly disturbed me, and I'm sure it.

MIRIAM: It disturbs the people he crashes into on the street, too.

LEONARD: Yes, I.

MIRIAM: Mark made his reputation as an adventurous. Now I'll tell you something that'll give you a turn and a twist, just dig this. He thinks he's made the discovery, the first discovery, of color.

LEONARD: Well, of course, there's always been some question as to whether or not color existed before there were eyes to see it.

MIRIAM: Crock! Don't make cornball remarks, pseudophilosophical cornball remarks like that to me that Mark's made to you.

35

LEONARD: I was merely.

MIRIAM: Yes, merely. Mark thinks he's discovered color and he's terrified of it. Says it's glorious but is terrified of it. How does that grab you or does it just bounce off you?

LEONARD: Painters must be allowed.

MIRIAM: You didn't hear me. I said he's *terrified* of it.

LEONARD: That, he told me that, too.

MIRIAM: You take him back to. His dependence on me is like a baby and a baby is something I never wanted, *never!*

LEONARD: Not so loud.

MIRIAM: I want you to hear me, Leonard.

LEONARD: Your intentions, what are they?

MIRIAM: Not continuing with him and not returning with him.

LEONARD: I thought you cared for Mark?

MIRIAM: Whom else have I spent a considerable part of my life with? But I'm not going to deprive myself of this trip. And there's a reason I won't, and I won't. And there's a reason.

LEONARD: Your desertion of him.

MIRIAM: There are sedations, stretchers, planes and.

LEONARD: Yes. Well, I see. I'll get some plane schedules and. [*He goes out through the arch.*]

MIRIAM: Some women grow suddenly old. They go to bed young, well, reasonably young women and when they wake up in the morning and go to the mirror, they face—what? —A specter! Yes, they face a specter! Themselves, yes, but not young, reasonably young, women, no, not any more! Oh, they

36

continue to pursue, if they are like me, the pursuit would continue! But the desired stranger would offer them no more than a minute of his time. A glance in a glistening bar. And I fear death, I know it would have to remove, wrench, tear! —the bracelets off my arms. Insignia of attraction still persisting. Then? In solitude, in a grove of afternoon trees or the bedroom of a hotel, the mortal pillbox—held still in reserve. To be old, suddenly old—*no!* Unacceptable to me on any terms. So I wait in dread. Terror, yes, I could say terror! [*She wrenches her brilliant bracelets up and down on her arms.*] No inner resources of serenity in me at all. A woman burning. Nothing to put the flames out. A woman condemned to the stake and. Oh, but that's later on. [*Leonard returns.*] Excuse me, Leonard. I was thinking of something. . . .

LEONARD: I was looking at schedules of planes, but frankly, Miriam, all your friends will be shocked.

MIRIAM: Tell them to go to Kyoto. And you, don't give me an argument about it. This trip, Leonard, has a special importance to me that, that I won't try to explain or justify or.

LEONARD: If you intend to.

MIRIAM: Back he goes to the States in your care, Leonard.

LEONARD: Who will finance your?

MIRIAM: Sometimes his dependence on me has been convenient. [*She removes a black leather case from her handbag, and opens it*].

LEONARD: Letter of credit for.

MIRIAM: Exactly. Made out in my name. He goes in a sanitarium and I continue as planned. Set free. Unencumbered. I love hotels. Room service in them and bars. I choose my choice.

LEONARD: Abandonment, at a time when.

37

MIRIAM: I have, under my own name, in Morgan Manhattan Storage, about, no less than two hundred of his best paintings before he discovered color with spray guns, and I also have a hell of a lot of his drawings.

LEONARD: You are a practical woman with an eye for.

MIRIAM: Any contingency, yes.

[*The Barman enters, crosses the stage, and notices the vase and flower on the floor. He picks them up, places them on the center table, and crosses behind the bar.*]

LEONARD: Yes, of course, I know that. Barman, I would like.

MIRIAM: Mark will ask you to exhibit this stuff. Oh, he will. What'll you say to that?

LEONARD: I'll say: "Mark, not yet."

MIRIAM: Well, he would have it exhibited in another gallery that would exhibit it because of his name.

LEONARD: That, I don't believe that.

MIRIAM: Don't believe it, Leonard, but I have an unalterable plan. The man is mad. He is mad!

LEONARD: Are you speaking of?

MIRIAM: Mark! Yes, Mark! I'm speaking of.

LEONARD: I wouldn't.

MIRIAM: You wouldn't but I would! You see the completed pictures, you never hear him at work. I do. I've heard him shout at the studio canvas. "You bitch, it's *you* or *me!* I'm getting, I've got you now! A burst of light in the."

LEONARD: Miriam, not so loud.

MIRIAM: I'd send the maid out at three or four with some food. "Get the fuck out of!" Once he struck with the tray!

38

You! You see the completed paintings. I? I hear the continual madness of his attack on the canvasses as he paints, and I can say with authority on the. Mark is mad! I am married to *madness!* I need some space between myself, and. —A man raging in dark! Constantly further away from.

[*A tinkling of the glass chimes is heard.*]

LEONARD [*seeing Mark in the arch*]: He's come down.

MIRIAM: Oh, God, I'm not going to look at him. Where's he standing?

LEONARD: I pretended not to see him. He's obviously ashamed of.

MIRIAM: He's past shame.

LEONARD: He's leaning against the wall, not looking at us.

MIRIAM: Covered with paint?

LEONARD: He's shaved and cut his face but he has on a clean summer suit. I'm looking at him from the corner of my eye.

MIRIAM: Let's go out in the garden, before he crashes into the table.

[*Mark goes out.*]

LEONARD: He's going into the lavatory to get off his face the blood.

MIRIAM: A primary color. A man that stinks like a goat and staggers into everything he.

LEONARD: He took a shower and fell on the shower floor. Caught hold of the shower curtains and tore them off the rod.

MIRIAM: If you value his past work, tell him it's necessary for him to go back to the States immediately.

39

LEONARD: No plane of any airline out of Tokyo would accept him as a passenger.

MIRIAM: On a stretcher under heavy sedation.

LEONARD: A doctor would have to sign a slip, a certification, that Mark is fit to travel, and I don't think a doctor would.

MIRIAM: What do you suggest, then?

LEONARD: He might be accepted as a passenger on a ship: That's all that I can suggest.

MIRIAM: Leonard? There's a limit to things and I want out.

LEONARD: You mean? Without you?

MIRIAM: Yes, I'm going to follow the plan I planned.

LEONARD: His dependence on you is.

MIRIAM: Yes, and on you.

LEONARD: Do you mean that, in spite of his complete dependence on you, you would consider?

MIRIAM: I don't want to spend my life with my feet in blocks of cement.

LEONARD: Miriam, I operate a gallery, I'm not a divorce attorney.

MIRIAM: The idea of the ship back to the States.

LEONARD: An excellent idea, but he'd have to accept it.

MIRIAM: I'm his wife. Temporarily. Any divorce lawyer would.

LEONARD: My gallery has exhibited the work of painters that painted with their toes. We even have one that paints with his penis.

MIRIAM: Erect or soft?

LEONARD: We are used to extremes. Our gallery is used to, you might say partial, to extremes of.

MIRIAM: To resurrect an old idiom, isn't that fine and dandy? Hmmm. Mark hasn't shown any marked preference for figurative or conventional styles of. He's gone through drip, fling, sopped, stained, saturated, scraped, ripped, cut, skeins of, mounds of heroically enduring color, but now he's arrived at a departure that's a real departure that I doubt he'll return from. Oh, I'm no fool about the. His sacred studio, talking to his. And his black and white period before he.

LEONARD: The, uh, the very early, exploratory phase of a new technique is not for exhibition, and that's what I told him. He took it well. He agreed. But most of the time I was holding him on his feet. I wish you would understand the seriousness of his.

MIRIAM [*sighting Mark offstage.*]: His face is covered with bloody tissue paper. When he comes to the table, if he can make it, I want you as his friend to tell him that. Leonard?

LEONARD: Yes.

MIRIAM: Why do you think I cabled you that he?

LEONARD: It isn't the extremes of. There are many wonderful ways to apply paint to canvas or wood or to a sheet of metal or slab of stone or.

MIRIAM: Leonard, I'm afraid I shouldn't have appealed to you.

LEONARD: Miriam, his chief concern right now is.

MIRIAM: Is?

LEONARD: A change that he feels or imagines in your attitude toward him.

41

[*Mark enters and crosses to the center table, with bloodied bits of tissue paper scattered over his face. He has on a clean white suit but has obviously lost weight so it doesn't fit him. His appearance is ravaged and fantastic: yet he has a childlike quality. When he speaks, his voice trembles.*]

MARK: Barman, another chair at the table, please, and.

[*The Barman sets the chair at the table. Miriam looks straight ahead coldly. Mark starts to sit down but pitches forward, hard, against the table. He laughs breathlessly.*]

MIRIAM: There, now! How does this little demonstration of his public appearance and behavior impress you, if you can imagine yourself in my place? The embarrassment of it is!

LEONARD: He may be embarrassed as you are, and possibly more.

MIRIAM: He's not at all, not in the least embarrassed. Not a bit in the. Don't you hear him laughing?

LEONARD: He's laughing out of embarrassment.

MIRIAM: I'm sorry that I can't laugh out of disgust. If I could laugh out of disgust, it would be the biggest "Ha-ha" you've ever heard, but unfortunately—*stop it!*—my disgust doesn't amuse me at all in the least. And the incident isn't unusual, it's usual, and now are you able to understand why I say that I've *had* it? And *meant* it?

LEONARD: Your voice is.

MIRIAM: Never mind my voice.

LEONARD: Shouting about it is.

MIRIAM: Totally justified!

LEONARD: But, uh.

MIRIAM [*first to Mark, then to Leonard*]: *Stop it, stop it!* And you, don't you say cool it, Goddam if I'll cool it!

LEONARD: It does no good to exaggerate an incident that's painful to us all.

MIRIAM: Your sympathy for him is just a little abnormal, yes, just a little, always calling him baby. Well, here's your baby, take out adoption papers. No difficulty about it, no opposition.

LEONARD: I've learned to have to.

MIRIAM: OK, ignore, ignore.

LEONARD: Yes, ignore and forget.

MIRIAM: Space!

LEONARD: What about?

MIRIAM: Space between two people is sometimes.

LEONARD [*to Mark*]: This, uh, these, uh, little attacks of, uh, disequilibrium have only troubled you recently, haven't they, Mark?

MARK: Since the. I knocked the breath out of. Let me get back my breath, and.

MIRIAM: Flying over here, he kept complaining that the plane cabins were not pressurized enough, and they were pressurized perfectly.

[*They sit in silence awhile as Mark struggles to catch his breath.*]

LEONARD: Mark, I think a. [*Mark nods.*] Barman, for Mr. Conley, please

MIRIAM: Lots of luck, if you expect him to deliver a drink to this table.

MARK: I found, I put on a. [*He draws a difficult breath.*] Clean summer suit, but, you see, I forgot my.

LEONARD: What did you forget, Mark.

MARK: My electric razor in Wetherbridge.

LEONARD: I think that unconsciously we resent shaving. I've often made trips and forgotten my razor. But this time Raymond packed for me, so I have my electric razor. Of course you're welcome to use it.

MIRIAM: Very relevant to the.

LEONARD [*grateful for a light topic*]: The Japanese make such lovely, compact electric appliances, such as their Sony transistors, and their, their. [*He keeps glancing nervously at Mark.*]—Do you like my star sapphire?

MIRIAM: I think it's an appropriate adornment.

LEONARD: From Raymond on my birthday.

[*Miriam snatches a small object from her handbag. Leonard's attitude during the snuff-box lines is detached, his attention remaining on Mark.*]

MIRIAM: How do you like my little Regency snuff-box?

LEONARD: Charming.

[*She shakes it.*]

You have something in it.

MIRIAM: Yes. Snuff.

LEONARD: Snuff doesn't rattle.

MIRIAM: It rattles when it's compressed.

LEONARD: Compressed snuff is something I've never heard of.

MIRIAM: Maybe you will. Snuff, snuff, enough.

44

MARK: I'll get my breath back.

LEONARD: Of course you will in a moment. —Miriam, Mark is a man of complexities that we.

MIRIAM: What an observation to make to a woman that's lived with him fourteen years.

MARK: If I imposed, I never meant to impose.

MIRIAM: Leonard, let's go straight to the point of your presence here in Japan.

MARK: I was.

LEONARD: What?

MARK: Always willing to.

LEONARD: What?

MARK: Die.

LEONARD: Mark means for you.

MIRIAM: He has a studio separate from the house, and as for dying for me, I prefer to have someone living for me, which I think is a natural preference.

MARK: The time.

LEONARD: It's twelve-fifteen.

MARK: Not what I meant. The time that you wait. To catch your breath, or *not* catch it.

MIRIAM: Nothing is being accomplished at this little round table conference.

MARK: The time you wait to recover. Or not to recover. And you're so revolted by the fear that you feel.

LEONARD: Fear is a built-in protection. Nothing to be ashamed of. I doubt that any living creature of the, the, uh, animal,

45

mammal species isn't provided with it. Possibly fish don't have it. No, I think even fish are frightened when they're.

MIRIAM: You have a remarkable facility for keeping things at sea level.

LEONARD: Sometimes it's the name of the game. Did the Barman make the?

MIRIAM: It's on the bar. Go get it.

LEONARD: The service in this bar is.

MIRIAM: No service.

LEONARD [*fetching the drink*]: Let me make a suggestion.

MIRIAM: Yes, do that. What is your suggestion?

LEONARD: —What an interminable plane flight from New York to Tokyo, with all the changes in time. To repeat it immediately, I mean in reverse, would be a little too much.

MIRIAM: Is that your suggestion?

MARK: Yes. Interminable.

MIRIAM: You don't have to repeat it at once, you can have my room next to Mark's while I visit Kyoto.

LEONARD: Your intention is to?

MIRIAM: Catch the evening clackety-clack to Kyoto alone.

MARK: Something has.

LEONARD: What, Mark?

MARK: Affected my.

LEONARD: Affected your?

MARK: —Vision. Our breathing and the, the—pulsation of our, our—arteries are things that we are so used to that we usually don't think about them, but—

LEONARD: Yes. We take them for granted.

MARK: As permanent possessions, but they're only loaned to us, and the loan of.

LEONARD: Mark, baby, you simply.

MARK: Yes. Was simply reminded that breath in my. Is something not given but loaned, and the loan is.

LEONARD: We've all had the breath knocked out of us for a few moments.

MIRIAM: Yes, that's right, Mark, baby.

MARK: The loan is subject to, to—unexpected.

LEONARD: Don't try to get up till.

MARK: Foreclosure? Is that the way that?

LEONARD: It's not important, but rest here a little longer.

MARK: I will. Has she left the room?

LEONARD: No. She's still in the room.

MARK: I—like—this—room. —My breath is—coming back, now.

LEONARD: Good. Good.

MARK: I'll tell you something about what's called—the breath of life in us. No, I don't have the breath to tell you.

MIRIAM: I have a few things more to attend to before.

MARK: Miriam?

MIRIAM: I wanted to come here alone but he wouldn't allow me a little time of space between us, oh, no, he followed me here like the tin can that children tie to the tail of a cat in an alley.

LEONARD: Let's.

MIRIAM: Not upset Mark baby.

MARK: I'm beginning to feel all right. Perfectly. Have the razor cuts stopped bleeding?

LEONARD: Oh, yes, they've stopped bleeding, now.

MIRIAM: Comparatively.

MARK [*rising, almost steady*]: Ladies and gentlemen, pardon me. . . . Lady and Leonard.

MIRIAM: He's decided to be offensive, now that he's got his breath back.

LEONARD: It's only the state of his.

MARK: You thought I was talking to you. I was talking to myself. A serious painter has two requirements—a long white beard and a—and a stepladder. [*He is talking to himself.*] Mark, you're talking about a thing that.

LEONARD: A thing that can't be clearly expressed at this point of.

MARK: Yep that's what you need to give you a constantly full quart of confidence in. A long white beard and a stepladder and a commission to paint—what did he paint on the ceiling of the Sistine Chapel.

LEONARD: Michelangelo painted the creation of the world on the ceiling of the.

MARK: The creation of the creation of the creation.

MIRIAM: Don't encourage him to.

[*Mark staggers a little. Leonard touches his shoulder.*]

MARK: Don't touch me—I can't stand to be touched!

48

LEONARD: I can't believe that a painter's dependence on the wealth of the Church would please you. Would it, Mark, baby? No. I—

MARK: Crock, as the lady would put it. I'm anyone's whore, including my own. The lady—where is she? Oh, there she is!— Christ! She looks like a three-masted schooner today, billowing out of a harbor with a cargo of that stuff made from coconuts. Copra? And a crew of some of them shanghaied, but the wind and the sea are favorable to her sailing around the Cape of, and if she's becalmed in equatorial waters she'll get the crew at the oars, oh, they'll row for the lady and live on hard tack.

MIRIAM: The hell with.

MARK: Suck my ass in Wetherbridge Square at noon on the Fourth of July.

[*He leans on the end of the bar and peers at Miriam's face. She doesn't look at him.*]

The lady knows an unabridged in-cyclone of ways to be intimate with. Oh pleasurable yes—the prices are widely variable —I found them not inexpensive once—once—once—[*He laughs.*] I forgot we were entertaining. It was one of those diaphanous afternoons in August. You know that seem to drift skyward to some clearer space and then to another space even higher and clearer.

MIRIAM: You love August because you were born in August.

MARK: I don't think that would prejudice me in its favor on the first ballot. But you remember.

MIRIAM: It was memorable yes.

MARK: A crowded, lively party was in progress and I burst out of the star-chamber, my studio, bare-assed as when I first added my cry of protest to the. Shambled dizzily to the.

49

Opened the sliding-glass doors, noticed the presence of no one but my wife. Shouted to her, "God damn but I think I've done a painting!" I never did more than *think* I'd done one, you see. —Why am I so tired? —Nobody ever gave me a magnum or a quart or a baby's bottle of confidence, and I didn't have a long, white beard and a stepladder to the vault of the Sistine Chapel to paint the creation of creation. —Well, anyway, pretension is the unpardonable offense.

[*His voice dies out; the wind chimes are heard.*]

Put the words back in a box and nail down the lid. *Fini.* —Wait for me just ten minutes. Watch the clock and clock me. I'll remove the tissue and talcum my face and be back in ten minutes, exactly.

[*He staggers and falls to the floor. Leonard crouches over him quickly, and feels his pulse. Leonard motions to the Barman.*]

LEONARD: Barman.

[*They carry the body of Mark out of the bar. Miriam appears to see and feel nothing. The wind chimes are heard. The Barman returns, replacing the overturned stool to its place. He crosses to the center table, takes the two glasses and returns to behind the bar. Leonard returns to the bar.*]

Miriam, he's.

MIRIAM: I know. —A long ten minutes.

LEONARD: The concierge is making the. Arrangements.

MIRIAM: Released!

LEONARD: —Yes, he's released from.

MIRIAM: I meant that I am released.

LEONARD: If that's your feeling, it's one that shouldn't be spoken even to me. —How do you know I won't repeat what you said? We live in a gossipy world. I might, accidentally, but.

MIRIAM: I'm sure that you will repeat but it doesn't concern me at all.

LEONARD: I think we should leave this room, and.

MIRIAM: I've never been to a mortuary and I'm not going to visit one now.

LEONARD: Let's get out of the bar and sit in the garden. The Barman hears and understands the savage things you're saying.

[*She lights a cigarette.*]

Miriam.

MIRIAM: Leonard.

[*The wind chimes are heard.*]

—There's an edge, a limit to the circle of light. The circle is narrow. And protective. We have to stay inside. It's our existence and our protection. The protection of our existence. It's our home if we have one.

LEONARD: Not to be trusted always.

MIRIAM: You know and I know it's dangerous not to stay in it. There's no reason to take a voluntary step outside of the. Do you understand that? [*He nods.*] Miriam Conley is not going to step outside the circle of light. It's dangerous, I don't dare to or care to. This well-defined circle of light is our defense against. Outside of it there's dimness that increases to darkness: never my territory. It's never been at all attractive to me. When someone at a party says, "Let's all go to the new club on something street, or even out of the country," I say, "Wonderful. Let's go." With Mark? No! Mark was bored with this party before it started. But oh I go. Do I go! The circle of light stays with me. Until. Until can be held off but not forever eluded. You've seen how fatal it is to step out of the.

LEONARD: I'm not sure I know what you mean.

MIRIAM: Animation. Liveliness. People at a smart restaurant talking gaily together. Interested in jewelry, clothes, shopping, shows. Leonard, you know it's imperative for us to stay inside of. As for the others. You know and I know incurably ill people, especially those with dreaded diseases such as. And people gone mad that need an acre of pacifying meadows, trees around them.

[*The tinkling chimes are heard.*]

A few perfunctory visits is all that they can expect and all they'll receive. Ask God if you don't believe me. It's like they'd violated a law that's.

LEONARD: Inviolable.

MIRIAM: Yes. Double yes. The circle of light won't be and can't be extended to include them. The final black needle is their visitor, Leonard.

LEONARD: Take this handkerchief and pretend to cry.

MIRIAM: I'll pretend to do nothing.

LEONARD: Let me tell you something that. When my grand-mother died, after an agony of several hours, my mother called a correct undertaker, and then said to us: "She put up a good fight. Now come downstairs and I will make us some cocoa and some cinnamon toast." We were children, but even so I thought the suggestion was shockingly inappropriate to the agony and death of her mother. Completed a minute before.

MIRIAM: She was in the circle that attends us faithfully as long as our bodies don't betray us and our minds don't make excursions of a nature that's incompatible with the.

LEONARD: Well.

MIRIAM: He was removed so quickly. If I should say that the circle of light is the approving look of God it would be romantic which I refuse to be. The program for today should not be changed except for the.

LEONARD: Absence of Mark.

MIRIAM: Mark that made the mistake of deliberately moving out of the.

LEONARD: Yes, Mark's absence.

MIRIAM: Of the man who has made a crossing that neither of us but each of us. I will bow my head to the table as an appearance of being stricken with. Then when we go to the street, put your arm about me as if I were overcome with the expected emotion.

LEONARD: Have you got everything, dear?

MIRIAM: It would be strange but possible if later I discovered that I cared for him deeply in spite of. He thought that he could create his own circle of light.

LEONARD: Miriam, what are your actual plans?

MIRIAM: I have no plans. I have nowhere to go.

[*With abrupt violence, she wrenches the bracelets from her arms and flings them to her feet. The stage darkens.*]

CURTAIN

I RISE IN FLAME, CRIED THE PHOENIX

A Play in One Act about D. H. Lawrence

AUTHOR'S NOTE

The action of this play, which is imaginary, takes place in the French Riviera where D. H. Lawrence died.

Not long before Lawrence's death an exhibition was held of his paintings in London. Primitive in technique and boldly sensual in matter, this exhibition created a little tempest. The pictures were seized by the police and would have been burned if the authorities had not been restrained by an injunction. At this time Lawrence's great study of sexual passion, *Lady Chatterley's Lover*, was likewise under the censor's ban, as much of his work had been in the past.

Lawrence felt the mystery and power of sex, as the primal life urge, and was the life-long adversary of those who wanted to keep the subject locked away in the cellars of prudery. Much of his work is chaotic and distorted by tangent obsessions, such as his insistence upon the woman's subservience to the male, but all in all his work is probably the greatest modern monument to the dark roots of creation.

T.W.
New Orleans, September, 1941.

CHARACTERS

LAWRENCE

FRIEDA

BERTHA [Brett]

I RISE IN FLAME,
CRIED THE PHOENIX

The scene of the play is at Vence in the Alpes Maritimes. It is late afternoon. Lawrence is seated on the sun porch, the right wall of which is a window that faces the sun. A door in this wall opens out on the high sea cliff. It is windy: the surf can be heard. Lawrence looks out that way. Behind him, on the left wall, woven in silver and scarlet and gold, is a large silk banner that bears the design of the Phoenix in a nest of flames—Lawrence's favorite symbol. He sits quite still. His beard is fiercely red and his face is immobile, the color of baked clay with tints of purple in it. The hands that gripped the terrible stuff of life and made it plastic are folded on the black-and-white checkered surface of an invalid's blanket. The long fingers of the Welsh coal miners, with their fine blond hairs and their knobby knuckles, made for rending the black heart out of the earth, are knotted together with a tightness that betrays the inner lack of repose. His slightly distended nostrils draw the breath in and out as tenderly as if it were an invisible silk thread that any unusual tension might snap in two. Born for contention, he is contending with something he can't get his hands on. He has to control his fury. And so he is seated motionless in the sunlight— wrapped in a checkered blanket and lavender wool shawl. The tiger in him is trapped but not destroyed yet. Frieda comes in, a large handsome woman of fifty, rather like a Valkyrie. She holds up a fancily wrapped little package.

LAWRENCE [*without even turning his head*]: What is it?

FRIEDA: Something left on the doorstep.

LAWRENCE: Give it here.

FRIEDA: The donor is anonymous. I only caught a glimpse of her through the window.

59

LAWRENCE: A woman?

FRIEDA: Yes. . . .

LAWRENCE: Yes. . . .

FRIEDA: Some breathless little spinster in a blue pea jacket. She stuck it on the porch and scuttled back down the hill before I could answer the doorbell.

LAWRENCE [*his voice rising querulously shrill*]: It's for me, isn't it?

FRIEDA [*in German*]: *Ja*, it's for you.

LAWRENCE: Well, give it here, damn you, you—!

FRIEDA: *Tch!* I thought that the sun had put you in a good humor.

LAWRENCE: It's put me in a vile humor. We've sat here making faces at each other the whole afternoon. I say to the sun, Make me well, you old bitch, give me strength, take hold of my hands and pull me up out of this chair! But the sun is a stingy *Hausfrau*. She goes about sweeping the steps and pretends not to hear me begging. Ah, well, I don't blame her. I never did care for beggars myself very much. A man shouldn't beg. A man should seize what he wants and tear it out of the hands of the adversary. And if he can't get it, if he can't tear it away, then he should let it go and give up and be contented with nothing. Look. [*He has unwrapped the package.*] A little jar of orange marmalade. [*He smiles with childish pleasure.*] This is the month of August put in a bottle.

FRIEDA: *Ja! Sehr gut.* You can have it for breakfast.

LAWRENCE [*drawing tenderly on the fine gold thread*]: Uh-huh. I can have it for breakfast as long as I live, huh, Frieda? It's just the right size for that.

60

FRIEDA: Shut up. [*She starts to take the jar from him. Quick as a cat he snatches her wrist in a steel grip.*]

LAWRENCE: Leave go of it, damn you!

FRIEDA [*laughing*]: My God, but you still are strong!

LAWRENCE: You didn't think so?

FRIEDA: I had forgotten. You've been so gentle lately.

LAWRENCE: Thought you'd tamed me?

FRIEDA: Yes, but I should have known better. I should have suspected what you've been doing inside you, lapping that yellow cream up, you sly old fox, sucking the fierce red sun in your body all day and turning it into venom to spew in my face!

LAWRENCE: No—I've been making a trap. I've been making a shiny steel trap to catch you in, you vixen! Now break away if you can!

FRIEDA [*grinning and wincing*]: Oh, God, how you hurt!

LAWRENCE [*slowly releasing her*]: Don't lie. . . . You with that great life in you—Why did God give you so much and me so little? You could take my arm and snap it like a dry stick.

FRIEDA: No. —You were always the stronger one. Big as I am, I never could beat you, could I?

LAWRENCE [*with satisfaction*]: No. You couldn't. [*His breath rasps hoarsely.*] Put the jar down on the sill.

FRIEDA [*complying*]: Ahh, there's a card stuck on it. "From one of your devoted readers." And on the other side it says— "I worship you, Mr. Lawrence, because I know that only a god could know so much about Life!"

LAWRENCE [*dryly*]: In looking for God so unsuccessfully myself, it seems that I have accidentally managed to create one

61

for an anonymous spinster in a blue pea jacket. Upon the altar of her pagan deity she places a dainty jar of orange marmalade! What a *cynical* little woman she is! Only the little ones of the earth, who scuttle downhill like pebbles dislodged by the rain, are really capable of such monumental disbelief. They find their god and they give him marmalade. If I find mine—ever— If I found mine, I'd tear the heart out of my body and burn it before him.

FRIEDA: Your health is returning.

LAWRENCE: What makes you think so?

FRIEDA: You are getting so sentimental about yourself and so unappreciated and so misunderstood. —You can't stand Jesus Christ because he beat you to it. Oh, how you would have loved to suffer the *original* crucifixion!

LAWRENCE: If only I had your throat between my fingers.

FRIEDA [*crouching beside him*]: Here is my throat. —Now choke me.

LAWRENCE [*gently touching her throat with the tips of his fingers*]: Frieda—do you think I will ever get back to New Mexico?

FRIEDA: You will do what you want to do, Lawrence. There has never been any kind of resistance you couldn't jump over or crawl under or squeeze through.

LAWRENCE: Do you think I will ever get back on a strong white horse and go off like the wind across the glittering desert? I'm not a literary man, I'm tired of books. Nobody knows what an ugly joke it is that a life like mine should only come out in books.

FRIEDA: What else should it come out in?

LAWRENCE: In some kind of violent action. But all that I ever do is go packing around the world with women and manuscripts and a vile disposition. I pretend to be waging a war with bourgeois conceptions of morality, with prudery, with intellectuality, with all kinds of external forces that aren't external at all. What I'm fighting with really's the little old maid in myself, the breathless little spinster who scuttles back down the hill before God can answer the doorbell. Now I want to get back on the desert and try all over again to become a savage. I want to stand up on the Lobos and watch a rainstorm coming ten miles off like a silver-helmeted legion of marching giants. And that's what I'm going to do, damn you!

FRIEDA: Whoever said that you wouldn't?

LAWRENCE: You! —You know that I won't. You know that the male savage part of me's dead and all that's left is the old pusillanimous squaw. Women have such a fine intuition of death. They smell it coming before it's started even. I think it's women that actually let death in, they whisper and beckon and slip it the dark latchkey from under their aprons—don't they?

FRIEDA: No—it's women that pay the price of admission for life. And all of their lives they make of their arms a crossbar at the door that death wants to come in by. Men love death—women don't. Men cut wounds in each other and women stop the bleeding.

LAWRENCE: Yes. By drinking the blood. Don't touch me so much! [*He releases his fingers.*] Your fingers, they make me feel weaker, they drain the strength out of my body.

FRIEDA: Oh, no, no, no, they put it back *in, mein liebchen.*

LAWRENCE: I want you to promise me something. If I should die, Frieda—the moment I'm dying, please to leave me alone! —Don't touch me, don't put your hands on me, and don't let anyone else. —I have a nightmarish feeling that while I'm dying I'll be surrounded by women. —They'll burst in the door and the windows the moment ·I lose the strength to push them away. —They'll moan and they'll flutter like doves around the burnt-out Phoenix. —They'll cover my face and my hands with filmy kisses and little trickling tears. —Alma the nymphomaniac and the virginal Bertha. —All of the under- and over-sexed women I've known, who think me the oracle of their messed-up libidos. —They'll all return with their suffocating devotion. —I don't want that. —I want to die like a lonely old animal does, I want to die fiercely and cleanly with nothing but anger and fear and other hard things like that to deal with at the finish. You understand, Frieda? I've still got a bit of the male left in me and that's the part that I'm going to meet death with. When the last bleeding comes, and it *will* in a little while now, I won't be put into bed and huddled over by women. I won't stay in the house, Frieda. I'll open this door and go outside on the cliff. And I don't wish to be followed. That's the important point, Frieda. I'm going to do it alone. With the rocks and the water. Sunlight—starlight on me. No hands, no lips, no women! —Nothing but—pitiless nature—

FRIEDA: I don't believe you. I don't think people want nothing but "pitiless nature" when they're—

LAWRENCE: Frieda! You mean you refuse?

FRIEDA: No. I consent absolutely.

LAWRENCE: You give me your promise?

FRIEDA [*in German*]: Yes, a hundred times, yes! Now think about something else. —I'll go fix tea. [*She starts to go out.*]

LAWRENCE [*suddenly noticing something*]: Ahh, my God.

FRIEDA: What's the matter?

LAWRENCE: Put the aquarium on the window sill.

FRIEDA: Why?

64

LAWRENCE: So I can keep an eye on it. —That detestable cat has attacked the goldfish again.

FRIEDA: How do you know?

LAWRENCE: How do I know? There used to be *four*, now there's *three! Beau Soleil!*

FRIEDA: She's gone outside.

LAWRENCE: To lick her chops, God damn her! Set the goldfish bowl on the window sill.

FRIEDA: You can't keep them there in the sun. The sun will kill them.

LAWRENCE [*furiously*]: Don't answer me back, put 'em *there!*

FRIEDA [*in German*]: All right, all right! [*She hastens to place the aquarium on the sill.*]

LAWRENCE: You know what I think? I think you *fed* her the fish. It's like you to do such a thing. You're both so fat, so rapacious, so viciously healthy and hungry!

FRIEDA: Such a fuss over a goldfish!

LAWRENCE: It isn't just a goldfish.

FRIEDA: What is it then?

LAWRENCE: —Now that my strength's used up I can't help thinking how much of it's been thrown away in squabbling with you.

FRIEDA [*suddenly covering her face*]: Oh, Lawrence.

LAWRENCE: —What are you doing? Crying? Stop it. I can't stand crying. It makes me worse.

FRIEDA: I think you *hate* me, Lawrence.

65

LAWRENCE [*shyly touching her arm*]: —Don't believe me. —I love you. *Ich liebe dich*, Frieda. Put some rum in the tea. I'm getting much stronger, so why should I feel so weak?

FRIEDA [*touching his forehead*]: I wish you would go back to bed.

LAWRENCE: The bed's an old tar baby. I'd get stuck. How do I know that I'd get loose again? —Is my forehead hot? [*Frieda places her hand tenderly over his eyes.*]

LAWRENCE [*in a childish treble*]: "Ladybug, ladybug, fly away home, thine house is on fire, thy children will burn!" [*He smiles slightly.*] My mother used to sing that whenever she saw one. —Simple. —Most people are so damned complicated and yet there is nothing much to them.

FRIEDA [*starting out, then pausing before the banner*]: Ahh, you old Phoenix—you brave and angry old bird in your nest of flames! —I think you are just a little bit sentimental.

LAWRENCE [*leaning suddenly forward*]: Tea for three!

FRIEDA: Who is it?

LAWRENCE: Bertha! —Back from London with news of the exhibition. [*He pulls himself out of his chair.*]

FRIEDA: What are you doing?

LAWRENCE: I'm going outside to meet her.

FRIEDA: Sit down, you fool! —I'll meet her. And don't you dare to ask her to stay in this house—if you do, I'll leave! [*She goes out.*]

LAWRENCE: Cluck-cluck-cluck-cluck! —You think I'm anxious to have more hens around me? [*He wriggles fretfully in his chair for a moment, then throws off the blanket and pushes himself to his feet. Stumbling with dizziness and breathing*

66

heavily, he moves to the inside rear door of the porch. He reaches it, and pauses with a fit of coughing. He looks anxiously back toward the chair—] No, no, damn you—I *won't!* [*He looks up at the Phoenix, straightens heroically and goes out. After a few moments Frieda returns with Bertha, a small, sprightly person, an English gentlewoman with the quick voice and eyes of a child.*]

FRIEDA: My God, he's got up!

BERTHA: He shouldn't?

FRIEDA: Another hemorrhage will kill him. The least exertion is likely to bring one on. Lorenzo, where are you?

LAWRENCE [*from the rear*]: Quit clucking, you old wet hen. I'm fetching the tea.

BERTHA: Go back to him, make him stop!

FRIEDA: He wouldn't.

BERTHA: Does he want to die?

FRIEDA: Oh, no, no, no! He has no lungs and yet he goes on breathing. The heart's worn out and yet the heart keeps beating. It's awful to watch, this struggle, I wish he would stop, I wish that he'd give it up and just let go!

BERTHA: Frieda!

FRIEDA: His body's a house that's made out of tissue paper and caught on fire. The walls are transparent, they're all lit up with the flame! When people are dying the spirit ought to go out, it ought to die out slowly before the flesh, you shouldn't be able to see it so terribly brightly consuming the walls that give it a place to inhabit!

BERTHA: I never have believed that Lorenzo could die. I don't think he will even now.

67

FRIEDA: But can he do it? Live without body, I mean, be just a flame with nothing to feed itself on?

BERTHA: The Phoenix could do it.

FRIEDA: The Phoenix was legendary. Lorenzo's a man.

BERTHA: He's more than a man.

FRIEDA: I know you always thought so. But you're mistaken.

BERTHA: You'd never admit that Lorenzo was a god.

FRIEDA: Having slept with him—no, I wouldn't.

BERTHA: There's more to be known of a person than carnal knowledge.

FRIEDA: But carnal knowledge comes first.

BERTHA: I disagree with you.

FRIEDA: And also with Lawrence, then. He always insisted you couldn't know women until you had known their bodies.

BERTHA: Frieda, I think it is you who kept him so much in his body!

FRIEDA: Well, if I did he's got that to thank me for.

BERTHA: I'm not so sure it's something to be thankful for.

FRIEDA: What would you have done with him if ever you got your claws on him?

BERTHA: Claws? —Frieda!

FRIEDA: You would have plucked him out of his body. Where would he be? —In the air? —Ahhhh, your deep understanding and my stupidity always!

BERTHA: Frieda!

FRIEDA: You just don't know, the meaning of Lawrence escapes you! In all his work he celebrates the body! How he despises the prudery of people that want to hide it!

BERTHA: Oh, Frieda, the same old quarrel!

FRIEDA: Yes, let's stop it! What's left of Lorenzo, let's not try to divide it!

BERTHA: What's left of Lorenzo is something that can't be divided!

FRIEDA: Shhh! —He's coming.

BERTHA [*advancing a few steps to the door*]: Lorenzo!

LAWRENCE [*out of sight*]: "Pussycat, pussycat, where have you been?"

BETTHA [*gaily*]: "I've been to London to look at the queen!"

LAWRENCE [*clear*]: "Pussycat, pussycat, what did you do there?"

BERTHA [*her voice catching slightly*]: "I chased a little mouse —under a chair!"

[*Laughing, he appears in the doorway, pushing a small tea-cart. Bertha stares aghast.*]

LAWRENCE: Yes, I know—I know. . . . I look an amateur's job of embalming, don't I?

BERTHA [*bravely*]: Lorenzo, you look very well.

LAWRENCE: It isn't rouge, it's the fever! I'm burning, burning, and still I never burn out. The doctors are all astonished. And disappointed. And as for that expectant widow of mine—she's almost given up hope.

[*Bertha moves to assist him with the table.*]

69

LAWRENCE: Don't bother me. I can manage.

FRIEDA: He won't be still, he won't rest.

LAWRENCE: Cluck-cluck-cluck-cluck! You better watch out for the rooster, you old wet hen!

FRIEDA: A wonderful Chanticleer you make in that lavender shawl!

LAWRENCE: Who put it on me? *You*, you bitch! [*He flings it off.*] Rest was never any good for me, Brett.

BERTHA: Rest for a little while. Then we go sailing again!

LAWRENCE: We three go sailing again!

> "Rub-a-dub-dub!
> Three fools in a tub!
> The Brett, the Frieda,
> the old Fire-eater!"

BERTHA [*tugging at his beard*]: The old Fire-eater!

LAWRENCE: Watch out! Now I'll have to comb it. [*He takes out a little mirror and comb.*]

FRIEDA: So vain of his awful red whiskers!

LAWRENCE [*combing*]: She envies my beard. All women resent men's whiskers. They can't stand anything, Brett, that distinguishes men from women.

FRIEDA: Quite the contrary. [*She pours the tea.*]

LAWRENCE: They take the male in their bodies—but only because they secretly hope that he won't be able to get back out again, that he'll be captured for good!

FRIEDA: What kind of talk for a maiden-lady to hear?!

LAWRENCE: There she goes again, Brett—obscene old creature! Gloating over your celibacy!

70

FRIEDA: Gloating over it? Never! I think how lucky she is that she doesn't have to be told a hundred times every day that man is life and that woman is just a passive hunk of protoplasm.

LAWRENCE: I never said passive. I always said malignant. [*He puts the comb away and stares in the mirror.*] Ain't I the devil to look at?

FRIEDA: I tell you, Brett, his ideas of sex are becoming right down cosmic! When the sun comes up in the morning—you know what he says? No, I won't repeat it! And when the sun's going down— Oh, well, you will hear him yourself.

LAWRENCE [*chuckling*]: Yes, I always make the same remark. You'll hear me yourself in just a few more minutes. . . . [*He puts the mirror away.*] Well, Brett!

BERTHA: Well, Lorenzo?

LAWRENCE: You haven't said anything yet.

BERTHA: Anything? About what?

LAWRENCE: What do you think that I sent you to London for?

BERTHA: To get me out of the way!

LAWRENCE: What else? Out with it, damn you! The show! How did they like my pictures?

BERTHA: Well—

FRIEDA: Go on, Brett, tell him the truth. The monster will not be satisfied till he hears it!

BERTHA: Well—

FRIEDA: The exhibition was a complete fiasco! Just as I said it would be!

LAWRENCE: You mean that they *liked* my dairies?

FRIEDA: *Liked* your pictures? They called your pictures *disgusting!*

LAWRENCE: Ah! —*Success!* They said that I couldn't paint? That I draw like a child? They called my figures grotesque? Lumpy, obscene, misshapen, monstrous, deformed?

BERTHA: You must have seen the reviews, you've read them yourself!

LAWRENCE: Why? Am I quoting exactly?

FRIEDA: Yes, you are quoting exactly!

LAWRENCE: And what did the public think? And what of the people?

FRIEDA: The people laughed!

LAWRENCE: They laughed?

FRIEDA: Of course they laughed! Lorenzo, you're not a painter, you're a writer! Why, you can't even draw a straight line!

LAWRENCE: No! But I can draw a *crooked* line, Frieda. And that is the reason that I can put *life* in my pictures! How was the attendance? How many came to look?

BERTHA: After the disturbance, the entrance had to be roped off to hold back the crowds.

LAWRENCE: Disturbance? What disturbance?

FRIEDA: Just look. The monster's exulting!

LAWRENCE: Go on, tell me what happened!

BERTHA: A group of ladies' club members attempted to slash the picture of Adam and Eve.

[*Lawrence shakes with laughter.*]

FRIEDA: Lorenzo! Stop that!

72

BERTHA: That was what called the attention of the police.

LAWRENCE: The police? [*He rises.*] What did they do to my pictures? Burn them? DESTROY THEM?

BERTHA: No. We got out an injunction to keep them from burning the pictures.

LAWRENCE: The pictures are safe?

BERTHA: The pictures are safe, Lorenzo.

FRIEDA: Sit down in that chair or I'll have to put you to bed! [*She tries to push him down; he slaps her fiercely.*]

BERTHA: Lorenzo!

LAWRENCE: Vaunting her power, gloating over my weakness! Put me to bed? Just try it—I dare you to touch me!

FRIEDA: Lawrence, sit down in the chair or you'll start the bleeding again.

[*He stares at her for a moment, then obeys slowly.*]

LAWRENCE [*weakly*]: Give me back that shawl. The sun's getting weaker. The young blond god is beginning to be seduced by the harlot of darkness. . . .

FRIEDA: Now he's going to make his classic remarks on the sunset. [*She puts the shawl about him.*]

LAWRENCE: Yes—the pictures—they weren't very good but they had a fierce life in them.

BERTHA: They had *you* in them. But why did you want to *paint*, Lawrence?

LAWRENCE: Why did I want to *write?* Because I'm an artist. —What is an artist? —A man who loves life too intensely, a man who loves life till he hates her and has to strike out with his fist like I struck at Frieda— to show her he knows her tricks, and he's still the master! [*The smoky yellow light is beginning to dim.*] Oh, Brett, oh, Frieda— I wanted to stretch out the long, sweet arms of my art and embrace the whole world! But it isn't enough to go out to the world with love. The world's a woman you've got to take by storm. And so I doubled my fist and I struck and I struck. Words weren't enough— I had to have color, too. I took to paint and I painted the way that I wrote! Fiercely, without any shame! *This* is life, I told them, life is like *this!* Wonderful! Dark! Terrific! They banned my books and they wanted to burn my pictures! That's how it is— When first you look at the sun it strikes you blind—Life's— blinding. . . . [*He stirs and leans forward.*] The sun's—going down. He's seduced by the harlot of darkness.

FRIEDA: Now he is going to say it— Stop up your ears!

LAWRENCE: Now she has got him, they're copulating together! The sun is exhausted, the harlot has taken his strength and now she will start to destroy him. She's eating him up. . . . Oh, but he won't stay down. He'll climb back out of her belly and there will be light. In the end there will always be light— And I am the prophet of it! [*He rises with difficulty.*]

BERTHA: Lorenzo!

FRIEDA: Lawrence, be careful!

LAWRENCE: Shut up! Don't touch me! [*He staggers to the great window.*] In the end there is going to be light— Light, light! [*His voice rises and he stretches his arms out like a Biblical prophet.*] Great light! —Great, blinding, universal *light!* And *I*—I'm the *Prophet* of it! [*He staggers and clutches his mouth.*]

FRIEDA: *Lawrence!*

BERTHA [*terrified*]: What *is* it?

FRIEDA: The *bleeding!*

BERTHA: *Lorenzo!* [*She would rush to him but Frieda clutches her arm.*]

LAWRENCE: Don't touch me, you women. I want to do it alone. —Don't move till it's finished. [*Gradually, as though forced down to the earth by invisible arms, he begins to collapse —his hands clutch onto the curtains—his knees collapse.*]

BERTHA [*struggling fiercely with Frieda*]: Let me go, let me go, I want to go to him!

FRIEDA: Not yet—not yet—one moment! [*His fingers let go. He slides to the floor. He is lifeless.*]

FRIEDA [*releasing the other woman*]: Now. —Go to him. —It's finished.
[*She covers her face. Bertha rushes moaning to Lawrence and crouches beside him. The sun disappears.*]

SLOW CURTAIN

THE MUTILATED

The Mutilated was first presented, as part of a double bill entitled *Slapstick Tragedy*, by Charles Bowden and Lester Persky in association with Sidney Lanier, at the Longacre Theatre, in New York City, on February 22, 1966. It was directed by Alan Schneider. The sets were designed by Ming Cho Lee; the costumes, by Noel Taylor; music was composed and selected by Lee Hoiby; and the lighting was by Martin Aronstein. Production was in association with Frenman Productions, Ltd. The cast, in order of appearance, was as follows:

CELESTE	KATE REID
HENRY	RALPH WAITE
TRINKET	MARGARET LEIGHTON
SLIM	JAMES OLSON
BRUNO	RALPH WAITE
MAXIE	DAVID SABIN
BIRD GIRL	RENEE ORIN
COP	JORDAN CHARNEY
BERNIE	TOM ALDREDGE
WOMAN AT BAR	ADELLE RASEY
PIOUS QUEEN	DAN BLY
TIGER	HENRY OLIVER
SHORE POLICE	HANK BRUNJES

PRODUCTION NOTE

The sets are as delicate as Japanese line drawings; they should be so abstract, so spidery, with the exception of Trinket Dugan's bedroom, that the audience will accept the nonrealistic style of the play.

The first set represents The Silver Dollar Hotel on South Rampart Street in New Orleans with the front wall lifted except for a doorframe to the lobby which contains only the desk and switchboard, stage left, a spring-ruptured old sofa, and a Christmas tree which has shed nearly bare of its needles. A few steps curve behind the back wall of the lobby indicating stairway to the floors above. The name of the hotel appears in pale blue neon above the skeleton structure a few moments after the curtain has risen on it.

The verses that appear preceding the play, after various scenes, and at the end of the play will be set to music and sung (probably *a cappella*) as "rounds" by a band of carollers. This band should comprise all the characters in the play and they will be signaled by a pitch pipe. Trinket and Celeste should sing in Trinket's room or as they descend the exterior stairs to the forestage.

*The Silver Dollar Hotel on South Rampart Street—the old
French Quarter in New Orleans. At the desk is seated the
night clerk, Bernie, in a swivel chair that leans way back, per-
mitting him to rest his feet on the low counter. He's reading a
comic book. If the switchboard buzzes, he can make a connection with very slight change of position. There is a spindling
outside staircase of gray wood to a landing on a level above.
For some reason, possibly because it used to be a private frame
residence, this stair-landing only has access to one room. This
favored room is Trinket Dugan's. As the curtain rises, we hear
the carollers sing the first verses of the carol.*

CAROLLERS:
I think the strange, the crazed, the queer
Will have their holiday this year
And for a while, A little while,
There will be pity for the wild.
A miracle, A miracle!
A sanctuary for the wild.

I think the mutilated will
Be touched by hands that nearly heal,
At night the agonized will feel
A comfort that is nearly real.
A miracle, a miracle!
A comfort that is nearly real.

The constant star of wanderers
Will light the forest where they fall
And they will see and they will hear
A radiance, A distant call.
A miracle, a miracle!
A vision and a distant call.

At last for each someone may come
And even though he may not stay,

It may be softer where he was,
It may be sweeter where he lay.
A miracle, a miracle!
Stones may soften where he lay.

[*The carollers finish and disperse. Celeste and her brother, Henry, appear before the hotel. Celeste is a short, plump little woman with a large bosom of which she is excessively proud, wearing low-cut dresses by night and day. She has hennaed hair with bangs and her muskrat jacket was discovered one lucky day in the window of a thrift shop. She has a passion for satins because they fit close and catch light, and pearls cannot be big enough to suit her. She has a very large purse, for shoplifting. Her age is fifty; her spirit, unconquerable.*]

CELESTE: Come on in with me, Henry.

HENRY: No.

CELESTE: Aw, just for a minute. I want you to meet the nice boy on the desk nights. [*She says this with eager cordiality which is rebuffed by her undertaker-brother.*]

HENRY: Look. [*He has produced a notebook and a Waterman pen which he received for Christmas when he was a child of ten.*] I'm gonna write down the address of the Rainbow Bakery for you and the name of the man to talk to when you get down there.

CELESTE: Oh, good, do that, Henry, dear! [*She squeezes his stiff arm against her.*] A girl never had a sweeter brother than you! Y'know that, Henry? How much I appreciate it?

HENRY: I know from experience how much good this'll do. You got no more idea of earning an honest living than flying to the moon.

CELESTE: I'm gonna surprise you, Henry.

HENRY: You got any decent clothes to go to work in?

CELESTE: Blood is thicker than water, ain't it, Henry?

HENRY: I'm not talkin' about blood. I asked if you got a suitable thing to wear to the bakery Monday after New Year's.

CELESTE: I know where I can pick up some real sweet little housedresses, for less than five dollars each and I'll pay you back out of my first week's wages, Henry.

HENRY: You think I'm fool enough to advance you cash for housedresses when right this minute you are staring over my shoulder at the bar on the corner? Now put this address in that suitcase you carry around like a purse. Hell. The size of that old purse would mark you as a shoplifter even if every store in town didn't already know you as one. [*He hands her the bakery address.*]

CELESTE: Don't have my "specs." What's it say?

HENRY: It says 820 Carondelet. That's on a corner, at Carondelet and Dauphine.

CELESTE: Rainbow Bakery, Carondelet and Dauphine, bright and early the first Monday after New Year's. Bless you, Henry, you old sweet thing, you!

HENRY: I'll see if the cook has some old white uniforms for you. You got to wear white in a bakery, I reckon. Well. . . . Oh, what name shall I tell this man when I phone him you're coming?

CELESTE: What name, why my own name of course, Celeste Delacroix Griffin! I'm not ashamed to work in a bakery, Henry, I don't have false pride about it.

HENRY: You don't have pride true or false about anything ever. That's not the point. The point is I don't want you using my name any more. Not there nor anywhere else. I got children growing up here. I don't want you using our name. So give me a madeup name for me to give Mr. Noonan.

CELESTE: —Oh! —Well, give him the name—Agnes Jones. . . .

HENRY: OK. Agnes Jones. [*He starts off abruptly, then stops at the exit and calls back to her.*] —I'll also tell Mr. Noonan that ten a week from your salary gets held back for me till I recover the full amount that it cost me to get you out of the jug.

CELESTE [*calling after him*]: See you for Xmas dinner tomorrow, Henry?

HENRY: I never want to see you again in my life, so bum your Xmas dinner off somebody else!

CELESTE: Henry, you don't mean that.

HENRY [*shouting back from a distance*]: Yes, I do!

CELESTE: —Yes, he does. Yes, I guess he does. . . . [*A cold wind whines: she raises her hands to her bosom, crossing her arms.*] Well, this time last year, on Xmas eve, Trinket Dugan and I were in her bedroom upstairs. [*On this cue, Trinket Dugan's bedroom is lighted at a low level and we see Trinket in a Japanese kimono, pale rose-colored, seated on the edge of a small, peeling-white, iron bed, holding a schoolchild's notebook on her lap, biting a pencil, about to make an entry in her diary. Her victrola is playing very softly by the bed. A gallon jug of California Tokay is on a tiny table: the wine catches the light with a delicate, jewel-like glow.*]

TRINKET [*aloud*]: Dear Diary! Dear Diary! —I have nothing to say. . . . [*She closes the book with a sigh and pours a glass of Tokay.*]

CELESTE: She's up in her room right now, and five will get you fifty, if I had five, that she's got herself a gallon jug of California Tokay. She's a terrible wino: can afford gin, drinks wine. . . . Well. She's rich and selfish. Purse-proud. But mutilated, oh, yes, ha ha, she's a mutilated woman. I know it, I'm the only one who knows it. —That's my ace-in-the-hole. I'm going up there now by these side stairs and offer the peace pipe to her, I'll tell her on the evening of Christ's birthday even a pair of old bitches like Trinket and Celeste should bury the hatchet, forget all past wounds that either's given the other, and drink a toast to the birth of the Babe in the Manger with a sweet golden wine, with Tokay. . . . [*The sound of drunk sailors singing is heard.*] Just a minute! —Business before pleasure. [*Bruno and Slim go by: she opens her mangy old fur to display her bosom but they pass right by, singing, as if she were invisible although she almost straddles the walk.*] Blind drunk! —Otherwise they would have noticed my bosom. Hell, even the sergeant on the desk when I checked out of the pokey took a good look at my bosom, didn't fail to observe it. Well, I'm mighty lucky to still be so firm-breasted when many women past forty or even thirty have boobs like a couple of mules hanging their heads over the top rail of a fence. [*She starts up the outside staircase but is distracted again by a street noise.*]

VOICE: *Bird-Girl, see the Bird-Girl, fifty cents, four bits to see the Bird-Girl!*

CELESTE: Oh-oh, oh-oh, Maxie and the Bird-Girl. [*She chuckles evilly.*] I can make out there if I play my cards right, he's gonna gather a crowd right on this corner, ah-*HAH!*

VOICE [*strident, approaching*]: See the Bird-Girl, two bits to see the Bird-Girl!

CELESTE: *OH*-oh! —Dropped the price! [*A fat man, Maxie, appears before the hotel with a cloaked and hooded companion who moves with a shuffling, pigeon-toed gait.*] Hi, Maxie! Merry Xmas, Bird-Girl!

MAXIE [*viciously, to Celeste*]: Git lost, yuh bum! —See the Bird-Girl, two bits to see the Bird-Girl uncovered, unmasked, the world's greatest freak attraction! [*A few drifters pause on the walk. A drunk staggers out of the Silver Dollar Hotel, digging in his pocket for a quarter.*]

85

CELESTE [*seeing the drunk is a live one*]: Shoot, that's no Bird-Girl, I know her personally. That's Rampart Street Rose with chicken feathers glued to her. It's a painful, dangerous thing, I know from experience, Mister. [*She turns to the Bird-Girl again.*] Hey, Rose, how much does Maxie pay you, how much is he payin' you, Rosie? [*Maxie raises a threatening hand over his head. The Bird-Girl makes angry bird noises.*] Maxie? Maxie? [*She rushes up close to him.*] I ain't gonna expose you, just give me five dollars, Maxie. I just got out of the pokey, gimme five bucks, will yuh? For a Xmas bottle? Huh, Maxie? To keep my mouth shut, Maxie?

MAXIE: I'll shut your fat mouth for you, for less'n five dollars!

CELESTE: Don't raise your hand at me, Maxie!

MAXIE: Go on, go on, get lost!

CELESTE: Why, I was the Bird-Girl myself! Have you forgotten I was the Bird-Girl myself? Got two-degree burns when you put that hot glue on me?

MAXIE: You want trouble? You want trouble, you want?

BIRD-GIRL: *Awk awk awk!*

CELESTE: No, I want two dollars and twenty cents to buy a half gallon of California Tokay.

[*A cop enters. The Bird-Girl whistles and croaks wildly as she flaps off.*]

COP: Break it up.

MAXIE: She's scared th' Bird-Girl away!

BIRD-GIRL [*offstage*]: AWK AWK AWK!

MAXIE [*running after her*]: Bird-Girl, hey, Bird-Girl! [*He whistles shrilly. The wind howls.*]

VERY FAST OVERLAPPED

86

CELESTE [*picking up a loose feather*]: Poor Rosie, she lost some feathers, ah, well that's life for you, tch, tch! If she was a bird, the humane society would be interested in her situation but since she's a human being, they couldn't care less. [*She turns to the Cop*]: How about that? I mean the irony of it? [*The wind whines coldly.*]

COP: Where you live?

CELESTE: My address? Here, right here! Hotel Silver Dollar.

COP: Get off the street. . . .

CELESTE: Aw, now really!

COP: I know you from night court, go in and stay off the street. [*He moves on. Another sailor appears: Celeste opens her coat, hopefully displaying her bosom.*]

CELESTE: Hello, there, Merry Christmas!

SAILOR [*shoving past her*]: Get lost. [*Her vivacious smile fades: she closes her coat like a book with a sad ending.*]

CELESTE: —I am. . . . [*She means lost.*] —When you're lost in this world you're lost and not found, the lost-and-found department is just the lost department, but I'm going in that lobby like I've just come back from the biggest social event of the Goddam season, no shit. . . . [*She starts to the door but freezes just outside it.*] Well, I'll count five and then enter. One. —Two. —Three. —Four. —Four and one-half. —Four and three-quarters. . . . [*Trinket starts a loud lively record on her victrola: four-four tempo—"Santiago Waltz."*] Hmm. Sounds like she's trying to boost her morale up there. I used to boost her morale. I'd say to her every day, forget your mutilation, it's not the end of the world for you or the world. Hell, I'd say, we all have our mutilations, some from birth, some from long before birth, and some from later in life, and some stay with us forever. Well, there's nothing like a week in the pokey to bring out the philosopher in you, but in me it's brought out the chicken in me, too. Scared to enter the lobby of a flea-bag. Four and seven-eighths. —No. Nope. —I need to be morally fortified before I count to five and face that lobby. . . . [*She turns to the outside staircase.*] —What'll I say to her? Well, I'll think of something when I—[*She goes on up to the landing and knocks at the outside door of Trinket's room.*]

TRINKET: Who's knocking at my door?

CELESTE: Me, Celeste, let's bury the hatchet for Christmas.

TRINKET: —We can't bury the hatchet. We hit each other too hard, and now it's too late to forget it.

CELESTE: Think of the wonderful times we had together!

TRINKET: They weren't wonderful times. We bummed around town together, I took you to breakfast, I took you to lunch, I took you to dinner. I took you to the movies. In return for all those favors, I just got envy, resentment, and sly insinuations that if I didn't go on sucking up to you, just for company in my time of despair, you'd give away my secret.

CELESTE: That's not true. No soul knows about your mutilation but me.

TRINKET: You kept reminding me of it. That no soul knew about my mutilation except Celeste. Why would you do that if you didn't mean to threaten me with exposure?

CELESTE: People don't trust each other. I was afraid you'd suddenly get tired of me, bored with me! Trinket? Let me in! I'm scared to pass through the lobby.

TRINKET: —They've checked you out, you've lost your room here, Celeste.

CELESTE: That's what I was afraid of: I suspected! —I see you're drinking Tokay. Let me in for a drink, it will give me the courage to face my situation in the lobby.

TRINKET: Celeste, we're through with each other. You know why. Remember the night you wanted to eat at Commander's Palace in the Garden District? I wanted to eat Chinese. . . . [*She starts addressing the audience instead of Celeste.*] I wanted some Moo Goo Gai Pan at the Chinese place on Dauphine Street. Oh, no, she said, no. If you want to eat boiled rats, go eat Chinese. —I wouldn't dream of it, I told her. Of course I knew two things: she couldn't afford a hamburger at the White Castle, and Moo Goo Gai Pan is made from water chestnuts, snow peas, and breast of chicken, one of the world's most famous and delicate dishes. I turned away from her and walked on without her toward the Chinaman's place. Pretty soon, in fact in less than a minute, I heard the rat-tat-tat of her high heels in pursuit. She caught my elbow. I faced her, her face was *livid* with *hate*. "Who knows except me about your mutilation? Have I ever exposed you?!" "Let me go, go, go, go," I said, "let me go! Go to Commander's Palace," I said, "or Galatoires and feast yourself on any dish you crave with imported wine, but go, go, go, let me go, I'm eating Chinese: I want to and I do what I want to!" —Know what she said, then, to me? *"Eat Chinese, you mutilated monster!"* —Well, that didn't improve our friendship. That terminated our friendship. Can you blame me? To taunt an old friend because of a mutilation in order to get a free meal in the place she wanted? [*Celeste resumes pounding at the stair-landing door.*] Go, go, go, go away, it's too late to bury the hatchet!

CELESTE: No, no!

TRINKET: Go, go!

CELESTE: Let me just pass through the room. People are kind at Christmas!

TRINKET: You just want to get in here because you can see this wine and you're a wino!

CELESTE: Me, a wino?

TRINKET: A notorious wino!

CELESTE: You call *me* a wino, sitting in there with your big economy jug of California Tokay, so big you can hardly carry it half a block down Rampart, you being too cheap to have it delivered to you? Ho-ho! [*She rattles the doorknob.*]

TRINKET [*springing up wildly*]: Go, go, go, go away, you merciless monster, before I call downstairs to get the police!

CELESTE: You fink, you freak! I'll get even with you, oh, will I ever get even with you, Trinket Dugan! Alias Agnes Jones! [*She rushes back downstairs and into the lobby with an air of bravado. Bernie, the night clerk, has his feet still propped on the desk and the comic book in his lap. Celeste is bold as brass.*] Hi, Bernie, Merry Xmas! Guess what's happened!

BERNIE: Yeah, you got sprung for Christmas.

CELESTE: Got what, Bernie, what, baby?

BERNIE: They let you out of the pokey for Xmas, did they?

CELESTE: Bernie, Bernie, you're lost in the comic-book world, God bless you and let me kiss you, you big sexy thing you, I could jump over this desk and just gobble you up. Oh, baby, let's have a quickie right now, in a vacant room.

BERNIE: —I got a message for you.

CELESTE: Boy, oh, baby, have I got a message for *you!*

BERNIE: Yeah, I bet, but the message I got for you is your stuff's locked up, and is gonna be held in storage till you've paid up your bill here.

CELESTE: —I don't understand this message.

BERNIE: Repeat it to yourself a couple of times and maybe you'll understand it.

90

CELESTE: You said my stuff—locked up? My personal belongings, no, I don't get this message, it's such a peculiar message that I could repeat it over and over and still be mystified by it.

BERNIE [*making switchboard connections*]: Aw, come off it, everyone knows that knows you that you've been in the House of Detention, because you got caught shoplifting at Goodman's department store Monday. You're coming down fast in the world, you used to shoplift at the Canal Street stores and—

CELESTE: What a lie, who said so?

BERNIE: It come out in the papers. *Picayune, Item* and *States.*

CELESTE: Show me the item so I can call my lawyer.

BERNIE: I don't save clippings, press clippings, for kleptos, sister.

CELESTE: It was a false accusation to begin with. My brother, Henry Delacroix Griffin, set them straight and also has got me a job, that's the news, the message, I rushed in here to let you be first to know of it.

BERNIE: It's about time you quit hustling, not because you think so but because the guys you hustle for the price of a bottle or a couple of drinks have eyes to see you with, sister, and what they see is a wino, long in the tooth.

CELESTE: Is this any way to talk to a girl at Xmas?

BERNIE [*with an amiable grin*]: Aw, no, face it, you can't make it, Celeste, can't even get away with a little shoplifting at Christmas.

CELESTE [*grandly*]: Give me the key to my room, I don't want to stay in this lobby.

BERNIE: You don't have a room here no more. You been checked out and your stuff locked up in the basement by order of Katz.

91

CELESTE: Katz wouldn't do this to me. When did he do this to me?

BERNIE: When it come out in the papers that a lady identifying herself as Miss Agnes Jones had been arrested shoplifting.

CELESTE: —Agnes Jones is who? Not me!—sounds like a made-up name. My name is Celeste Delacroix Griffin.

BERNIE: Yeah, but we were tipped off that you give a made-up name when the cops picked you up and it's Agnes Jones.

CELESTE: —Who told you such a false story?

BERNIE: Trinket, your old friend, Trinket, saw the newspaper item about your shoplifting rap and said, "Agnes Jones? It's Celeste!"

CELESTE: Me? Agnes Jones? Not me! Agnes Jones is the name she gave at Mercy Hospital when she—I never spoke of it before. She used the name Agnes Jones for her secret operation. [*There is a pause: contemplation.*] I got to go upstairs, I got to go to the little girls' room a minute.

BERNIE: Use the toilet down here.

CELESTE: Get crabs for Christmas? I don't want crabs for Christmas. You use it if you want to be infested with crabs but I'm going to the upstairs john. [*She crosses to the stairs off the lobby and goes up. Bernie answers a switchboard call.*]

BERNIE: Silver Dollar Hotel. —No, gone. —I said GONE. — People *go!* —Checked out of here and left no forwardin' address. Sorry, Merry Christmas. . . . [*The switchboard rings again as Bernie is plugging out. He answers this second ring.*]

TRINKET [*at the phone in her room*]: Bernie, is she down there? I mean Celeste.

BERNIE: She's not in the lobby right now.

TRINKET: Good! Then I can come down. I don't want to run into her. [*Bernie plugs out. He unpeels a candy bar and starts munching on it slowly with lazy enjoyment. Celeste returns to the desk with an oddly accomplished smile, more than a mere visit to the "loo" would account for.*]

CELESTE [*excitedly malicious*]: —I see there's been a Christmas celebration. Was it organized by Trinket Dugan? Did she put on her Santie Claus suit and ring a cowbell under that sorry tree? I never seen a worse-decorated tree, broken ornaments on it and needles already shedding, it sure looks sad. —Sample bottles of cheap perfume for the ladies and dime-store ties for the gents? Ha ha! Christmas is something you got to do big or don't do it. [*There is a pause. Bernie munches his candy bar. Celeste hugs her bosom as if she were still on the chilly street. She watches him munching slowly at his candy bar as he reads a book of cartoons.*] Whatcha eatin', Bernie, a candy bar? [*Bernie barely grunts.*] What kind of candy bar is it? O Henry? Baby Ruth? [*Picking up the candy wrapper.*] Aw. A Mr. Goodbar. I never have had one of them. I'm a Hershey milk-chocolate girl. The only thing better than a Hershey milk-choc-late bar is a Hershey almond bar, Bernie. They used to come in the fifty-cent size, when I was in convent school. A girlfriend of mine and me would buy us that fifty-cent bar and eat away on it all afternoon. —Dibs on the last bite, Bernie. Huh? Dibs on the last bite, Bernie? They give me the cold-turkey treat-ment in the pokey, and that, that—treatment, it—it leaves you with an awful craving for sweets. . . —My mouth is watering, Bernie!

BERNIE: —Yeh, well, swallow or spit. . . . [*He finishes the bar and leans back in his swivel chair, eyes falling shut.*]

CELESTE: —In summer the chocolate sticks to the candy wrapper but in the winter, the wrapper comes off clean . . . [*She licks a tiny bit of chocolate off the candy wrapper.*] —It sure comes off clean in winter. . . .

93

BERNIE [*sleepily*]: Why don't you give up?

CELESTE: Give up, did you say? An easy piece of advice to give but not to follow. [*She moves back to the ruptured sofa under the Christmas tree, removes from the tree a garland of popcorn, and munches it as she speaks.*] Give up? My life? Oh, no. I still have longings, and as long as you have longings, satisfaction is possible. Appetites? —Satisfaction's always possible, Bernie. Cravings? Such as a craving for sweets or liquor or love? Satisfaction is still possible, Bernie, and on a give-and-take basis. Why, just today a man was talking to me. He didn't look in my eyes. He kept his eyes on my breasts. At last I laughed, I said, "Touch 'em, they won't break, they're not soap bubbles and they're not a padded brassiere." —Bernie? —Bernie! —How would you like a quickie in my old room? It wouldn't be the first time, would it, Bernie?

BERNIE: Give up.

CELESTE [*sitting back down*]: —Give up is something I never even think of. I'll go on—not to the Rainbow Bakery after New Year's, that's not for me. —I'm too imaginative to fool with bread. Bread is something that has to be broken in kindness, in friendship or understanding as it was broken among the Apostles at Our Lord's Last Supper. Gee, the cold-turkey treatment sure does leave you hungry and with such a craving for sweets that if I was employed right now at the Rainbow Bakery, the doughnuts and pastry and fruitcakes, cream puffs and—last year Trinket Dugan had some little fancy cornucopias full of hard candy on the tree, now just stale popcorn. —Katz is a long man to wait for. . . . When do you think he'll —[*Trinket enters the lobby by the interior stairway, she is wild-eyed, shaken. Celeste has snatched up an old copy of the* Saturday Evening Post; *she has raised it to cover her face but is peeking over the top of the dirty cover.*]

BERNIE [*making a switchboard connection*]: Silver Dollar.

TRINKET [*faintly*]: Bernie?

CELESTE [*giggling*]: —What a funny cartoon! You can't beat the cartoons in the *Saturday Evening Post!*

BERNIE [*into the phone*]: No such party here. Nope, no such party. [*He unplugs.*]

TRINKET [*louder*]: Bernie! May I speak to you, please?

BERNIE: Sure. What?

TRINKET: Come outside for a moment. This is private, Bernie.

BERNIE: I can't leave the switchboard, Miss Dugan.

TRINKET: I think you'd better. This is a serious matter. I can't speak to you about it in front of that woman.

CELESTE: What a funny cartoon, it's a scream, ho ho ho!

TRINKET: This is something that may call for legal action.

CELESTE [*turning a page*]: Here's another funny one, ho ho ho!

TRINKET: On several occasions I found signs that my bedroom had been entered while I was out. Not by the hall door but by the outside entrance, from the stairs outside. The lock wasn't broken. It was entered by someone who held a key to that entrance. Only one person did. Consequently I knew who'd been coming in. Still I refrained from reporting it to the police: out of pity, Bernie, I made no report, no complaint, although the sneak had been drinking up my wine and picking up money that I deliberately left on the bureau, out of pity. This is a person, Bernie, that I have befriended over a long, long period. You might say supported, even. Bernie, you know that I could afford to stay at a first-class hotel but I've stayed here out of loyalty and friendship. I dressed that Christmas tree. I bought a gift for everyone registered here and put them under the tree.

95

To all employees I passed out a five-dollar gold piece. I pity transients at Christmas. This hotel is full of derelicts, Bernie, lost, lonely, homeless at Christmas. [*Her voice is high and shaky.*] Heaven knows what secret sorrows they carry with them! And very few care!

CELESTE [*throwing down the magazine*]: Bernie, get her some music to go with that speech!

TRINKET [*her voice rising*]: I've been lucky, financially. I'm not boasting about it. I feel humbly grateful about it. My daddy left me three oil wells in West Texas; one is bone-dry right now, one comes in now and then but the number three well is a gusher, it's a continual gusher. Now, Bernie. I'm not purse-proud. See this? [*She removes a large wad of paper money from her purse.*] —I never walk out of the Silver Dollar Hotel without a wad of money that you could choke a horse with. That's not what I do with it, though. I have a horde of friends in financial trouble. As long as they're loyal to me, I'm devoted to them. I give out gifts called loans, expecting no repayment, except in friendship, Bernie. Bernie, go up to the stair landing and see what some vicious person has scratched on the wall up there. It has to come off right away.

BERNIE: Something's written up there?

TRINKET: No, not written, scratched, I said, scratched, probably with a nail file.

BERNIE: Well, I'll go take a look.

TRINKET [*breathlessly*]: Yes, please do, thank you, Bernie. [*He goes up the few steps that curve behind the back wall of the lobby.*]

CELESTE [*in a fierce whisper*]: I told you I'd get even. This is just the beginning.

TRINKET: Yes, I knew who did it.

CELESTE: I spent every day for years, for years!

TRINKET: Living off me!

CELESTE: Cheering you up, getting you out of depression, distracting you from your mutilation, you know it! [*Bernie comes back to the lobby.*]

BERNIE: Miss Dugan, I seen it but I don't know how to remove it because it's scratched in the wall.

TRINKET: Cover it with something, with a, with a—with a "no smoking" sign.

BERNIE: The only sign we got's a "no loitering" sign in the downstairs washroom and it wouldn't make sense on the landing.

TRINKET: Cover it up with this calendar. [*She points to a pictorial calendar over the desk.*]

BERNIE: I don't have no thumbtacks here.

TRINKET: Use adhesive tape, then.

BERNIE: Don't have that neither.

TRINKET [*putting money in his hands*]: Run to the drugstore next door and get some adhesive tape, fast as you can. Nobody must go up or down those stairs till that vicious lie about me is covered up. Hurry. Otherwise the Silver Dollar Hotel will lose its only good tipper. And for New Year's I'm planning to pass out presents again!

BERNIE: OK, OK.

TRINKET: I'll watch the switchboard for you. [*Bernie goes out. There is a dead silence in lobby. Trinket speaks without looking at Celeste.*] If I were you, I wouldn't sit there much longer.

CELESTE: The calendar won't stay up.

97

TRINKET: If it doesn't, I'll know who's taken it down and I'll take action.

CELESTE: What action?

TRINKET: *Action!*

CELESTE: How do you know it won't appear other places? There's other places, it might break out like a plague.

TRINKET: Yes, in the House of Detention! Print it on the walls in the House of Detention, cover the prison walls with it!

BERNIE [*returning*]: Got it.

TRINKET: Here's the calendar: *hurry!* [*Bernie goes up the short curving flight of steps and disappears behind the back wall of the lobby. The two women are silent.*]

CELESTE [*rising from sofa*]: How much a discount do you get on a Xmas tree from last year? I'm covered with needles off it. [*She brushes herself elaborately.*]

TRINKET: I would like for you to return me the key to my outside entrance. I'd be much obliged if you hand it back to me right now so I won't have to put a padlock and a burglar alarm on that door.

CELESTE: I thrown it away long ago.

TRINKET: You know I know that's a lie, and let me warn you that if tonight I discover any evidence that you've been in my room while I'm out, you'll find yourself right back in the House of Detention, yes, right back there tonight.

CELESTE: Tonight I'll be at my brother's for eggnog and fruit-cake. Huey P. Long will be there. I love the Kingfish and he seems to find me amusing.

TRINKET: Who *doesn't* find you *absurd!*

CELESTE: Uh-huh, well, I won't be alone with a continual gusher of jealousy in my heart, tonight and all other nights, forever and ever, Amen. [*Bernie returns to the lobby.*]

BERNIE: OK, I got it covered.

CELESTE: So long, Agnes Jones. [*She exits to the street.*]

TRINKET [*to Bernie*]: You don't believe it, do you? That vicious lie about me?

BERNIE: Hell, Miss Dugan, I got my own business to mind.

TRINKET: —I—*can't imagine! Impossible to imagine*—malice like *that!* [*The lobby dims out as she goes out to the street and the carollers sing.*]

On the forestage is a bench in Jackson Park. Behind it, on the scrim, is a projection of the equestrian statue of Andrew Jackson. Trinket enters and sits on the bench, stiffly.

TRINKET: It's going to take me a little while to recover from that shock. I'm still shivering from it. Yes, I felt close to panic, but now I'll get hold of myself. —Why do I care so much? There's nothing shameful, nothing criminal about an affliction, a—mutilation. . . . [*She shakily lights a cigarette.*] I am *not* Agnes Jones, I am Trinket Dugan, and *I have absolutely no intention of giving up, not a bit in the world, wouldn't dare to or—care to!* —Tonight I'll drive out Agnes Jones, I'll do it right now. How? I'll walk around this bench and when I've walked around it, Agnes Jones will be out of me and never get back in! [*She springs up. The sudden action makes her dizzy: she falls back onto the bench and gasps for breath. Then she rises and starts a slow march about the bench.*] Out, Agnes Jones, out, Agnes Jones, out Agnes Jones. [*She has returned to the front of the bench.*] There, now. It's such a clear, frosty night, I can see my breath in the air and, yes, I'm calming down now. I knew I would and I am. [*She sways a bit and falls back onto the bench. Now she speaks in a different voice: harsh with anger and self-contempt.*] —In the afternoons, old people with nothing else to do come here and stay and stay till the sun is fading away. When they leave here, I come here. I'm the night bench-sitter of Jackson Square. The gates are closed at midnight. It's nearly midnight. My hands are still shaky. It's time for me to go to the Cafe Boheme and have my absinthe frappé at a corner table with an empty chair across from me. Over-tipping as if it was necessary to apologize for sitting alone at a table meant for two. *Two!* In life there *has* to be two! —The old winter voice of Agnes Jones is still in me. I said OUT, Agnes Jones, out, out, out and stay out! Once more around the

100

bench. [*She marches around the bench again.*] —But of course
I do have to prepare myself for the possibility that Celeste will
be in the Cafe Boheme tonight, and when I come in, is likely
to make a vicious remark of some kind. Oh, I'd—sink through
the floor, I'd never be able to enter the place again! —OUT,
AGNES JONES! [*She arrives in front of the bench.*] —Such
a clear, frosty night. Andrew Jackson is all wet, shiny green
like he'd rode up out of the sea. Oh, with so much beauty
around me, yes, still, even now, why should I have room in me
for the ugly, cowardly voice of Agnes Jones. Too much solitude can be corrected, yes, it *must* be corrected. I will correct
solitude by—what? —Why not enter the Cafe Boheme tonight
like a gladiator, shouting: "Here I am, the mutilated Trinket
Dugan alias—Agnes Jones!" No! Impossible! Couldn't! Not
necessary! She can't prove the mutilation unless I expose it to
someone. Oh, but not daring to expose the mutilation has made
me go without love for three years now, and it's the lack of
what I need most that makes me speak to myself with the
bitter-old, winter-cold voice of—Agnes Jones: LOVE! —a
hand on my *breast.* . . . [*She makes a sound like a hooked fish
would make if it could make a sound. She rises, then sits back
down: she gives way not to despair but to some inner convul-
sion which makes her produce these dreadful soft cries. They
are accompanied by abrupt, indecisive movements to rise or
reach out or— Gradually they subside: she pulls herself together.*] No. No more negative thoughts. Tonight I'll give
myself the Christmas gift of a lover, yes, I'll find him tonight
and he will be—beautiful! Perfect! —Perhaps he'll be kind,
even, so kind I can tell him about my—mutilation. [*She acts out
the admission.*] "There's something I feel I should tell you before I—before we—" COULDN'T—get the words out! —Oh,
but I'll think of something, if I find him tonight, if that miracle
happens tonight at the Cafe Boheme!

VOICE [*offstage*]: Gates closing!

101

TRINKET: Gates closing, must go. . . .

[*She leaves as the bench is dimmed out. The carollers enter.*]

CAROLLERS:
The lost will find a public place
Where their names are not unknown
And there, oh, there an act of grace
May lift the weight of stone on stone.
A miracle, a miracle!
The finding of a love unknown.

Oh, but to love they need to know
How to walk upon fresh snow
And leave no footprint where they go,
Walking on new-fallen snow.
A miracle, a miracle!
No footprint on new-fallen snow.

The wounded and the fugitive,
The solitary ones will know
Somewhere a place that's set apart
A place of stillness cool as snow.
A miracle, a miracle!
A place that quiets the outraged heart.

It may be in a public park
That has a bench that's set apart,
And not by daylight, after dark,
With winter mist upon the park.
A miracle, a miracle!
A mist that veils a winter park.

The park bench is removed and the scene becomes the interior of the Cafe Boheme. The bar is shaped like a horseshoe; inside is standing Tiger, the proprietor, who was formerly a boxer and a seaman and who is now in his fifties. About the bar are several patrons. The sound of an ambulance is now receding into the distance. Trinket Dugan appears in the lighted area.

TRINKET: Merry Christmas! [*She gets no response. Has Celeste been there, talking against her? She is uncertain whether to stay in the bar, but where else is there to go? Nowhere. She slips quietly, then, to a solitary table, beside the bar. . . . There is a slight pause.*]

WOMAN AT BAR: I can't believe it! Can you? Alive and laughing one second, dead the next!

PIOUS QUEEN [*at the bar*]: He told a very sacrilegious story.

TIGER: Hell, don't you think that God has a sense of humor? Ted just laughed a little too loud and bust a blood vessel. Maybe God laughed too.

WOMAN AT BAR: And "bust a blood vessel" too?

TIGER: —It wasn't a bad way to go.

TRINKET [*sitting up straight and stiff and calling out shrilly*]: WHO DIED? DID SOMEBODY DIE?

TIGER: Yeah, somebody died, so he died. Somebody always dies, don't he? What yours, Trinket? Name your drinks, everybody, it's all on the house in memory of the deceased. [*They murmur their drinks. Trinket calls out hers as loudly as if she was furious over something: a hand has risen to her mutilated bosom.*]

TRINKET: Absinthe frappé, please, Tiger! [*The old electric piano is started again: it plays another ragtime tune or medley, starting with "Under the Bamboo Tree," as two sailors enter. One is short, named Bruno, one tall, called Slim. Everyone turns to glance at them: it's the tall one they look at, because he shines like a star. Suddenly, Trinket calls shrilly.]* "Tiger, Tiger, burning bright!"—I need my absinthe frappé!

SLIM: Is this the place?

BRUNO: Yeh, yeh, this is the place.

SLIM: Where is he?

BRUNO: What're you shouting about?

SLIM: Why should I whisper, what's there to whisper about?

BRUNO: Don't make you'self conspicuous in this place.

SLIM: Why? Is they somethin' wrong with it?

BRUNO: No. They's nothin' wrong with it except it's special. You notice how quiet people are?

SLIM: Yeah. The place is spooky. Why's a place so quiet on Xmas Eve?

BRUNO: Sit down at the bar.

SLIM: Where's your rich friend, is he here or not here? I want to go if he ain't.

BRUNO: We are ten minutes early.

TIGER: Boys, you can't stay here. This place is off limits to the Navy.

BRUNO: We're just lookin' for someone.

TIGER: Who're you lookin' for, Mac?

BRUNO: —A—a—fellow I met on my last liberty here.

TIGER: What's his name?

104

BRUNO: His name was Ted.

TIGER: If you mean Ted Dinwiddie, Ted Dinwiddie is dead.

BRUNO: No kidding.

SLIM: Jesus, come on, let's go. I knew somebody had died here.

WOMAN AT BAR: He died here tonight. Screamed and fell off that barstool an hour ago.

PIOUS QUEEN: This one, right next to me.

WOMAN: Th' coroner said he was probably already dead when he hit the floor. . . .

TRINKET [*rising and crossing to the bar*]: That is no way to break the news of a death!

SLIM: He died and he's dead, let's go.

BRUNO: Hell, I need a drink first.

TRINKET: The news of a death is shocking to anyone living and it ought to be broken more gently.

BRUNO: Gimme a C.C. and Seven.

TIGER: I told you, you're off limits here.

PIOUS QUEEN [*rising from the barstool*]: Boys, boys, I have a room next door and I can provide you both with civilian outfits. In civvies, you know, you can go anywhere in town.

TRINKET: Your clothes wouldn't fit these boys. I have a better suggestion. [*She grips Bruno's elbows.*] Get your buddy outside, I'll wait by the door. [*She goes out of the bar. The electric piano starts up and the voices fade as Trinket departs. She waits tensely on the forestage, then suddenly runs back into the bar, calling out—*] Shore Police are coming!

SLIM: I got no liberty pass.

TIGER: Go out the back way.

BRUNO: I got a liberty pass, I'll go out front. Slim, you go in the "head." [*The light on the bar area dims out as the sailors run in separate directions. Bruno, the short sailor, comes out and stands beside Trinket.*]

TRINKET: Here they come. [*She means the Shore Police: she advances to intercept them as the lights dim out.*] Merry Christmas, boys.

As the scrim closes and lights come up on forestage, the Shore Police ignore Trinket and ask to see Bruno's liberty pass which he produces very slowly.

TRINKET: —He's got his pass: he is my little brother, we are just standing here discussing where to go next.

SHORE POLICE: Yeah, well, don't go in here, this place is off limits.

TRINKET: Oh, we're not going in that bar, we're going to the —the cathedral for the midnight candlelight service. Aren't we, Buddy?

BRUNO: Yes, ma'am. —Sister. [*The Shore Police "case" the bar; they look offstage and then depart.*]

TRINKET: —That's that. Now get your buddy.

BRUNO: I don't wanna insult you, but we're not out looking for whores.

TRINKET: Oh, I'm not insulted, I'm—flattered, but you couldn't be more mistaken. Here, looky here. [*She opens her purse and produces a roll of large bills.*] —See this roll of greenbacks? You could choke a horse with it, if you wanted to choke a horse, but who wants to choke a horse. So money isn't my problem, my problem is not economic, my problem is— [*She raises a trembling hand to her left breast.*]

BRUNO: Is what?

TRINKET: —Human, a human problem. Only one person knows it besides myself. Only one other person in the world knows about it but me.

BRUNO: What's your problem?

TRINKET: This other person who knows it was a person I trusted, but now, just tonight, she betrayed me: in such a horrible way, she— [*She clenches a gloved fist in the air.*]

BRUNO: Are you scared to tell me this problem?

TRINKET: It's a thing, it's a thing, a— [*She can't force herself to confess it.*]

BRUNO [*chuckling*]: Everything is a thing.

TRINKET: This is a thing that—

BRUNO: You got a nice little body—have you ever done it outdoors?

TRINKET: What? No!

BRUNO: I've done it outdoors in the Quarter. You just slip between two buildings, out of the light, and it's just as private as it would be in your room.

TRINKET: You're talking about alley cats, and you don't understand: I'm attracted to your friend, I'm waiting out here for him. Get him out of the bar before the wolves snatch him away.

BRUNO: Him? Slim? He's ignorant like a baby. I'm experienced at it.

TRINKET: Slim, his name's Slim?

BRUNO: Forget him.

TRINKET [*calling out*]: Slim! Slim! [BRUNO *makes another effort to put his hand under her cape. She cries out in panic.*] Stop it! I'm mutilated! [*At this exact moment Celeste's loud, drunken voice is heard.*]

CELESTE: Jingle bells, jingle bells, jingle bells, jingle—bells— jingle—bells. . . . [*It seems to be all she remembers of the song.*]

TRINKET: Oh, God, it's her, it's Celeste, stand in front of me, hide me! [*She clutches Bruno by the lapels of his pea jacket and draws them about her, pressing her face to his chest as Celeste appears and stalks across the forestage, still tonelessly singing.*]

CELESTE: Jingle bells, jingle bells, jingle bells, jingle bells, jingle all the—jingle all the—*wayyyyy!* [*On the word "wayyyyy," she arrives at the lamp post and turns front, opening her coat, her eyes very wide in a farcically lascivious way. She must be trying to attract the attention of someone across the street. Then she resumes the hoarse, toneless chant and stalks off.*]

TRINKET: —Ahhh, God, has she gone? That awful demented creature goes singing at night through the Quarter to catch the attention of near- and far-sighted drunks, and when they hear her in the Cafe Boheme, they all laugh, they all say, "There goes old Madame Goat." Did she see me, she didn't see me, did she? If she'd seen me, she would have shouted a criminal slander about me for which I would have her locked up. Now! Quick! Find your buddy! It's him that I want for Christmas! [*She moves a few steps from Bruno, so that the rest of the speech will seem addressed to herself, rhapsodically.*] Tall, crowned with gold that's so gold it's like his head had caught fire, and I know, I remember the kind of skin that goes with flame-colored hair, it's like snow, it's like sunlight on snow, I remember, I know! [*Slim appears with Celeste, entering from the left. She is stoutly supporting his tall, wobbly frame. Trinket cries out—*] Oh, God, he's been snagged by an old wino, get him away from her, quick! That woman's criminal, a shoplifter, a convicted klepto, evicted, takes old men up alleys for the price of a drink!

CELESTE: *I heard that remark, Agnes Jones!* [*She squares off like a bull about to charge. There should be flashes of bluish-white light on the stage as if an acetylene torch, a soundless one, was drilling the street, throwing fantastically long, tall shadows over the street-fronts. Inside the bar, the electric piano plays a paso-doble.*]

TRINKET: Just out of jail, less than an hour ago, I swear, I swear! Get him away from her quick, quick! She is infested with vermin, lice, LICE!

CELESTE: *I heard that remark!* [*She stamps like a bull pawing the earth before charging.*]

BRUNO: Slim? Hey, Slim! [*But Bruno doesn't approach Celeste who stands guarding Slim.*]

TRINKET [*in a transport, an ecstasy of fury*]: Don't just *call* him, go *GET* him!

CELESTE: *Try.* He's felt my *bosom!* He's felt my *breasts, both* of them!

TRINKET [*wildly*]: *Shut up, for God's sake, be still!* [*Celeste spits at her from a distance.*] SHE SPITS! —Where's the toad? Wherever a witch spits it produces a *toad!* [*Bruno is amused, now, chuckling drunkenly. Slim rests against the proscenium, with a weak, vague grin.*]

SLIM: Cat-fight.

BRUNO: C'mon, this one here's got money.

SLIM: Aw, frig 'em all.

TRINKET: Oh, I—have a *warning* for you! Celeste? Let me give you this warning! I have engaged the biggest lawyer in town, a criminal lawyer, that never loses a case and I will spare no expense, *no expense!* —to have you committed to the State Hospital for the CRIMINAL INSANE! —Bread and water, not wine! That's what you'll— [*Celeste suddenly charges forward and snatches Trinket's purse from her.*] *Thief, thief, stop thief!* [*With an Indian war whoop, Celeste has dashed offstage.*

110

Slim slides slowly down the proscenium edge till he sits against it. There is a change of light and music. The electric piano goes into a number such as "Please Don't Talk About Me When I'm Gone."] Hah! She snatched an empty purse! I had my money out, look, here, in my hand! [*She holds up her roll of bills.*] —Now, hurry, catch us a taxi before I die on this corner! [*Bruno is getting Slim onto his feet, with soothing, affectionate murmurs as the carollers assemble on the forestage and sing.*]

CAROLLERS:

For dreamers there will be a night
That seems more radiant than day,
And they'll forget, forget they must,
That light's a thing that will not stay.
A miracle, a miracle!
We dream forever and a day.

Now round about and in and out
We will turn and we will shout.
Round about and in and out
Again we turn, again we shout.
A miracle, a miracle!
A magic game that children play.

[*The forestage dims out as the carollers disperse.*]

Trinket's bedroom is lighted, as she comes up the outside stairs with Slim, who is leaning heavily on her.

TRINKET: Well, here we are. Did you think we'd ever make it?

SLIM: Yeh, I thought we'd make it.

TRINKET: I wasn't so sure. I mean that we'd make it together. But here we are, together. This is my—little home. . . .

SLIM: Not much to it.

TRINKET: No, there's not much to it, but it's—familiar, it's—home. I lived here before my father's good luck in the oilfields and I became so attached to this room that I stay on and on. You know, you can love a room you live in like a person you live with, if you live with a person. I don't. I live alone here. I have the advantage of a private, outside entrance, and that's an important advantage, especially if I, when you—have a guest with you at night. I don't, you, uh, don't—always want to have to go through the hotel lobby which I'd have to do at any big hotel with—

SLIM: —With house dicks in it?

TRINKET: With anyone, everyone in it.

SLIM: [*suspiciously*]: Hmmmm.

TRINKET: You're so tall you make the ceiling seem low. Take off your coat and sit down.

SLIM: Not till I make up my mind if I want to stay here or not.

TRINKET [*nervously*]: Oh.

112

SLIM: "Oh." I can take care of myself in this situation or any Goddam situation that that wop Bruno's ever gotten me into. Las' week-en' he innerduced me to a rich ole freak that had a two-story apartment at the Crescent Hotel. I looked around and I was alone with this freak. I said to the freak, "Something's not natural here," an' the freak said to me: "I'm your slave! I'm your slaaaa-ve!" —I said "OK, slave, show me the color of your money!"

TRINKET [*sadly*]: Oh.

SLIM: What do you mean by "oh"?

TRINKET: I just mean oh.

SLIM [*broodingly*]: Oh. Then the rich freak says, "Master, I am your slave. My money is green as lettuce and as good as gold." I said, "Slave, forget the description, lemme see it. — Show me the color of your money!"

TRINKET: —Are you speaking to me, or—?

SLIM: I'm telling you something that happened las' week-en' which cost me home leave for Chris'mas. This character, this freak, fell down on her knees an' said: "You hit me, oh, boo, hoo, you hit me." I hadn't touched this freak. But then I got the idea. The freak wanted me to hit her. "OK, slave, get up." The freak got up and I shoved her into a gold frame mirror so hard it cracked the glass. "Now, slave, I don't wanna hear a description of your money, I wanta see it." —What're you messing aroun' with over there?

TRINKET: Me?

SLIM: You.

TRINKET: I'm boiling some water to make you some instant coffee. [*She comes from behind an ornamental screen or hanging.*]

113

SLIM: Are you having a heart attack?

TRINKET: Oh, no! Why? Why?

SLIM: You keep a hand over your chest. [*He reaches out to pull her hand away. She gasps and retreats.*]

TRINKET: *No, no, no, no, no!* [*In panic, to divert him, she snatches a photograph from the dresser.*] Look at this! Would you recognize me? In this newspaper photo I am standing between the Mayor and the president of the International Trade Mart. Then, at that time, I was in the field of public relations, I was called the Texas Tornado. I planned and organized the funeral of Mr. Depression, yes, I had the idea of burying Mr. Depression, holding an exact imitation of a funeral for him. All civic leaders backed me. There was a parade, I mean a funeral procession—*no, no, no, no, no!* [*He has stretched his hand out again to remove her hand from her chest.*] —For, for Mr. Depression! [*It should be apparent that this was the climax of her life.*]

SLIM: There's something not natural here.

TRINKET: Oh? No! —Mr. Depression was carried along Canal Street and up Saint Charles with big paper lilies on his twelve-foot coffin and there was a band playing a funeral march and I led the band, I walked in front of it dressed like a widow sobbing in a black veil. [*He reaches again for her hand still clasped in panic to her chest.*] *No, no, no, no, no!* —It went, the procession went, all the way to Audubon Park: and then can you guess what happened? [*Slim, weaving, pays no attention to this.*] —It rained like rain had never fallen before upon the earth! Cats, dogs, crocodiles—ZEBRAS! The procession broke up, band quit, everything dissolved, dispersed in the cloudburst!—Kettle's whistling. . . . [*She rushes back of the screen or hanging.*]

SLIM: Morbid!

TRINKET [*rushing back out*]: Here, but let it cool first before you— [*He takes the cup and empties it on the floor.*] —Oh, you spilt it, I'll— [*She rushes back of the screen and back out with a towel, mops up the spilt coffee.*] —Now I'm no longer in public relations at all, it seems like another life in another world to me. It's hard to imagine the energy, confidence, drive I had when I first hit this town. Personalities go through such radical changes when something happens to change the course of their lives. Don't they? Haven't you noticed? [*There is a pause between them. Celeste appears before the hotel. She has two purses: Trinket's and hers. She stands at the foot of the outside stairs to Trinket's room and stamps her foot twice.*]

SLIM: There's somethin' Goddam wrong here, peculiar, not natural, morbid.

TRINKET: —I don't know what it could be except that you won't sit down and you won't take coffee. —Is it something about me? I'm a simple, ordinary person, and you're my guest and I'm your friend, not your slave. I've always maintained that this city is hard on the unformed characters of young people that come here, especially if they, oh, now, please sit down! Do! I'd be so happy!

SLIM: I don't sit down and stay down in any morbid place till I know if I want to stay in it. Be my slave. And show me the lettuce color of your money. —Good as—gold. . . .[*Celeste remains at the foot of the stairs. She stamps her foot twice more.*]

TRINKET [*in a shamed voice.*]: It's green as lettuce and it's— good as my father's continual gusher in Texas. . . . [*Celeste stamps her feet twice more and tosses Trinket's purse onto the sidewalk. She stamps on the purse.*]

CELESTE [*in a strange chanting voice, separating each syllable*]: Sa-rah Bern-hardt had one leg.
The oth-er was a wood-en peg.

115

But good she did, yep, she did good,
Clump-ing on a STUMP OF WOOD!

[*She throws back her head and laughs at the sky.*]

TRINKET: It's a pity so many people choose the night of Our Savior's birth to behave in such a— [*Celeste kicks Trinket's purse into the orchestra pit as a policeman comes on.*]

POLICEMAN: Move along.

CELESTE: That's just what I'm doing. [*She goes off one way, the policeman the other.*]

SLIM: What've you got to drink here?

TRINKET: You don't want more to drink, Slim.

SLIM: Don' argue with me or I'll throw you across a room an'—

TRINKET: Oh, Slim, you don't mean that. You only say that because I'm afraid your friend has led you into the wrong kind of company, Slim. Oh, your hair is red gold, red gold, your skin is like—sunlight on snow. . . .

SLIM: Liquor! Out with it! Quick, before I—

TRINKET: I have nothing but wine here.

SLIM: Produce it, out with it, quick, before I—break you a —mirror!

TRINKET: No one can frighten me, Slim, but— [*She pours a glass of wine from her crystal decanter.*] —here!

SLIM: You take a drink of it, first, I'm takin' no chances.

TRINKET: Why, thank you, I will, I can use it. [*She sips the wine, then offers the glass to him.*]

SLIM: Pour me a clean other glass. I don't wanna drink outa yours an' catch somethin' morbid.

116

TRINKET: You mustn't talk like that to me, even though you don't mean it. Do you know how long it's been since a man has been in this room? Several years. And it seemed like a lifetime—a *death* time. [*Celeste marches into sight again, stops at the foot of the stairs, and stamps her foot twice as if about to commence the formal parade of a palace guard.*]

SLIM [*falling onto the bed*]: I'm paralyzed here in a morbid —situation. . . .

[*Celeste opens her huge purse and removes a key: then she mounts the stairs, saying "Clump!" with each step. Trinket gasps and rushes to bolt the outside door. Celeste tries the door with her key: no luck: then she throws back her head like a dog yowling at the moon and she cries out—*]

CELESTE: Agnes—*JOOOOOO—OOOOOnes!*

TRINKET: Yes, it's the whore that snatched my purse on the street! [*She gasps and turns out the light as if that would protect her from Celeste's maniacal siege.*]

CELESTE: You'll find your empty purse outside in the gutter where I kicked it, you FINK! It's got your rosary in it an' your father's picture standin' next to his GUSHER! You better come out an' get it before the trash-man sweeps it into a sewer!

TRINKET: Celeste, go back to the House of Detention and ask for medical help there. You are out of your mind, howling like a mad dog on my stairs!

CELESTE: You told Bernie and Katz I'd been to jail, you fink.

TRINKET: You scratched a hideous lie on the stairs about me!

CELESTE: I scratched the truth about you! You got two mutilations, not one! The worse mutilation you've got is a crime of the Christian commandments, STINGINESS, CHEAPNESS, PURSE PRIDE! Your rosary's in the gutter with your

117

GUSHER! Goddam, you got me thrown out, out, out! [*She stamps her foot with each "out."*] And everything that I owned locked up in a basement!

TRINKET: You know what you did, I don't have to remind you, and now go back down the stairs before I— I have the phone in my hand! [*She has picked up the telephone.*]

CELESTE: FINK, MUTILATED FINK!

TRINKET [*into the telephone*]: BERNIE! [*Celeste runs down the stairs. At the bottom, she stops and looks up sobbing at the sky, weeping like a lost child. There is a pause, a silence. Celeste approaches the orchestra pit, stoops, her hand extended. The purse is handed back to her from below. She returns sobbing to the bottom of the outside staircase; she removes the rosary from Trinket's purse and begins to "tell her beads," sobbing.*] I believe she—

SLIM: —I'd a-been home for Christmas an' not broke Mom's heart if I hadn' gone AWOL las' week-en' but 'stead of home I'm paralyzed here in a morbid situation with a morbid hooker an' Goddam Bruno's gone where?

TRINKET [*at the telephone*]: Bernie? Trinket! [*Bernie is lighted dimly at the switchboard in the lobby.*] —Be a doll, Bernie, and fetch me two hamburgers from the White Castle and a big carton of black coffee, and hurry back with it. This is a five-dollar tip night for you, Bernie. [*Celeste stands shivering in a blue spotlight at the foot of the outside stairs.*]

CELESTE: Anyhow, I'm not mutilated. She is. [*Bernie walks past her to the White Castle.*] Bernie? —Sweetheart? [*He ignores her as he goes. Slim falls back onto the bed, Trinket unties his shoes.*]

SLIM [*falling asleep*]: Morbid, unnatural—slave. . . .

TRINKET: Oh, please stay awake with me!

118

SLIM: Ah-gah-wah. . . . [*He rolls away from her and begins to snore.*]

TRINKET: —Well, anyhow, I have somebody here with me. Celeste's alone but I'm not, I'm not alone but she is.

CELESTE [*sinking onto the bottom step of the outside stairs*]: No, I'm not mutilated. She is. [*Trinket switches on the radio: it's soundless.*]

TRINKET: —The candlelight service is over. —The Holy Infant has been born in the manger. Now He's under the starry blue robe of His Mother. His blind, sweet hands are fumbling to find her breast. Now He's found it. His sweet, hungry lips are at her rose-petal nipple. —Oh, such *wanting* things lips are, and such *giving* things, breasts! [*The carollers have quietly assembled before the hotel. As the bedroom scene dims out, they begin to sing.*]

CAROLLERS:
I think for some uncertain reason
Mercy will be shown this season
To the wayward and deformed,
To the lonely and misfit.
A miracle! a miracle!

The homeless will be housed and warmed.

SINGLE CAROLLER [*stepping out of the group*]:
I think they will be housed and warmed
And fed and comforted a while.
And still not yet, not for a while
The guileful word, the practiced smile.

CAROLLERS:
A miracle! a miracle!
The dark held back a little while.

[*They disperse.*]

Daylight comes. Celeste is on the sofa under the Christmas tree, snoring and sighing, her huge purse in her lap. Then Trinket's bedroom is lighted. She is in a kimono, seated on the bed. Slim enters from the hall.

TRINKET: Good morning. I thought you'd gone. [*He grunts disdainfully and turns away from her to comb his hair.*]

SLIM: —You got some free publicity on the bathroom wall down the hall there. It says if you don't mind sex with a mutilated woman, knock at room #307, which is this room number.

TRINKET: Oh. —How horrible of someone. I think I know who it is, the monster that did it.

SLIM: —Where's my wallet?

TRINKET: I *know* I know who did it, the monster last night.

SLIM: You're talking about one thing, I'm talking about another. You being mutilated is your own business except it's a stinking trick to take a fellow to bed without letting him know he's going to bed with someone mutilated. [*She begins to gasp "Ah," first very softly, then building to a scream. He claps his hand over her mouth as Bruno rushes into the room. Slim releases Trinket.*] Hey, Bruno, this Goddam lunatic rolled me! [*Trinket plunges toward the open wall of the room. The sailors drag her back. She writhes grotesquely in their grasp, then collapses to the floor.*] She's got my wallet with eighty-six dollars!

BRUNO: Have you got rocks in your head?

SLIM: I got no rocks in my head, she's got my wallet.

BRUNO: Lady, are you okay? [*Trinket moans, crouching by the bed. Bruno hisses at Slim.*] You lack decent human feelings!

120

—You lack—[*He picks up Trinket and puts her on the bed.*] Are you all right? Are you all right? Huh, Miss?

TRINKET [*faintly*]: —Yeah. . . .

BRUNO [*to Trinket*]: Are you sure you're all right?

TRINKET: Get him out of here, will you?

BRUNO [*to Slim*]: Come out in the hall, rock-head.

SLIM: I got no rocks in my head, she's got my wallet, that mutilated whore has got my wallet, hid somewhere in this fly-trap!

BRUNO: That woman ain't got your wallet, you gave your wallet to me to hold for you, rock-head.

SLIM: I'll count the money left in it. [*They have started to leave.*]

BRUNO: This is the last time I go out on liberty with you, never again, never under any conditions, no time, ever! [*During this, Trinket has been slowly lifting a trembling hand to her breast.*]

TRINKET: —Ahhhh! [*She opens her diary.*] —Dear Diary, the pain's come back.

[*The singers enter from the wings. The pitch pipe is blown but no one sings. They're waiting for someone. He enters from the upstage door of the hotel lobby, in a black cowboy's suit, with diamond-like brilliants outlining his shirt pockets, belt, holster and the edge of his wide-brimmed hat. The pitch pipe is blown again.*]

CAROLLERS:
I think—

[*There is a long pause: the pitch pipe is blown.*]

I think—

121

[*Long pause: the leader blows long and hard on the pitch pipe.*]

I think—

[*The leader hurls his pitch pipe to the floor. Then the black-clad cowboy, Jack In Black, steps forward and sings alone with a hand on his holster.*]

JACK IN BLACK:
I think the ones with measured time
Before the tolling of the bell
Will meet a friend and tell their friend
That nothing's wrong, that all goes well.

CAROLLERS:
A miracle, a miracle!
Nothing's wrong and all goes well.

JACK IN BLACK:
They'll say it once and once again
Until they say it to themselves,
And nearly think it may be true,
No early tolling of the bell.

CAROLLERS:
A miracle, a miracle!
Nothing's wrong, all is well!

Later that day: it is silver dusk; there is a murmur of rain. Trinket is dimly lighted in her bedroom: Bernie is back at the switchboard. Celeste is still on the sofa.

TRINKET [*at the telephone*]: Is she still down there, Bernie?

BERNIE: Her? [*He leans forward in his swivel chair to look.*] —Yeah. . . .

TRINKET: What's she doing, Bernie?

BERNIE: Nothin'. Sittin'.

TRINKET: She can't sit down there forever, or can she, Bernie?

BERNIE: No. Katz don't like it. He told me to git her out and I said then git me a stick of dynamite, will yuh.

TRINKET: —I have been thinking things over this afternoon, Bernie, and Celeste is not a mentally grown-up person. She's mentally retarded. You know that, Bernie? Irresponsible. Childish. She doesn't examine her actions, she can't distinguish between a right and wrong thing, she acts impulsively, Bernie, like children do. You know how children act. Impulsively, thoughtlessly, Bernie? Her shoplifting, for instance, is the act of a child. She sees a thing, she wants it, she picks it up. Like a child picks a flower. . . .

CELESTE [*rousing slightly*]: What's she sayin' about me?

TRINKET: Bernie, you can't hold malice against a child for bad actions. No matter how much it hurts you, you know the limitations and you forgive. —Bernie, tell her to come on up to my room and have a glass of wine with me. I want to bury the hatchet.

CELESTE [*rising heavily*]: What's she saying, huh, Bernie?

123

BERNIE: Excuse me, Miss Dugan. [*He turns to Celeste.*] You got a invitation. Miss Dugan wants you to have a glass of wine upstairs with her.

CELESTE: —Never! —I still have pride!

BERNIE: Yeah, she's comin', Miss Dugan.

CELESTE: Never! I'd sooner die!

BERNIE: G'bye, Miss Dugan. [*He hangs up and leans back again with his comic book.*]

CELESTE [*She draws her ratty fur coat about her and stalks outside. There is no hesitation. She goes straight up the outside stairs to Trinket's. Hearing her approaching footsteps, Trinket unlocks the outside door. Celeste enters with an air of dignity.*] I just come up here to tell you my friendship isn't for sale. [*But her eyes gravitate to a cut-glass decanter of Tokay on the table. She stops speaking, her eyes gleam and jaws hang ajar. . . .*]

TRINKET: —It must be raining out there. Your coat looks wet. Let me hang it up by the heater to dry.

CELESTE: Aw, yeah. Thanks. [*Her eyes glitter, fastened on the California Tokay.*]

TRINKET: Sit down, dear. Would you like a glass of Tokay?

CELESTE: Aw, yeah! Thanks!

TRINKET: Help yourself, please. I filled the cut-glass decanter. There's more in the jug.

CELESTE: Where's the jug?

TRINKET: It's right under the table.

CELESTE: Aw, yeah—thanks!

TRINKET: —Well, it seems like old times.

124

CELESTE: You used to keep those little sweet biscuits, you know, the—

TRINKET: The vanilla cream wafers? Nabiscos?

CELESTE: Yes, yes, Nabiscos!

TRINKET: It's possible I still have some.

CELESTE [*half rising with excitement*]: You kept them in a tin box, a round—

TRINKET: Yes, in this round tin box. Let's see if there's any left in it.

TRINKET: Why, yes!

CELESTE: Aw! Good! It's hard to beat a Nabisco vanilla wafer in the way of a sweet cake or cookie.

TRINKET [*with a little shuddering cry of horror*]: There's a dead cockroach in the box!

CELESTE: Now, now, now, now, it's just a dead bug in a box, give me the box, I'll get rid of the bug! [*Celeste picks the bug out of the box.*]

TRINKET: Not in the room, out the door!

CELESTE: OK, OK, out the door! [*She tosses the bug out the door and immediately starts munching a wafer.*]

TRINKET [*sadly, imploringly*]: Oh, Celeste! You mustn't eat after a cockroach, you can't eat after a cockroach! Don't, please, eat after a cockroach!

CELESTE: Honey, in the best restaurants people eat after cockroaches! Hey! Let's bum around town tomorrow! Huh? Huh? Yeah, we'll bum around town and have lunch together at Arnaud's. Oysters Rockefeller? Yeah, yeah, to begin with! Then a shrimp bisque and—

125

TRINKET: TODAY I FOUND!

CELESTE: —What? You said you found something today?

TRINKET: Today I found! —A *scorpion* in my bed. . . .

CELESTE: —Is that a insect? Forget it. —Well, then, after Arnaud's—a movie? An afternoon at the movies with a large size Hershey, a big Hershey almond bar, huh? Then home together. Trinket, we got to pick up the thread of our old lives together. It's essential, necessary, we got to! —And go on and on and on and on, like it was! —Because we were happy together before we hurt each other and all that's finished, we won't hurt each other again as long as we live, will we, dear? Uh-uh! —Music? A little radio music?

TRINKET: —I think we ought to go out after while to hear the boys' choir sing at the cathedral. The Christmas afternoon Mass.

CELESTE: M'clothes are too wet to go out again tonight, Trinket. Get the boys' choir on the radio, honey.

TRINKET: The cathedral service is peaceful.

CELESTES Well, light a candle and let the boys' choir sing on the radio, dear.

TRINKET: No, it's not the same thing. Christ is present, Christ and Our Lady are present in the cathedral, but here. . . . [*A drunken sailor stumbles up the steps. Hearing their voices, he stops, tries the door and knocks.*]

CELESTE: —Somebody's at the door, Trinket . . . [*Her voice is already slurred by the Tokay.*]

TRINKET: —The hotel is full of drunk sailors on leave. Don't let him in, he'll drink the wine up on us.

CELESTE: I'll just peek out.

126

TRINKET: No, don't *you*, let *me*. I won't admit a drunk sailor after last night. [*She peeks out but the sailor has stumbled back off. She shuts the door.*] —Nobody.

CELESTE: But you opened the door for someone that knocked and how do you know that that someone didn't come in?

TRINKET: Make sense, please. How could he? Where would he be? We'd see anybody that entered.

CELESTE: Not necessarily, Trinket. I've always believed in invisibility. I've always had faith in invisi-*bee*-able *presence!* [*She rises and faces the audience with a mysterious air.*]

TRINKET: [*skeptically*]: Oh, Celeste, I—

CELESTE: Not so loud.

TRINKET: I remember when you used to see colored aureoles around people's heads, and—

CELESTE: Not aureoles, *auras.*

TRINKET: Yes, auras, different-colored auras and you'd tell their fortunes and characters by the color of the aura. You said mine was purple.

CELESTE: Stop talking. Be still. Act naturally. Give the presence a chance to manifest itself. It will. It's still in the room. Have a little wine, dear. [*She refills their glasses. Jack In Black enters the lobby from the upstage opening. He lounges, smiling, in the downstage entrance. A distant bell starts tolling. Celeste's voice and manner become even more mysterious.*] There was an elderly sister at Sacred Heart Convent School that received invisible presences, and once she told me that if I was ever cut off and forgotten by the blood of my blood and was homeless alone in the world, I would receive the invisible presence of Our Lady in a room I was in. She said that I would smell roses.

127

I smell roses. She said I would smell candles burning. I smell burning candles. She said I would smell incense. I smell incense. I would hear a bell ringing. I hear a bell ringing. [*More singers appear from the wings.*] —I feel it, yes, I feel it, I know it! Our Lady's in the room with us. She entered the room invisible when you opened the door. You opened the door of your heart and Our Lady came in! [*She falls to her knees.*] MARY? MARY? OUR LADY? [*Then, in a loud whisper*]: Trinket, kneel beside me! [*Trinket hesitates only a moment, then kneels beside Celeste. There has been a gradual change of light in the room: it now seems to be coming through stained glass windows —a subjective phenomenon of the trance falling over the women. Celeste stretches out a hand as if feeling for the invisible presence. She suddenly cries out and draws back her hand as if it had touched the presence.*]

TRINKET: *What, what?*

CELESTE [*sobbing and rocking on her knees*]: I touched Her robe, I touched the robe of Our Lady!

TRINKET: *Where is it, where is the robe of Our Lady?*

CELESTE: *Here!* [*She seizes Trinket's hand and draws it forward.*]

TRINKET [*fallen into the trance*]: *Here?*

CELESTE: *Yes, there! Kiss the robe of Our Lady!* [*Both women stretch their hands out and draw them back to their mouths as if kissing the robe.*]

TRINKET [*crying out wildly*]: *The pain in my breast is gone!*

CELESTE: *A miracle!*

TRINKET: *Finally!*

CELESTE & TRINKET [*Together*]: *Finally, oh, finally!*

128

JACK IN BLACK [*singing alone*]:
And finally, oh, finally
The tolling of a ghostly bell
Cries out farewell, to flesh farewell,
Farewell to flesh, to flesh farewell!

OTHER SINGERS [*with him*]:
A miracle, a miracle!
The tolling of a ghostly bell.

[*Celeste and Trinket begin to sing with them*]:

SINGERS [*without soloist*]:
The tolling of a ghostly bell
Will gather us from where we fell,
And, oh, so lightly will we rise
With so much wonder in our eyes!
A miracle, a miracle!
The light of wonder in our eyes.

[*Jack In Black crosses through them, smiling and lifting his hat.*]

But that's a dream, for dream we must
That we're made not of mortal dust.
There's Jack, there's Jack, there's Jack In Black!

JACK IN BLACK:
Expect me, but not yet, not yet!

CHORUS:
A miracle, a miracle!
He's smiling and it means not yet.

[*The bell stops tolling.*]

JACK IN BLACK [*singing alone*]:
I'm Jack In Black who stacks the deck,
Who loads the dice and tricks the wheel.

129

The bell has stopped because I smile.
It means forget me for a while.

CHORUS:
A miracle, a miracle!
Forget him for a little while.

[*Jack In Black moves his lifted hat from left to right in the style of a matador dedicating his fight to the audience.*]

THE CURTAIN FALLS

I CAN'T IMAGINE TOMORROW

CHARACTERS

ONE, *a woman*

TWO, *a man*

I CAN'T IMAGINE TOMORROW

One and Two are, respectively, a woman and a man approach-
ing middle age: each is the only friend of the other. There are
no walls to the set, which contains only such pieces of furniture
(a sofa, a chair, another chair on the landing of a low flight of
stairs, a lamp table and a card table) that are required by the
action of the play. There is a doorframe far down stage left.
Soft blue evening dusk is the lighting of the play, with soft
amber follow spots on the players. The sofa and chairs should
be upholstered in satin, pastel-colored, perhaps light rose and
turquoise. Beside the chair on the stair landing there might be
a large potted palm or fern. The woman, One, stands down-
stage, near the doorframe, with her arms spread apart as if she
were dividing curtains to look out a window. She wears a white
satin robe with a wine stain on it. The man, Two, appears
before the doorframe; the woman draws back and covers her
face with her hands. Two raises an arm as if to knock at a
door. This action is repeated two or three times before the
woman crosses to the doorframe and makes the gesture of
opening the door.

ONE: Oh, it's you.

TWO: Yes, it's me.

ONE: I thought so. [*There is a strangely prolonged silence,*
during which neither moves.] You have on your ice-cream
suit. [*Two laughs at this, embarrassed.*] Well, don't just stand
there like a delivery boy without anything to deliver.

TWO: You didn't say come in.

ONE: Come in, come in—enter!

TWO [*entering*]: Thank you. [*There is another strange pause.*]
As I came up the drive I saw you at the window. Then you
closed the curtains.

133

ONE: What's wrong with that?

TWO: I had to knock and knock before you—opened the door.

ONE: Yes, you nearly broke the door down.

TWO: I wondered if—

ONE: If what?

TWO: You didn't want to—to—

ONE: Want to what?

TWO: —to see me this—this evening.

ONE: I see you every evening. It wouldn't be evening without you and the card game and the news on TV.

TWO: But—

ONE: It's not getting any better, is it?

TWO: What?

ONE: I said it's not getting any better, your difficulty in speaking.

TWO: It will. It's—temporary.

ONE: Are you sure? It's been temporary for a long time now. How do you talk to your students at the high school, or do you say nothing to them, just write things on the blackboard?

TWO: No, I—

ONE: What?

TWO: I've been meaning to tell you. It's been five days since I've met my high-school classes.

ONE: Isn't that strange. I thought so. I thought you'd stopped. What next? Something or nothing?

TWO: There's always—

ONE: What?

TWO: Got to be something, as long as—

ONE: Yes, as long as we live.

TWO: Today. Today I did go.

ONE: To the clinic?

TWO: Yes. There.

ONE: What did you tell them? What did they tell you?

TWO: I only talked to the girl, the—

ONE: Receptionist?

TWO: Yes, she gave me a paper, a—

ONE: An application, a—

TWO: Questionnaire to—

ONE: Fill out?

TWO: I— I had to inform them if I—

ONE: Yes?

TWO: Had ever before had—

ONE: Psychiatric?

TWO: Treatment, or been— hospitalized.

ONE: And you?

TWO: Wrote no to each question.

ONE: Yes?

TWO: No.

ONE [*impatiently*]: Yes, I know, you wrote no.

135

TWO: Then the receptionist told me—

ONE: Told you what?

TWO: There wasn't an opening for me now, right now, but— I'd be informed as soon as— one of the—

ONE: Doctors?

TWO: Th— *therapists* could— fit me into his— *schedule.*

ONE: Did you tell her you were a teacher and the situation was desperate because you can't talk to your classes?

TWO: She was just the receptionist so I— didn't go into that. But I put on the, the—

ONE: Questionnaire?

TWO: That there was only one person that I—could still talk to—a little. I underlined desperately and I underlined urgent.

[*He pauses. Abashed, he turns away slightly.*]

ONE [*gently*]: In this dim light you could pass for one of your students, in your ice-cream suit, just back from the cleaners.

[*She drifts away from him.*]

TWO: On the way coming over I passed a lawn, the lawn of a house, and the house was dark and the lawn was filled with white cranes. I guess at least twenty white cranes were stalking about on the lawn.

ONE: Oh? So?

TWO: At first I thought I was seeing things.

ONE: You were, you were seeing white cranes.

TWO: I suppose they were migrating on their way further south.

136

ONE: Yes, and stopped off on the lawn of the dark house, perhaps to elect a new leader because the old one, the one before, was headed in the wrong direction, a little disoriented or losing altitude, huh? So they stopped off on the lawn of the dark house to change their flight plans or just to feel the cool of the evening grass under their feet before they continued their travels.

TWO: It's only a block from here. Would you like to go over and see them?

ONE: No. Your description of them will have to suffice, but if you would like to go back over and have another look at them, do it, go on. I think they'd accept you in your lovely white suit.

TWO: The maid didn't come today?

ONE: She came but couldn't get in, the door was bolted.

TWO: Why?

ONE: I didn't want her fussing around in the house. She knocked and called, and called and knocked and finally gave up and—went away. . . .

TWO: Everything's just like it was yesterday evening. The cards are still on the table. You still have on your white robe with the wine stain on it.

ONE: I've stayed down here since last night. I haven't gone upstairs. I finished the wine and I slept on the sofa. Oh. No supper tonight. None for me. I did go into the kitchen and opened the Frigidaire, but the sight and smell of the contents made me feel sick. So go in the kitchen and make yourself a sandwich or whatever you want while I deal the cards.

TWO: I'll make something for us both.

137

ONE: No, just for yourself! Do you hear me? And eat it out there, in the kitchen. [*He goes out of the lighted area. She wanders back to the windowframe and draws her hands apart as if dividing curtains.*]—Dragon Country, the country of pain, is an uninhabitable country which is inhabited, though. Each one crossing through that huge, barren country has his own separate track to follow across it alone. If the inhabitants, the explorers of Dragon Country, looked about them, they'd see other explorers, but in this country of endured but unendurable pain each one is so absorbed, deafened, blinded by his own journey across it, he sees, he looks for, no one else crawling across it with him. It's uphill, up mountain, the climb's very steep: takes you to the top of the bare Sierras. —I won't cross into that country where there's no choice anymore. I'll stop at the border of the Sierras, refuse to go any further. —Once I read of an old Eskimo woman who knew that her time was finished and asked to be carried out of the family home, the igloo, and be deposited alone on a block of ice that was breaking away from the rest of the ice floe, so she could drift away, separated—from—all. . . . [*Two returns with a plate of sandwiches.*] Back, back, take it back or I'll send you away!

TWO: Are you—?

ONE: I am, I told you!

TWO: If you won't eat, I won't either. I'm not hungry tonight.

ONE: *I can't!*

TWO: What?

ONE: Play cards. I can't, I can't. Sorry, forgive me, I can't.

TWO: —I think you—

ONE: What?

TWO: —want me to go. . . .

ONE: Where to, where would you go?

TWO: I could—go to my room.

ONE: You say it's not air-conditioned, there's no TV, it's so small you feel suffocation when you're in it.

TWO [*sadly*]: There's a TV set in the lobby of the hotel.

ONE: You've told me you can't stand the lobby of the hotel, it's full of dying old women that crowd around the TV as if they got their blood and their oxygen from it. The lobby of that hotel, just passing through it, its atmosphere rubs off on you and you come here carrying it with you, you come here like a sick dog after passing through that lobby, it's in your eyes, your voice, your, your—manner. When you knock and I open the door, you have a sick, frightened look as if you thought I'd slam the door shut in your face. You poor, dear little man! [*She suddenly catches hold of him with a sobbing intake of breath.*] I don't have the strength any more to try to make you try to save yourself from your—paralyzing—depression! Why don't you stop looking like a middle-aged lost little boy? It makes it so hard for me to talk honestly to you! [*She catches a loud breath and pushes him away, turning her back to the table.*] Every evening you have a frightened, guilty expression. I always say, "Oh, it's you," and you always say, "Yes, it's me." And then you put on that painful, false, sickly grin, blinking your eyes, your hands stuffed in your pockets. You teach school, but you've never got out of school, you're still in the—primary grades of—grammar school, or still in kindergarten. Oh, it's you, yes, it's me. My God, can't there be some other greeting between us? It would be better if you just stepped in and sat down to eat and then dealt out the cards or turned on television. But, no. We have to repeat the ritual, oh, it's you and yes, it's me, there's almost nothing else said, at least nothing else worth saying. I force myself to carry on a sort of monologue, with a few interjections from you, such as

"Mmmm" or "Mmm-hmmm." And I tell you things I've told you so often before I'm ashamed to repeat them. But I have to repeat them or we'd just sit together in unbearable silence, yes, intolerable silence. Yes, and in summer, you say, "It's so nice and cool in here," and in winter you say, "It's so nice and warm in here." Oh, God, God. . . . [*She catches his shoulders, presses her head a moment to his back: then thrusts him away.*]

TWO: It never was easy for me to—

ONE: To talk?

TWO: As long as I can remember it was difficult for me.

ONE: To talk?

TWO: —To put what I think and feel into speech.

ONE: And even to look in the eyes of another person?

TWO: —Yes. To look in the eyes of another person, that, too.

ONE: You always look a little to the side with a guilty expression. What makes you feel guilty? Is it just being alive?

TWO: —I—

ONE: —You?

TWO: —don't really know. . . .

ONE: Take this piece of paper and this pencil and write me the first thing that comes into your mind. Quick. Don't stop to think. [*Two scratches something on the paper.*] Good. Let me see what you wrote. "I love you and I'm afraid." —What are you afraid of? Quick. Write it down. [*He scratches something on the paper again. She snatches the paper from him.*] "Changes." —Do you mean changes in yourself or in me or changes in circumstances affecting our lives? Quick, write it down, don't think. [*He writes again.*] "Everything. All." —Yes, well, I knew that about you from the beginning. Now

140

I'll be it; I'll write down the first thing that comes in my mind. Pencil. Quick! [*She writes rapidly on the sheet of paper and thrusts it toward him across the card table.*] Read it, read it out loud.

TWO: [*reading aloud*]: "If there wasn't a thing called time, the passing of time in the world we live in, we might be able to count on things staying the same, but time lives in the world with us and has a big broom and is sweeping us out of the way, whether we face it or not."

ONE: Well? Why don't you say something? —Nothing? Take the pencil and paper, write down anything, something, quick, don't stop to think. [*He writes.*] "I love you and I'm afraid." —That's what you began with.

TWO: You said not to stop to think.

[*She reaches out to caress his face across the table. He catches hold of her hand and presses it to his mouth, then goes around the table to kiss her. She clutches his head against her for a moment, then thrusts him away.*]

ONE: Sit back down where you were. There's no way back there, believe me. [*He drops his face into his hands.*] —Are you crying? [*He shakes his head.*] Let me see. Look up. [*He drops his face into his hands.*] Don't look so tortured. —Did you eat in the kitchen? —No? —Then stop by the drugstore on your way back to the hotel mortuary and have a sandwich or something. It might be a good change for you, better than nothing. People need little changes now and then, and have to make them or accept them. I know some people are terrified of changes, hang on to repeated routines. I think it gives them a sense of being protected. But repetition doesn't make security, it just gives a feeling of it. It can't be trusted. You can walk one street every day and feel secure on that street, and then one day it collapses under your feet and the sky goes black.

141

TWO: —We have to—

ONE: We have to what?

TWO: —try not to—

ONE: What?

TWO: —think about that. It doesn't—

ONE: What?

TWO: —help to—

ONE: What?

TWO: —think about that, it's better to—

ONE: What?

TWO: —to feel—

ONE: What?

TWO: —protected, even if—

ONE: What?

TWO: —the feeling can't be—

ONE: What?

TWO: —trusted.

ONE: You completed a sentence. It wasn't easy for you, but you got through it. Now please get me a glass of water for my drops. [*Two crosses from the card table into a dim area.*]

TWO: [*to himself*]: I can't imagine tomorrow. [*He returns with a glass of water.*] —Shall I put the drops in the water for you?

ONE: Yes. Thank you.

TWO: It says on the bottle five drops.

142

ONE: Tonight it has to be more.

TWO: Are you—

ONE: What?

TWO: —sure?

ONE: Give me the glass, the bottle, I'll do it myself. [*Two counts the drops aloud. One goes on. He seizes the bottle from her and places it on the table out of the lighted area.*] All right, come back, sit down. [*He returns to the card table.*] I'm going to tell you a story. [*She drinks the glass of water as she speaks.*] —It's about a small man. Well? Aren't you going to sit down? [*He takes a chair at the table.*] —A small man came to the house of Death and the uniformed guard at the gate asked him what he wanted. He said that he wanted Death. The guard said that's a very large order for a small man like you. The small man said yes, he knew it was a large order, but it was what he wanted. The guard asked for his documents. The only document he had was his birth certificate. The guard looked at the date on the birth certificate and said: Too early, you've come too early, go back down the mountain and don't come up here again for twenty years. The small man started to cry. He said: If you won't let me in for twenty years, I'll wait twenty years at the gate, I can't go back down the mountain. I have no place down there. I have no one to visit in the evening, I have no one to talk to, no one to play cards with, I have no one, no one. But the guard walked away, turned his back on the small man and walked away, and the small man, who was afraid to talk, began to shout. For a small man he shouted loudly, and Death heard him and came out himself to see what the disturbance was all about. The guard said the small man at the gates had come twenty years too early, and wouldn't go back down the mountain, and Death said: Yes, I understand, but under some circumstances, especially when they shout their heads off at

143

the gates, they can be let in early, so let him in, anything to stop the disturbance. Well? What do you think of the story?

TWO: It's, uh—

ONE: It's uh what?

TWO: Did you make up the story?

ONE: No. You made it up. You've been making it up for a long time now. It's time to send it out for publication. Don't you think so?

TWO: I, uh—

ONE: I uh what?

TWO: Let's—

ONE: Let's what?

TWO: Tonight you—

ONE: Tonight I what?

TWO: —you seem—

ONE: What?

TWO: —not as well as you—

ONE: Not as well as I what?

TWO: —not as well as, not as well as— [*He springs up with a soft, tortured outcry.*]

ONE: Yes. I know. I know. You didn't eat anything, did you? No. You must stop at the drugstore on your way back and have something to eat at the soda fountain. They serve all kinds of things there and it's a popular place. You might even strike up an acquaintance with someone else eating there. When I go there for my prescriptions, I notice there's usually several people eating there at the soda fountain. I've heard them talk

144

to each other. They seem to be acquainted with each other. It's easier to become acquainted with someone at a soda fountain than at a table in a restaurant because you're sitting beside them and a restaurant table is separate. And I think it's important for you to strike up some new acquaintances. Because it's possible that some evening I won't hear you when you knock at the door. I might be upstairs and not want to come down or not feel able to come down to the door when you knock, and in that— [*She closes her eyes and clenches her teeth in a spasm of pain.*] —in that—possible—eventuality—you should —have—other—acquaintances—to fall back on, in that case, if it comes.

TWO: I think you're still in pain. Aren't you?

ONE: If I am, it's my pain, not yours, and I have the right not to discuss it, don't I? I think a person in pain has the privilege of keeping it to himself. But try out the drugstore tonight and don't go in there with a long face, go in there with a bright attitude and sit next to someone that seems to have an extrovert air about them. Say something first, don't wait for them to say something to you because they might not do it. I know you will hate to talk, but you have to do things sometimes that are difficult for you, so go in there and sit at the soda fountain and have a milk shake and talk, speak, open your mouth even if you just open your mouth to say you heard an owl tonight, imitating your voice in a palm tree. Of course they won't believe you, but that could lead to an interesting conversation.

TWO: I think what you mean is—

ONE: What I mean is—things have to change in life.

TWO: The changes don't have to be sudden.

ONE: The changes are much easier to accept when you've already prepared yourself for them. That's why I mentioned the drugstore soda fountain.

145

TWO: It's bright and noisy and I would never be able to strike up an acquaintance at a bright, noisy soda fountain, I wouldn't know how and wouldn't want to attempt it.

ONE: Up till a year ago—

TWO: What?

ONE: What was I saying? Oh. Up till a year ago—

TWO: What?

ONE: Never mind. Whatever I was saying has flown out of my head.

TWO [*after a pause*]: Do you want me to slip away now?

ONE: Slip away is a way of saying dying. [*She sits up.*] I've changed my plans for the night. I'm going upstairs, after all. I can still get up them if I take my time about it and hold onto the banisters. I can get up to the landing and rest there a while and then climb the rest of the way. And as for you, don't forget my advice to strike up some new acquaintances. It doesn't have to be at the soda fountain, it could be at a bar. Say something to somebody. That's my advice, but I can see it's wasted.

TWO: An acquaintance isn't a friend.

ONE: Who is a friend? Let it go. But eat something at the drugstore on your way back.

TWO: Shall I help you upstairs before I—?

ONE: Lately I've been sleeping down here on the sofa. The stairs have gotten much steeper. But tonight I think I'll get up them. I'll climb to the landing first and then I'll rest there a while before I go on. There's a fairly comfortable chair on the landing that I can rest in till I feel able to go up the second flight. [*She goes up three or four steps to a platform and a chair.*] Yes, I can rest here a while.

146

TWO: I'll stay till you've gone to your bedroom. Then I'll slip out.

ONE: No, don't wait. Slip out now. I like to talk to myself a little before I sleep.

TWO: You mustn't sleep on the landing, you can't sleep on the landing.

ONE: I'll do what I want to do!

TWO: I'm sorry, I—didn't mean to tell you what you—

ONE: Go on, slip out now. Fasten the bolt on the door.

TWO: The bolt is inside the door.

ONE: Oh. —Yes. You're right. That changes my plans a little, yes, I'll have to bolt it myself.

TWO: I don't think you ought to be left alone here at night.

ONE: That's your opinion, not mine. Good night, go on, slip away now, the evening has been an effort.

TWO: I'm—sorry, I—feel as if you'd lost all feeling for me. . . .

ONE: That isn't true. I wouldn't have let you enter the house tonight if I didn't still love you. I did and still do. But we've gone into different countries, you've gone into a strange country and I've gone into another.

TWO: Could I stay on the sofa?

ONE: No, no, I'm sorry, no. You have to go, now.

TWO: You are—

ONE: I am what?

TWO: —my life: all of it: there's nothing else. I'll go to the clinic, I'll go back to the school, I'll—

ONE: Don't make it so hard for me.

TWO: Please! Let me stay on the sofa!

ONE: No!

TWO: But—

ONE: No, I said *no!* Open the door, go out!

TWO: When I come back tomorrow, you'll—

ONE: What?

TWO: Let me in?

ONE: If you go now, yes, but if you—

TWO: I'm going now. [*He opens the door.*] The air is—the sky is—

ONE: What are they?

TWO: —unusually light tonight. Like very clear shallow water, like, like—

ONE: The roosters will crow all night because they'll think it's near daybreak. Good night. Have a nice walk back. Perhaps the white cranes will still be on the lawn you passed coming over. Rest well. Don't ever doubt I care for you, but remember we're going into separate countries. [*He shuts the door silently from inside, walks back to the sofa.*]

ONE [*to herself*]: Gone—better alone. It's hard because he has nobody but me and I have nobody but him, but in the Dragon Country, you leave your last friend behind you and you go on alone. —Oh. —The door. —Not bolted—I'd better go down and bolt it or the maid will get in tomorrow. Get up, get up, I said up! [*She rises with great difficulty and descends the stairs, clinging to the banisters. She doesn't see Two at the card table. She crosses to the door and bolts it: then to the windowframe and looks out. Two lifts a card as if to shield his face with it. She turns to the room and sees the man by the sofa.*] Oh. —You stayed, didn't go. —I can't imagine tomorrow. —Help me back up the stairs, please help me back up to my chair on the landing. [*He catches her as she seems about to fall and supports her up to the landing.*] Let me rest here, please. I'll go on up to my bedroom in a while, even if I have to crawl up the rest of the stairs. . . .

TWO: Let me help you up now.

ONE: No. Here. Stop. Impossible—further—right now. [*She sits in the chair on the landing.*] Now. Go back down.

TWO: Let me—

ONE: *No, no, go back down, down, down!*

TWO: —I—you—

ONE: Sorry. I have to be alone here. [*Two returns to the card table.*] If I wake up and come downstairs tomorrow, it won't surprise me to find you still here. I think you've always wanted to stay in my house. Well, now's your chance, so make yourself at home. You know where everything is: the TV set, the liquor, the Frigidaire, the downstairs bedroom and bathroom. I leave you with all these delights. I'm going to sleep in a minute. I suppose it's still possible that tomorrow you'll pull yourself together and meet your classes. I wouldn't bet on it, though. Anyway it's likely that you've been replaced at the Junior High School. You've probably been expelled from the Junior High School like some—incorrigible—student. They just haven't bothered to notify you about it, or you've been scared to pick up the phone if they called you at the hotel mortuary. Haven't you always wanted to move in here? You've paid so many compliments to the place, the evenings you've come here from the hotel mortuary you live in. You always tell me how lovely something is, the warm air in winter, the cool air in summer,

149

the palm garden, even the sky, as if it belonged to the house. All right, now, you can stay here if you want to. You wouldn't get in my way, I wouldn't get in yours. After a couple of days we'd hardly notice each other. It would be like talking to ourselves, or hearing a bird or a cricket somewhere outside. Of course you have the alternative of creeping back to that mortuary called a hotel, but there's a time limit, a pretty short time limit, on your acceptance there in your present circumstances. They probably already know you're out of a job. Well, such things happen to people, all people, no exceptions, the short time limit runs out, it runs out on them and leaves them high and dry— [*There is a pause. Two collects the cards, puts them in the pack. Then One continues.*] If I sleep well tonight, I'll be better tomorrow, and if you're still here, we'll drive out or take a cab to the Food Fair Market and stock up the Frigidaire for you, and then we'll go by your hotel and collect your things and check you out of that awful mortuary. After that? I can't think. Perhaps it's not necessary to think past that. That's far enough for thinking and planning the future. So make yourself at home here. Take a drink out on the screen porch, enjoy the sky and the sea that belong to the house. I'm going on upstairs now. [*But she sits back down.*] —Not quite yet. Going on up is like climbing a peak in the Alps.

TWO: Stay down a little while longer.

ONE: All right, just a little while longer. . . .

TWO: [*softly, after a pause*]: Are you asleep now? Are you asleep now?

ONE: —I can't imagine tomorrow.

CURTAIN

150

CONFESSIONAL

CHARACTERS

LEONA

DOC

MONK

BILL

VIOLET

STEVE

YOUNG MAN

BOY FROM IOWA

A POLICEMAN

The scene is a somewhat nonrealistic evocation of a bar on the beach-front in one of those coastal towns between Los Angeles and San Diego. It attracts a group of regular patrons who are nearly all so well known to each other that it is like a community club, and most of these regulars spend the whole evening there. Ideally, the walls of the bar, on all three sides, should have the effect of fog rolling in from the ocean. A blue neon outside the door says: "Monk's Place." The bar runs diagonally from upstage to down; over it is suspended a large varnished sailfish, whose gaping bill and goggle-eyes give it a constant look of amazement. There are about three tables, with hurricane lamps, each of which is turned on only when that particular table is being used in the play. Near the entrance is the juke box, and in the wall at left are doors to the ladies' and gents' lavatories. A flight of stairs ascends from behind the back table, giving access to the bar-owner's living quarters. The stairs should be "masked" above first few steps.

Ideally, there should be a forestage, projecting a few feet in front of the proscenium; if that isn't practical, then there should be an area in the downstage center that can be lighted in a way that sets it apart from the bar at those points in the play when a character disengages himself from the group to speak as if to himself. This area is the "confessional"; it is used by everyone in the bar at some time in the course of the play.

The first few minutes of the play are given over to a tirade by a drunk female patron named Leona, a large, ungainly woman who paces the floor in the slightly crouched, menacing posture of a "villain" wrestler. She wears white clam-digger slacks and a woolly pink sweater. On her head of dyed corkscrew curls is a sailor's hat which she occasionally whips off her head to slap something with it—the bar, a table-top, somebody's back—to emphasize a point. A few moments before the curtain rose,

*she had apparently exchanged blows, or rather given a blow
to another female "regular," Violet, who has taken refuge in
the locked ladies' room from which she keeps shouting for
Monk, the owner and barman, to "call the wagon." This sobbing appeal should be repeated at intervals during Leona's
tirade. The "regulars" are a fairly raffish bunch. Leona and
Violet are in their late thirties. Steve, and Monk, the bar-owner,
and Doc—who lost his license for heavy drinking but still
practices more or less clandestinely, are middle-aged. Bill is
still in his twenties and is crudely attractive. At the rise of the
curtain, Leona is in the midst of a declamation against Violet.*

LEONA: —with no respect for herself, and that I don't blame
her for. What could she possibly find to respect in herself?
She lives like an animal in a room with no bath that's directly
over the amusement arcade at the foot of the pier, yeah, right
over the billiards, the pinball games and the bowling alleys at
the amusement arcade, it's bang, bang, bang, loud as a TV
western all day and all night, it would drive a sane person crazy
but she couldn't care less. I know, I been there, I seen it and
I heard it, bang, bang, till two or three in the morning, then
bang, bang again at eight A.M. when it opens for the next day.
She don't have a closet, she didn't have a bureau so she hangs
her dresses on a piece of rope that hangs across a corner between two nails, and her other possessions she keeps on the
floor in boxes.

BILL: What business is it of yours?

LEONA: None, not a Goddam bit! When she was sick? I went
there to bring her a chicken. I asked her, where is your silver?
Get up, sit at the table, where's your silver? She didn't have
any silver, not a fork, spoon or knife, hell, not even a plate,
but she ate the chicken, aw, yeah, she ate the chicken like a
dog would eat it, she picked it up in her paws and gnawed at

154

it just like a dog. Who came to see if she was living or dead? ME! ONLY! I got her a bureau, I got her a knife, fork and spoon, I got her some china, I got her a change of bed linen for her broken-down cot, and ev'ry day after work I come by that Goddam rat-hole to see what she needed and bring it, and then one time I come by there to see what she needed and bring it. The bitch wasn't there. I thought my God she's died or they put her away. I run downstairs and I heard her screaming with joy in the amusement arcade; she was having herself a ball with a shipload of drunk sailor-boys: she hardly had time to speak to me.

BILL: Maybe she'd gotten sick of you: that's a possible reason.

LEONA: It's a possible reason I was sick of her, too, but I'd thought that the bitch was dying of malnutrition so I'd come by her place ev'ry day with a bottle of hot beef-bouillon or a chicken or meatloaf for her because I thought she was human and a human life is worth saving or what the shit *is* worth saving. But is she human? She's just a parasite creature, not even made out of flesh but out of wet biscuit dough, she always looks like the bones are dissolving in her, that's what she—

BILL [*banging his beer-bottle on the table*]: DO YOU THINK I BELONG TO YOU? I BELONG TO MYSELF, I JUST BELONG TO MYSELF.

LEONA: Aw, you pitiful piece of—worthless—conceit! [*She addresses the bar.*] —Never done a lick of work in his life. —He has a name for his thing. He calls it Junior. He says he takes care of Junior and Junior takes care of him. How long is that gonna last? How long does he figure Junior is going to continue to provide for him, huh? HUH! —Forever or *less* than forever? —Thinks the sun rises and sets between his legs and that's the reason I put him in my trailer, feed him, give him beer-money, pretend I don't notice there's five or ten bucks

155

less in my pocketbook in the morning than my pocketbook had in it when I fell to sleep, night before.

BILL: Go out on the beach and tell that to the seagulls, they'd be more in'trested in it.

VIOLET [*shrilly, from the ladies room*]: Help me, help me, somebody, somebody call the po-liiiiice!

LEONA: Is she howling out the ladies' room window?

VIOLET: How long do I have to stay in here before you get the police!?

LEONA: If that fink is howling out the ladies' room window, I'm going out back and throw a brick in at her.

MONK: Leona, now cool it, Leona.

LEONA: I'll pay the damage, I'll pay the hospital expenses.

MONK: Leona, why don't you play your violin number on the multi-selector and settle down at a table and—

LEONA: When I been insulted by someone, I don't settle down at a table, or nowhere, NOWHERE!

[*Violet sobs and wails as Steve comes into the bar.*]

STEVE: Is that Violet in there?

LEONA: Who else do you think would be howling out the ladies' room window but her, and you better keep out of this, this is between her and me.

STEVE: What happened? Did you hit Violet?

LEONA: You're Goddam right I busted that filthy bitch in the kisser, and when she comes out of the ladies', if she ever comes out, I'm gonna bust her in the kisser again, and kiss my ass, I'm just the one that can do it! MONK! DRINK! BOURBON SWEET!

156

MONK: Leona, you're on a mean drunk, and I don't serve liquor to anyone on a mean drunk.

LEONA: Well, you can kiss it, too, you monkey-faced mother. [*She slaps the bar-top with her sailor hat.*]

STEVE: Hey, did you hit Violet?

[*Bill laughs at this anticlimactic question.*]

LEONA: Have you gone deaf, have you got wax in your ears, can't you hear her howling in there? Did I hit Violet? The answer is *yes*, and I'm not through with her yet. [*Leona approaches the door of the ladies' room.*] COME ON OUT OF THERE, VIOLET, OR I'LL BREAK IN THE DOOR! [*She bangs her fist on the door, then slaps it contemptuously with her cap, and resumes her pacing. Bill keeps grinning and chuckling.*]

STEVE: Why did she hit Violet?

LEONA: Why don't you ask *me* why?

STEVE: Why did you hit Violet?

LEONA: I hit Violet because she acted indecent with that son of a bitch I been supporting for six months in my trailer, that's the reason I hit her and I'll take another crack at her when she comes out of the ladies' if I have to wait here all night.

STEVE: What do you mean "indecent"?

LEONA: Jesus, don't you know her habits? Are you unconscious ev'ry night in this bar and in her rat-hole over the amusement arcade? I mean she acted indecent with her dirty paws under the table, hell, and I'd even bought the mother a drink and told her to sit down with us. She sat down. I looked at her hands on the table. The red enamel had nearly all chipped off the nails and the fingernails, black, I mean *black*, like she'd spent every day for a month without washing her hands after

157

making mud-pies with filthy motherless kids, and I thought to myself, it's awful, the degradation a woman can sink down into without respect for herself, so I took her hand and pulled it up under the lamp on the table, and said to her, Violet, will you look at your hand, will you look at your fingernails, Violet?

STEVE: Is that why you hit Violet?

LEONA: Goddam it, NO! Will you listen? I told her to look at her nails and she said, oh, the enamel is peeling, I know. I mean the dirtiness of the nails was not a thing she could notice, just the chipped red enamel.

STEVE: Is that why you hit Violet?

LEONA: Shit, will you shut up till I tell you why I hit her? I wouldn't hit her just for being unclean, unsanitary, I wouldn't hit her for nothing that affected just her. And now, if you'll pay attention, I'm going to tell you exactly why I did hit her. I got up from the table to play "Souvenir."

STEVE: What is she talking about? What are you talking about?

LEONA: A violin number I like to play on the box. And when I come back to the table her hands had disappeared off it. I thought to myself, I'm sorry, I made her ashamed of her hands and she's hiding them now.

STEVE: Is that why you hit Violet?

LEONA: Why do you come in a bar when you're already drunk? No! Listen! It wasn't embarrassment over her filthy nails that had made her take her hands off the table-top, it was her old habit, as filthy as her nails, and you know what I'm talking about if you've ever known her at all. The reason her pitiful hands had disappeared off the table was because under the table she was acting indecent with her hands in the lap of that ape that moved himself into my trailer and tonight will

158

move himself out as fast as he moved himself in. And now do you know why I hit her? If you had balls, which it doesn't look like you do, you would've hit her yourself instead of making me do it.

STEVE: I wasn't here when it happened, but that's the reason you hit her?

LEONA: Yeah, now the reason has got through the fog in your head which is thick as the fog on the beach.

[*Violet wails from the ladies' room.*]

STEVE: I'm not married to Violet, I never was or will be. I just wanted to know who hit her and why you hit her.

LEONA [*slapping at him with her cap*]: Annhh!

STEVE: Don't slap at me with that cap. What do I have to do with what she done or she does?

LEONA: No responsibility? No affection? No pity? You stand there hearing her wailing in the ladies' and deny there's any connection between you? Well, now I feel sorry for her. I regret that I hit her. She can come back out now and I won't hit her again. I see her life, the awfulness of her hands reaching out under a table, automatically creeping under a table into the lap of anything with a thing that she can catch hold of. Let her out of the ladies', I'll never hit her again. I feel too much pity for her, but I'm going out for a minute to breathe some clean air and to get me a drink where a barman's willing to serve me, and then I'll come back to pay up whatever I owe here and say good-bye to the sailfish, hooked and shellacked and strung up like a flag over—over—lesser, much lesser—creatures that never, ever sailed an inch in their—lives. . . .

[*The pauses at the end of this speech are due to a shift of her attention toward a Young Man and a Boy who have entered the bar. Her eyes have followed them as they walked past her*

159

to a table in the front. She continues speaking, but now as if to herself.]

LEONA: —When I leave here tonight, none of you will ever see me again.

BILL: Is anyone's heart breaking?

LEONA: Not mine, not mine.

BILL: The heartbreak of a slob makes a lot of noise over nothing.

LEONA: Over nothing is right, and the nothing is you. When I leave here tonight, I'm going to stop by the shop, let myself in with my passkey and collect my own equipment, which is enough to open a shop of my own, write a good-bye note to Flo, she isn't a bad old bitch, I doubled her trade since I been there, she's going to miss me, poor Flo, then leave my passkey and cut back to my trailer and pack like lightning and move on to—

BILL: —Where?

LEONA: Where I go next. You won't know, but you'll know I went fast.

[*Now she forgets her stated intention of going out of the bar and crosses to the table taken by the Young Man and the Boy. The Boy wears khaki shorts, and a sweatshirt on the back of which is lettered "Iowa to Mexico." The Young Man is dressed effetely in a yachting jacket, maroon linen slacks, leather sandals and a silk neck-scarf. Despite this costume, he has a quality of sexlessness, not effeminacy. Some years ago, he must have been remarkably handsome: now his face seems to have been burned thin by a fever that is not of the flesh.*]

LEONA [*suddenly very amiable*]: Hi, boys!

YOUNG MAN: Oh. Hello. Good Evening.

160

BOY [*with shy friendliness*]: Hello.

[*Bill is grinning and chuckling. Violet's weeping in the ladies room no longer seems to interest anyone in the bar.*]

LEONA [*to the Boy*]:How's the corn growing out there where the tall corn grows?

BOY: Oh, it's still growing tall.

LEONA: Good for the corn. I'm from the corn country, too. What town or city are you from in Iowa?

BOY: Dubuque.

LEONA: Oh, from Dubuque, no shoot. I could recite the telephone book of Dubuque, but excuse me a minute, I want to play a selection on the box, and I'll come right back to discuss Dubuque with you. Huh? [*She moves as if totally pacified to the juke box and removes some coins from a pocket. They fall to the floor. She starts to bend over to pick them up, then decides not to bother, gives them a slight kick, gets a dollar bill out of a pocket, calling out—*] Monk, gimme change for a buck.

YOUNG MAN: Barman? —Barman? —What's necessary to get the barman's attention here, I wonder.

MONK: I heard you. You've come in the wrong place. You're looking for the Jungle Bar, half a mile up the beach.

YOUNG MAN: Does that mean you'd rather not serve us?

MONK: Let me see the kid's draft card.

BOY: I just want a coke.

YOUNG MAN: He wants a plain Coca-Cola, I'd like a vodka and tonic.

[*Bill has left his table and walked casually onto the forestage, the lighted "confessional." As he begins to speak, the confessional is lighted and the rest of the bar is dimmed.*]

161

BILL: Y' can't insult 'em, there's no way to bring 'em down except to beat 'em and roll 'em. I noticed him stop at the door before he come in. He was about to go right back out when he caught sight of me. Then he decided to stay. A faggot that dresses like that is asking for it. After a while, say about fifteen minutes, I'll go in the gents' and he'll follow me in there for a look at Junior. Then I'll have him hooked. He'll ask me to meet him outside by his car or at the White Castle. It'll be a short wait and I don't think I'll have t'do more than scare him a little. I don't like beating 'em up. They can't help the way they are. Who can? Not me. Left home at fifteen, and like Leona says, I've never done a lick of work in my life and I never plan to, not as long as Junior keeps batting on the home team, but my time with Leona's run out. She means to pull out of here and I mean to stay. . . .

[*As he slouches back to his table, the forestage spot is dimmed out and the bar is brought up. Leona is still at the multi-selector: she lights it up with a coin and selects a violin number, "Souvenir." A look of ineffable sweetness appears on her face, at the first note of music.*]

MONK [*rapping at the ladies'*]: Violet, you can come out, now, she's playing that violin number.

[*Bill and Steve laugh. As he laughs, Steve leaves the bar-stool and walks to the confessional area where he is lighted as the bar is dimmed.*]

STEVE: I guess Violet's a pig, all right, and I ought to be ashamed to go around with her. But a man unmarried, forty-seven years old, employed as a short-order cook at a salary he can barely get by on alone, he can't be choosy. Nope, he has to be satisfied with the Goddam scraps in this world, and Violet's one of those scraps. She's a pitiful scrap, but—[*He shrugs sadly and lifts the beer-bottle to his mouth.*]—something's better than nothing and I had nothing before I took up with her. She gave

162

me a clap once and tried to tell me I got it off a toilet seat. I asked the doctor, Is it possible to get a clap off a public toilet seat, and he said, Yes, you can get it that way but you *don't!* [*He grins sadly and drinks again, wobbling slightly.*]—Oh, my life, my miserable, cheap life! It's like a bone thrown to a dog! I'm the dog, she's the bone. Hell, I know her habits. She's always down there in that amusement arcade when I go to pick her up, she's down there as close as she can get to some navy kid, playing a pinball game, and one hand is out of sight. Hustling? I reckon that's it. I know I don't provide for her, just buy her a few beers here, and a hot dog on the way home. But Bill, why's he let her mess around with him? One night he was braggin' about the size of his tool, he said all he had to do to make a living was wear tight pants on the street. Life! —Throw it to a dog. I'm not a dog, I don't want it. I think I'll sit at the bar and pay no attention to her when she comes out. . . .

[*He turns back upstage and takes a seat at the bar. During his speech in the confessional area, the violin number has been heard at a very low level. Now the light in the bar and the violin selection are brought up to a normal level. After a moment, Violet comes out of the ladies' room slowly with a piteous expression. She is dabbing her nostrils with a bit of toilet tissue. She has large, liquid-looking eyes and her lips are pursed in sorrow so that she is like a travesty of a female saint under torture. Nothing said about her could prepare for her actual appearance. She has a kind of bizarre beauty although her two-piece velvety blue suit has endured several years—since its acquisition at a thrift shop—without darkening the door of a cleaner. She gasps and draws back a little at the sight of Leona; then, discreetly sobbing, she edges onto a bar-stool and is served a beer. Steve glares at her. She avoids looking at him. Bill grins and chuckles at his table. Leona ignores the fact that Violet has emerged from her retreat: she goes on pacing the bar but is enthralled by the music.*]

163

LEONA: My God, what an instrument, it's like a thing in your heart, it's a thing that's sad but better than being happy, in a— crazy drunk way. . . .

VIOLET [*piteously*]: I don't know if I can drink, I feel sick at my stomach.

LEONA: Aw, shit, Violet. Who do you think you're kidding? You'll drink whatever is put in the reach of your paws. [*She slaps herself on the thigh with the sailor cap and laughs.*]

VIOLET: I do feel sick at my stomach.

LEONA: You're lucky you're sick at your stomach because your stomach can vomit but when you're sick at your heart, that's when it's awful, because your heart can't vomit the memories of your lifetime. I wish my heart could vomit, I wish my heart could throw up the heartbreaks of my lifetime, my days in a beauty shop and my nights in a trailer. It wouldn't surprise me at all if I drove up to Sausalito alone this night. With no one. . . .

[*She glances at Bill who grins and chuckles. Violet sobs piteously again. Leona gives Violet a fairly hard slap on the shoulders with her sailor's cap. Violet cries out in affected terror.*]

Shuddup, I'm not gonna hit you. Steve, take her off that bar-stool and put her at a table, she's on a crying jag and it makes me sick.

STEVE [*to Violet*]: Come off it, Violet. Sit over here at a table, before you fall off the bar-stool.

LEONA: She hasn't got a mark on her, not a mark, but she acts like I'd nearly kilt her, and turns to a weeping willow. But as for that ape that I put up in my trailer, him I could blast out of my trailer and out of my life and out of all memory of him. I took him in because a life in a trailer, going from place to place

164

any way the wind blows you, gets to be lonely, sometimes, and you make the mistake of taking in somebody that don't respect you for anything but his tendency in your trailer, I mean the tenancy of it . . .

STEVE: Violet, I told you to come over to this table.

LEONA: Take her over before she falls off the stool.

[*Steve supports Violet's frail, weeping figure to a table. Monk receives a phone call.*]

MONK: Doc, it's for you.

DOC [*crossing to the end of the bar*]: Thanks, Monk.

MONK: The old Doc's worked up a pretty good practice for a man in retirement.

LEONA: Retirement your ass, he was kicked out of the medical profession for performing operations when he was so loaded he couldn't tell the appendix from the gizzard.

MONK: Leona, go sit at your table.

LEONA: You want responsibility for a human life, do you?

MONK: Bill, I think she's ready to go home now.

LEONA: I'll go home when I'm ready and I'll do it alone.

BILL: I seen a circus with a polar bear in it that rode a three-wheel bicycle. That's what you make me think of tonight.

LEONA: You want to know something, McCorkle? I could beat the shit out of you.

BILL: Set down somewhere and shut up.

LEONA: I got a suggestion for you. Take this cab fare—[*She throws a handful of silver on the table.*]—And go get your stuff out of my trailer. Clear it all out, because when I go home to-

165

night and find any stuff of yours there, I'll pitch it out of the trailer and bolt the door on you. I'm just in the right mood to do it.

BILL: Don't break my heart.

LEONA: What heart? We been in my trailer together for six months and you contributed nothing.

BILL: Shit, for six months I satisfied you in your trailer!

LEONA: You never satisfied nothing but my mother complex. Never mind, forget it, it's forgotten. Just do this. Take this quarter and punch number six three times on the juke box.

BILL: Nobody wants to hear that violin number again.

LEONA: I do, I'm somebody. My brother, my young brother, played it as good if not better than Heifetz on that box. Y'know, I look at you and I ask myself a question. How does it feel to've never had anything beautiful in your life and not even know you've missed it? [*She crosses toward the multi-selector.*] Walking home with you some night, I've said, Bill, look at the sky, will you look at that sky? You never looked up, just grunted. In your life you're had no experiation—experience! Appreciation!—of the beauty of God in the sky, so what is your life but a bottle of, can of, glass of—one, two, three! [*She has punched the violin selection three times.*]

MONK: The Doc's still on the phone.

LEONA: "Souvenir" is a soft number.

DOC [*returning to the bar*]: I've got to deliver a baby. Shot of brandy.

LEONA [*returning to Bill's table*]: It wouldn't be sad if you didn't know what you missed by coming into this world and going out of it some day without ever having a sense of, experience of and memory of, a beautiful thing in your life such as I

166

have in mine when I remember the violin of and the face of my young brother. . . .

BILL: You told me your brother was a fruit.

LEONA: I told you privately something you're repeating in public with words as cheap as yourself. My brother who played this number had pernicious anemia from the age of thirteen and any fool knows a disease, a condition, like that would make any boy too weak to go with a woman, but he was so full of love he had to give it to someone like his music. And in my work, my profession as a beautician, I never seen skin or hair or eyes that could touch my brother's. His hair was a natural blond as soft as silk and his eyes were two pieces of heaven in a human face, and he played on the violin like he was making love to it. I cry! I cry! —No, I don't, I *don't* cry! —I'm proud that I've had something beautiful to remember as long as I live in my lifetime. . . .

[*Violet sniffles softly.*]

LEONA: When they passed round the plate for the offering at church, they'd have him play in the choir stall and he played and he looked like an angel, standing under the light through the stained glass window. Um-hmmm. [*Her expression is rapt.*] —And people, even the tightwads, would drop paper money in the plates when he played. Yes, always before the service, I'd give him a shampoo-rinse so that his silky hair, the silkiest hair I've ever known on a human head in my lifetime as a beautician, would look like an angel's halo, touched with heavenly light. Why, people cried like I'm crying, why, I remember one Easter, the whole choir started crying like I'm crying and the preacher was still choked up when he delivered the sermon. "Angels of Light," that was it, the number he played that Easter. . . . [*She sings a phrase of the song.*] Emotions of people can be worse than people but sometimes better than people, yes, superior to them, and Haley had that gift of

167

making people's emotions uplifted, superior to them! But he got weaker and weaker and thinner and thinner till one Sunday he collapsed in the choir stall and after that he failed fast, just faded out of this world. Anemia—pernicious. . . .

VIOLET [*sobbing*]: Anemia, that's what I've got!

LEONA: Don't compare yourself to him, how dare you compare yourself to him. He was too beautiful to live and so he died. Otherwise we'd be living together in my trailer. I'd train him to be a beautician, to bring out the homeliness in—I mean the, I mean the— [*She is confused for a moment; she lurches into a bar-stool and knocks it over.*] I mean I'd train my young brother to lay his hands on the heads of the homely and lonely and bring some beauty out in them, at least for one night or one day or at least for an hour. We'd have our own shop, maybe two of 'em, and I wouldn't give you— [*She directs herself to Bill.*] —the time of the day, the time of the night, the time of the morning or afternoon, the sight of you never would have entered my sight to make me feel pity for you, no, *noooo!* [*She bends over Bill's table, resting her spread palms on it, to talk directly into his face.*] The companionship and the violin of my brother would be all I had any need for in my lifetime till my death-time! Remember this, Bill, if your brain can remember. Everyone needs! One beautiful thing! In the course of a lifetime! To save the heart from colluption!

BILL: What is "colluption," fat lady?

LEONA: *CORRUPTION!* —Without one beautiful thing in the course of a lifetime, it's all a death-time. A woman turns to a slob that lives with a slob, and life is disgusting to her and she's disgusting to life, and I'm just the one to—

BILL [*cutting in*]: If you'd rather live with a fruit—

LEONA: *Don't say it! Don't say it!* [*She seizes hold of a chair and raises it mightily over her head. Violet screams. Leona hurls*

168

the chair to the floor.] Shit, he's not worth the price of a broken chair! [*Suddenly she bursts into laughter that is prodigious as her anger or even more: it's like an unleashed element of nature. Several patrons of the bar, involuntarily, laugh with her. Abruptly as it started, the laughter stops short: there is total silence except for the ocean sound outside.*]

DOC [*rising from his bar-stool*]: Well, I better be going. Somebody's about to be born at Treasure Island.

LEONA: That's my trailer court where I keep my trailer. A baby's about to be born there?

BILL: Naw, not a baby, a full-grown adult's about to be born there, and that's why the Doc had t' brace himself with a coupla shots of brandy.

DOC [*turning about on his bar-stool, glass in hand*]: You can't make jokes about birth and you can't make jokes about death. They're miracles, holy miracles, both, yes, that's what both of them are, even though, now, they're usually surrounded by—expedients that seem to take away the dignity of them. Birth? Rubber gloves, boiled water, forceps, surgical shears. And death? —The wheeze of an oxygen tank, the jab of a hypodermic needle to put out the panic light in the dying-out eyes, tubes in the arms and the kidneys, absorbent cotton inserted in the rectum to hold back the bowels discharged when the—the *being* stops. [*During this speech, or possibly before it, he has moved into the pool of light, at the center front, which serves as a confessional for the characters.*] —It's hard to see back of this cloud of—irreverent—paraphernalia. But behind them both are the holy mysteries of—birth and—death. . . . They're dark as the face of God whose face is dark because it's the face of a black man; yes, that's right, a Negro, yes. I've always figured that God is a black man with no light on his face, He moves in the dark like a black man, a Negro miner in the pit of a lightless coal mine, obscured completely by the—

169

irrelevancies and irreverencies of public worship—standing to sing, kneeling to pray, sitting to hear the banalities of a preacher —[*The pool of light dims out and he returns to the bar to put his glass down.*]

LEONA: [*as light comes up on the bar*]: I want to know: is nobody going to stop him from going out, in his condition, to deliver a baby? I want to know quick, or I'll stop him myself!

DOC: Monk, did I give you my—?

MONK: Bag? Yeah, here. [*Monk hands a medical kit across the bar.*]

DOC: Thanks. And I'll have a shot of brandy to wash down a benzedrine tablet to steady my hands.

LEONA: NOBODY, HUH?

DOC: Tonight, as I drove down Canyon Road, I noticed a clear bright star in the sky, and it was right over that trailer court, Treasure Island, where I'm going to deliver a baby. So now I know: I'm going to deliver a new Messiah tonight.

LEONA: The hell you are, you criminal, murdering quack, leggo of that bag!

[*She tries to snatch the bag from him. Bill and Steve hold her back. The Doc leaves: the boom of surf is heard through the door left open after Doc's departure.*]

You all, all of you, are responsible, too, if he murders that baby and the baby's mother. Is life worth nothing in here? I'm going out. I'm going to make a phone call!

[*Bill makes a move to stop her.*]

DON'T!—you *dare* to!

MONK: Who're you going to call?

170

LEONA: That's my business, I'm not gonna use your phone. [*She charges out of the bar, leaving the door open.*]

BILL: I know what she's up to. She's gonna call the office at Treasure Island and tell 'em the Doc's comin' out there to deliver a baby.

MONK: Go and stop her, she could get the Doc in serious trouble.

BILL: Shit, they know her too well to pay her any attention when she calls.

VIOLET [*plaintively*]: Last week she give me a perm and a rinse for nothing, and then tonight she turns on me, threatens to kill me.

BILL: Aw, she blows hot and cold, dependin' on whichever way her liquor hits her.

VIOLET: She's got two natures in her. Sometimes she couldn't be nicer. A minute later she—

MONK [*at the telephone*]: Shut up a minute. Treasure Island? This is Monk speaking from Monk's Place. Just a minute. [*He turns to the table.*] Close that door, I can't hear the talk over the surf. [*Steve shuts the door on the surf's boom. Bill takes Steve's seat next to Violet.*] —Yeah. Now. If you get a phone call out there from Leona Dawson, you know her, she's got a trailer out there, don't listen to her; she's on a crazy mean drunk, out to make trouble for a capable doctor who's been called by someone out there, an emergency call. So I thought I'd warn you, thank you. [*Monk hangs up the telephone.*]

[*Violet comes downstage and the light is focused on her.*]

VIOLET: It's perfectly true that I have a room over the amusement arcade facing the pier. But it's not like Leona describes it. It took me a while to get it in shipshape condition because I was not a well girl when I moved in there, but now it's clean

171

and attractive. It's not luxurious but it's clean and attractive and has an atmosphere to it. I don't see anything wrong with living upstairs from the amusement arcade, facing the pier. I don't have a bath or a toilet but I keep myself clean with a sponge bath at the washbasin and use the toilet in the amusement arcade. Anyhow, it's a temporary arrangement, that's all it is, a temporary arrangement. . . .

[*Leona returns to the bar. Bill rises quickly and walks over to the bar.*]

LEONA: One, two, button my shoe, three, four, shut the door, five, six, pick up sticks. . . . [*No one speaks.*] —Silence, absolute silence. [*She goes to the table of the Young Man and the Boy from Iowa.*] Well, boys, what went wrong?

YOUNG MAN: I'm afraid I don't know what you mean.

LEONA: Sure you know what I mean. You're not talking to each other, you don't even look at each other. There's some kind of tension between you. What is it? Is it guilt feelings? Embarrassment with guilt feelings?

YOUNG MAN: I still don't know what you mean, but, uh—

LEONA: "But, uh" what?

YOUNG MAN: Don't you think you're being a little presumptuous?

LEONA: Naw, I know the gay scene. I learned it from my kid brother. He came out early, younger than this boy here. I know the gay scene and I know the language of it and I know how full it is of sickness and sadness; it's so full of sadness and sickness, I could almost be glad that my little brother died before he had time to be infected with all that sadness and sickness in the heart of a gay boy. This kid from Iowa, here, reminds me a little of how my brother was, and you, you remind me of how he might have become if he'd lived.

172

YOUNG MAN: Yes, you should be relieved he's dead, then.

[*She flops awkardly into a chair at the table.*]

YOUNG MAN [*testily*]: Excuse me, won't you sit down?

LEONA: D'ya think I'm still standing up?

YOUNG MAN: Perhaps we took your table.

LEONA: I don't have any table. I'm moving about tonight like an animal in a zoo because tonight is the night of the death-day of my brother and—Look, the barman won't serve me, he thinks I'm on a mean drunk, so do me a favor, order a double bourbon and pretend it's for you. Do that, I'll love you for it, and of course I'll pay you for it.

YOUNG MAN [*calling out*]: Barman? I'd like a double bourbon.

MONK: If it's for the lady, I can't serve you.

[*Bill laughs heartily at the next table.*]

YOUNG MAN: It isn't for the lady, it's for me.

LEONA: How do you like that shit? [*She shrugs.*] Now what went wrong between you before you come in here, you can tell me and maybe I can advise you. I'm practically what they call a faggot's moll.

YOUNG MAN: Oh. Are you?

LEONA: Yes, I am. I always locate at least one gay bar in whatever city I'm in. I live in a home on wheels, I live in a trailer, so I been quite a few places. And have a few more to go. Now nobody's listening to us, they're having their own conversation about their own situations. What went wrong?

YOUNG MAN: Nothing, exactly. I just made a mistake, and he did, too.

173

LEONA: Oh. Mistakes. How did you make these mistakes? Nobody's listening, tell me.

YOUNG MAN: I passed him riding his bicycle up Canyon Road and I stopped my car and reversed it till I was right by his bike and I—spoke to him.

LEONA: What did you say to him?

BOY: Do you have to talk about it?

YOUNG MAN: Why not? I said: "Did you really ride that bike all the way from Iowa to the Pacific Coast," and he grinned and said, yes, he'd done that. And I said: "You must be tired?" and he said he was and I said: "Put your bike in the back seat of my car and come home with me for dinner."

LEONA: What went wrong? At dinner? You didn't *give* him the dinner?

YOUNG MAN: No, I gave him drinks, first, because I thought that after he'd had dinner, he might say: "Thank you, good night."

BOY: Let's shut up about that. I had dinner after.

LEONA: After what?

YOUNG MAN: After—

BOY: I guess to you people who live here it's just an old thing you're used to, I mean the ocean out there, the Pacific, it's not an *experience* to you any more like it is to me. You say it's the Pacific, but me, I say *THE PACIFIC!*

YOUNG MAN: Well, everything is in "caps" at your age, Bobby.

LEONA [*to the Young Man*]: Do you work for the movies?

YOUNG MAN: Naturally, what else?

174

LEONA: Act in them, you're an actor?

YOUNG MAN: No. Script-writer.

LEONA [*vaguely*]: Aw, you write movies, huh?

YOUNG MAN: *Re*-write them. My specialty is sophisticated chatter at cocktail parties—*you* know. . . .

LEONA [*still vaguely*]: No, I don't know.

YOUNG MAN: Politely bitchy remarks between smartly gowned ladies such as—

LEONA: No. No, I don't know. Never mind. I've known many a bitch but no polite ones. I don't think that monkey-faced mother is gonna serve us that bourbon. —I've never left this bar without leaving a dollar tip on the table, and this is what thanks I get for it, just because it's the death-day of my brother and I showed a little human emotion about it. Now what's the trouble between you and this kid from Iowa where the tall corn blows, I mean grows?

YOUNG MAN: I only go for straight trade. But this boy—look at him! Would you guess he was gay? —I didn't, I thought he was straight. But I had an unpleasant surprise when he responded to my hand on his knee by putting his hand on mine.

BOY: I don't know the word *gay*. What does that word mean?

LEONA: Don't tell him—he's got plenty of time to learn the meanings of words and cynical attitudes. Why, he's got eyes like my brother's! Have you paid him?

YOUNG MAN: For disappointment?

LEONA: Don't be a mean-minded mother. Give him a five, a ten. If you picked up what you don't want, it's your mistake and pay for it.

BOY: I don't want money from him. I thought he was nice, I liked him.

175

LEONA: Your mistake, too. [*She turns to the Young Man.*]: Gimme your wallet. [*The Young Man hands her his wallet.*]

BOY: He's disappointed. I don't want anything from him.

LEONA: Don't be a fool. Fools aren't respected, you fool. [*She removes a bill from the wallet and stuffs it in the pocket of the Boy's shirt. The Boy starts to return it.*] OK, I'll hold it for you till he cuts out of here to make another pickup and remind me to give it back to you when he goes. He wants to pay you, it's part of his sad routine. It's like doing penance—penitence. . . . [*She turns to the Young Man.*] Do you like being alone except for vicious pickups? The kind you go for? If I understood you correctly? —Christ, you have terrible eyes, the expression in them! What are you looking at?

YOUNG MAN: That fish over the bar. . . .

LEONA: You're changing the subject.

YOUNG MAN: No, I'm not, not a bit. —Now suppose some night I woke up and I found that fantastic fish—what is it?

LEONA: Sailfish. What about it?

YOUNG MAN: Suppose I woke up some midnight and found that peculiar thing swimming around in my bedroom? Up the Canyon?

LEONA: In a fish bowl? Aquarium?

YOUNG MAN: No, not in a bowl or aquarium: free, unconfined.

LEONA: Impossible.

YOUNG MAN: Granted: it's impossible. But suppose it occurred just the same as so many impossible things *do* occur just the same. Suppose I woke up and discovered it there, swimming round and round in the darkness over my bed, with a faint phosphorescent glow in its big goggle eyes and its gorgeously

176

iridescent fins and tail making a swishing sound as it circles around and about and around and about right over my head in my bed.

LEONA: Hah!

YOUNG MAN: Now suppose this admittedly preposterous thing did occur.

LEONA: All right. Suppose it occurred. What about it?

YOUNG MAN: What do you think I would say?

LEONA: Say to who? To the fish?

YOUNG MAN: To myself and the fish.

LEONA: —I'll be raped by an ape if I can imagine what a person would say in a situation like that.

YOUNG MAN: I'll tell you what I would say, I would say: "Oh, well. . . ."

LEONA: —That's all you would say, just "Oh, well"?

YOUNG MAN: "Oh, well" is all I would say before I went back to sleep.

LEONA: What I would say is: "Get the hell out of here, you goggle-eyed monstrosity of a mother," that's what I'd say to it.

MONK: Leona, you got to quiet down.

LEONA: But what's the point of your story?

YOUNG MAN: You don't see the point of my story?

LEONA: Nope.

YOUNG MAN [to the Boy]: Do *you* see the point of my story? [*The Boy shakes his head.*] Well, maybe I don't either.

LEONA: Then why'd you tell it?

177

YOUNG MAN: What is the thing that you mustn't lose in this world before you're ready to leave it? The one thing you mustn't lose ever?

LEONA: —Love?

[*The Young Man laughs.*]

BOY: Interest?

YOUNG MAN: That's closer, much closer. Yes, that's almost it. The word that I had in mind is surprise, though. The capacity for being surprised. I've lost the capacity for being surprised, so completely lost it, that if I woke up in my bedroom late some night and saw that fantastic fish swimming right over my head, I wouldn't be really surprised.

LEONA: You mean you'd think you were dreaming?

YOUNG MAN: Oh, no. Wide awake. But not really surprised. [*He rises casually and moves to the "confessional": the light concentrates on him.*] There's a coarseness, a deadening coarseness, in the experience of most homosexuals. The experiences are quick, and hard, and brutal, and the pattern of them is practically unchanging. Their act of love is like the jabbing of a hypodermic needle to which they're addicted but which is more and more empty of real interest and surprise. This lack of variation and surprise in their—"love life"— [*He smiles harshly.*] —spreads into other areas of—"sensibility?"—[*He smiles again.*] —Yes, once, quite a long while ago, I was often startled by the sense of being alive, of being *myself, living!* Present on earth, in the flesh, yes, for some completely mysterious reason, a single, separate, intensely conscious being, *myself: living!*—Whenever I would feel this—*feeling*, this—shock of— what?—self-realization?—I would be stunned, I would be thunderstruck by it. And by the existence of everything that exists, I'd be lightning-struck with astonishment. . . . It would do more than astound me, it would give me a feeling of panic,

178

the sudden sense of—I suppose it was like an epileptic seizure, except that I didn't fall to the ground in convulsions; no, I'd be more apt to try to lose myself in a crowd on a street until the seizure was finished. —They were dangerous seizures. One time I drove into the mountains and smashed the car into a tree, and I'm not sure if I *meant* to do that, or. . . . In a forest you'll sometimes see a giant tree, several hundred years old, that's scarred, that's blazed by lightning, and the wound is almost obscured by the obstinately still living and growing bark. I wonder if such a tree has learned the same lesson that I have, not to feel astonishment any more but just go on, continue for two or three hundred years more? —This boy I picked up tonight, the kid from the tall corn country, still has the capacity for being surprised by what he sees, hears and feels in this kingdom of earth. All the way up the canyon to my place, he kept saying, *I can't believe it, I'm here, I've come to the Pacific, the world's greatest ocean!*—as if nobody, Magellan or Balboa or even the Indians had ever seen it before him; yes, like he'd discovered this ocean, the largest on earth, and so now, because he'd found it himself, it existed, now, for the first time, never before. . . . And this excitement of his reminded me of my having lost the ability to say: "My God!" instead of just: "Oh, well." I've asked all the questions, shouted them at deaf heaven, till I was hoarse in the voice box and blue in the face, and gotten no answer, not the whisper of one, nothing at all, you see, but the sun coming up each morning and going down that night, and the galaxies of the night sky trooping onstage like chorines, robot chorines: one, two, three, kick, one two three, kick. . . . Repeat any question too often and what do you get, what's given? —A big carved rock by the desert, a— monumental symbol of wornout passion and bewilderment in you, a stupid stone paralyzed Sphinx that knows no answers that you don't but comes on like the oracle of all time, waiting on her belly to give out some outcries of universal wisdom, and if she woke up some midnight at the edge of the desert

179

and saw that fantastic fish swimming over her head—y'know what she'd say, too? She'd say: "Oh, well"—and go back to sleep for another five thousand years. [*He turns back; the "confessional light" fades out and the bar is re-lighted. He returns to the table and adjusts his neck-scarf as he speaks to the boy.*] —Your bicycle's still in my car. Shall I put it on the sidewalk?

BOY: I'll go get it. [*He turns to Leona*] Good night.

LEONA: You could put your bike in my trailer and go up the Coast with me. I've got two bunks in my trailer.

BOY: Thank you, but I—

LEONA: Why not? It wouldn't cost you nothing and we'd be company for each other.

BOY: I, uh, I—

LEONA: Why *not?* Are you afraid I'd put the make on you, Sonny?

BOY: I, uh, I've got my trip planned. I'm headed for Mexico.

LEONA: Mexico's dangerous country for a kid that don't know the score, and you could get sick there. You'd be better off with me. I can teach you the gay scene if you want to learn it.

BOY: It's nice of you, but I—better get my bicycle.

BILL [*to Steve*]: She wants that young fruit in her stinking trailer but the offer has been turned down.

LEONA: You can't understand one person wanting to give protection to another, it's way past your understanding.

[*The Boy moves downstage, pulling on a sweater he carried into the bar. The bar is dimmed and the voices fade out. Light comes up in the confessional as the Boy enters that area.*]

180

BOY: —In Goldenfield, Iowa, there was just one man like that. He ran a flower shop and I heard boys talk about him. They said you went in a back room of the flower shop and it was decorated Chinese with incense and naked pictures. I was afraid to go there. I was afraid to even walk down the street it was on. These kids made fun of the man, they said he was a—bad word—but he'd give 'em two dollars any time they went there. One time there was a discussion of what made a man like that and I remember Clay Rivers said that they had something in their throats, something different from normal throats, which made them need to—bad word—and I felt my face turning hot and my throat choked up so I couldn't say anything in that discussion, at all. One time, one winter night, I rode down the street the flower shop was on, and I saw it was closed—for rent—and I heard he'd been run out of town because he'd—bad word—had immoral relations with a kid still in grade school. That's all I've known of that world until tonight. Tonight was —initiation. It scares me because I liked it, and liked him, too. I'll never turn into the bad-word flower shop man, but I'll probably have an experience like that again, and next time I won't make the mistake of showing any excitement and pleasure. —I think I'll ride my bike all night tonight, I've got a lot to think over.... [*He leaves the area of the confessional and goes out of the bar.*]

LEONA [*suddenly*]: *Aw, the money!* [*She rushes to the door.*] HEY, IOWA TO MEXICO, HEYYY!

BILL: He don't want a lousy five bucks, he wants everything in the wallet. He'll roll the faggot and hop back on his bike looking sweet and innocent as your brother fiddling in church.

[*Leona rushes out, calling.*]

STEVE: The Coast is over-run with 'em, they come running out here like animals out of a brushfire.

181

MONK [*crossing into the confessional*]: I've got no moral objections to them as a part of humanity, but I don't encourage them here. One comes in, others follow. First thing you know you're operating what they call a gay bar and it sounds like a bird cage, they're standing three deep at the bar and lining up at the men's room. Business is terrific for a few months. Then in comes the law. The place is raided, the boys hauled off in the wagon, and your place is padlocked. And then a cop or a gangster pays you a social visit, big smile, all buddy-buddy. You had a good thing going, a real swinging place, he tells you, but you needed protection. He offers you protection and you buy it. The place is re-opened and business is terrific a few months more. And then? It's raided again, and the next time it's re-opened, you pay out of your nose, your ears, and your ass. Who wants it? I don't want it. I want a small steady place that I can handle alone, that brings in a small, steady profit. No buddy-buddy association with gangsters and the police. I want to know the people that come in my place so well I can serve them their brand of liquor or beer before they name it, soon as they come in the door. And all their personal problems, I want to know that, too.

[*Violet begins to hum softly, swaying to and fro like a water-plant.*]

I'm fond of, I've got an affection for, a sincere interest in my regular customers here. They send me postcards from wherever they go and tell me what's new in their lives and I am interested in it. Just last month one of them I hadn't seen in about five years, he died in Mexico City and I was notified of the death and that he'd willed me all he owned in the world, his personal effects and a two-hundred-fifty-dollar savings account in a bank. A thing like that is beautiful as music. These things, these people, take the place of a family in my life. I love to come down those steps from my room to open the place for the evening, and when I've closed for the night, I love climbing

182

back up those steps with my can of Ballantine's ale, and the stories, the jokes, the confidences and confessions I've heard that night, it makes me feel not alone. —I've had heart attacks, and I'd be a liar to say they didn't scare me and don't still scare me. I'll die some night up those steps, I'll die in the night and I hope it don't wake me up, that I just slip away, quietly.

[*During his speech, the light has been concentrated on him, the rest of the bar very dim. Leona has returned. The light in the bar comes up but remains at a low level.*]

LEONA: —Is there a steam engine in here? Did somebody drive in here on a steam engine while I was out?

MONK [*returning from his meditation*]: —Did what?

LEONA: I hear something going huff-huff like an old loco-motive pulling into a station. [*She is referring to a sound like a panting dog: it comes from the unlighted table where Violet is seated between Bill and Steve.*] —Oh, well, my home is on wheels. —Bourbon sweet, Monk.

MONK: Leona, you don't need another.

LEONA: Monk, it's after midnight, my brother's death-day is over, I'll be all right, don't worry. [*She goes to the bar.*] —It was selfish of me to wish he was still alive.

[*A pin-spot of light picks up Violet's tear-stained and tranced face at the otherwise dark table.*]

—She's got some form of religion in her hands. . . .

[*The lights dim slowly for a time passage.*]

DIM OUT OR CURTAIN

An hour later. "Group singing" has been in progress at the back table. Leona is not participating. She is leaning moodily against the bar in front.

VIOLET: I like the old numbers best. I bet none of you know this one, this one's a real, real oldie I learned from Mother. [*She opens her eyes very wide and assumes a sentimental look.*]
"Lay me where sweet flowers blos-som,
Where the whitest lily blows
Where the pinks and violets min-gle,
Lay my head beneath the rose."

LEONA [*disparagingly*]: Shit.

VIOLET: "Life is from me fastly fa-ding,
Soon I'll be in sweet re-pose.
Ere I die I ask this fa-vor—
Lay my head beneath the rose. . . ."
—Now how is that for a sweet, sentimental old number?

[*No one offers any comment but Leona.*]

LEONA: Y'don't need a rose to lay her, you could lay her under a cactus and she wouldn't notice the diff-rence.

[*Bill crosses to the bar for a beer.*]

I guess you don't think I'm serious about it, hitting the highway tonight.

[*Bill shrugs and crosses to a downstage table.*]

Well, I am, I'm serious about it. [*She sits at his table.*] An experienced expert beautician can always get work anywhere.

BILL: Your own appearance is a bad advertisement for your line of work.

184

LEONA: I don't care how I look as long as I'm clean and decent—and *self-supporting*. When I haul into a new town, I just look through the yellow pages of the telephone directory and pick out a beauty shop that's close to my trailer camp. I go to the shop and offer to work a couple of days for nothing, and after that couple of days I'm in like Flynn, and on my own terms which is fifty percent of charges for all I do, and my tips, of course, too. They like my work and they like my personality, my approach to customers. I keep them laughing.

BILL: You keep me laughing, too.

LEONA: —Of course, there's things about you I'll remember with pleasure, such as waking up sometimes in the night and looking over the edge of the upper bunk to see you asleep in the lower.

[*Bill leaves the table. She raises her voice to address the bar-at-large.*]

Yeah, he slept in the lower cause when he'd passed out or nearly, it would of taken a derrick to haul him into the upper bunk. So I gave him the lower bunk and took the upper myself.

BILL: As if you never pass out. Is that the idea you're selling?

LEONA: When I pass out I wake up in a chair or on the floor, but when you pass out, which is practically every night, I haul you onto your bunk. I never would dream of leaving you stoned on the floor, I'd get you into your bunk and out of your shoes when you passed out on the floor, and you know Goddam well you never done that for me, oh, no, the floor was good enough for me in your opinion, and sometimes you stepped on me even, yeah, like I was a rug or a bug, and that's the God's truth and you know it, because your nature is selfish. You think because you've lived off one woman after another woman after eight or ten other women you're something superior, special. Well, you're special but not superior, baby. I'm going to worry

185

about you after I've gone and I'm sure as hell leaving tonight, fog or no fog on the highway, but I'll worry about you because you refuse to grow up and that's a mistake that you make, because you can only refuse to grow up for a limited period in your lifetime and get by with it. —I *loved* you! —I'm not going to cry.

[*Violet starts weeping for her.*]

When I come to a new place, it takes me two or three weeks, that's all it takes me, to find somebody to live with in my home on wheels and to find a night spot to hang out in. Those first two or three weeks are rough, sometimes I wish I'd stayed where I was before, but I know from experience that I'll find somebody and locate a night spot to booze in, and get acquainted with—friends. . . . [*The light has focused on her. She moves downstage with her hands in her pockets, her face and voice very grave as if she were less confident that things will be as she says.*] And then, all at once, something wonderful happens. All the past disappointments in people I left behind me, just disappear, evaporate from my mind, and I just remember the good things, such as their sleeping faces, and—Life! Life! I never just said, "Oh, well," I've always said "Life!" to life, like a song to God, and when I die, I'll say "death" like a song to God, too, because I've lived in my lifetime and not been afraid of—changes. . . . [*She goes back to the table.*] —However, y'see, I've got this pride in my nature. When I live with a person I love and care for in my life, I expect his respect, and when I see I've lost it, I GO, GO! —So a home on wheels is the only right home for me. Now what is she doing here?

[*Violet has weaved to the table and taken a chair.*]

Hey! What are *you* doing here?

VIOLET: You're the best friend I ever had, the best friend I— [*She sways and sobs like a religieuse in the grip of a vision.*]

LEONA: What's that, what're you saying?

[*Violet sobs.*]

She can't talk. What was she saying?

VIOLET: —BEST—!

LEONA: WHAT?

VIOLET: —*Friend!*

LEONA: I'd go further than that, I'd be willing to bet I'm the *only* friend that you've had, and the next time you come down sick in that room upstairs from the amusement arcade, nobody will bring you nothing, no chicken, no hot beef-bouillon, no chinaware, no silver, and no interest and concern about your condition, and you'll die in your rattrap with no human voice, just bang, bang, bang from the bowling alley and billiards. And when you die you should feel a relief from the conditions you lived in. Now I'm leaving you two suffering, bleeding hearts together, I'm going to sit at the bar. I had a Italian boyfriend that taught me a saying, "Meglior solo que mal accompanota," which means that you're better alone than in the company of a bad companion.

[*She starts to the bar, as the Doc enters.*]

Back already, huh? It didn't take you much time to deliver the baby. Or did you bury the baby? Or did you bury the mother? Or did you bury them both, the mother and baby?

DOC [*to Monk*]: Can you shut up this woman?

LEONA: Nobody can shut up this woman. Quack, quack, quack, Doctor Duck, quack, quack, quack, quack, quack!

DOC: I'M A LICENSED PHYSICIAN!

LEONA: *SHOW me your license. I'll shut up when I see it!*

187

DOC: A doctor's license to practice isn't the size of a drunken driver's license, you don't put it in a wallet, you hang it on the wall of your office.

LEONA: Here is your office! Which wall is your license hung on? Beside the sailfish or where? Where is your license to practice hung up, in the gents', with other filthy scribbles?!

MONK: Leona, you said your brother's death-day was over and I thought you meant you were—

LEONA: THOUGHT I MEANT I WAS *WHAT?*

DOC: You were ready to cool it. BILL! —Take Leona home, now.

LEONA: Christ, do you think I'd let him come near me?! Or near my trailer?! Tonight?! [*She slaps the bar several times with her sailor-cap, turning to right and left as if to ward off assailants, her great bosom heaving, a jungle-look in her eyes.*]

VIOLET [*sweet and sadly*]: —Steve, it's time to leave. [*Violet, Steve and Bill start out.*]

LEONA [*stomping the floor with a powerful foot*]: Y'WANT YOUR ASS IN A SLING? BEFORE YOU'RE LAID UNDER THAT ROSE?

VIOLET [*shepherded past Leona by Steve and Bill*]: If we don't see you again, good luck wherever you're going.

[*They go out the door.*]

LEONA [*rushing after them*]: *Yes, she does, she wants her ass in a sling!*

[*She charges out of the door. A moment or two later are heard, above the boom of the surf, the shrill outcries of Violet.*

[*Monk crosses toward the door: Violet collides with him, screeching, blood flowing from her nose. She utters several,*

188

wild cries, then dashes into the ladies' room and bolts the door.]

VIOLET [*shrilly, from the ladies' room*]: They're calling the wagon for her, she's like a wild animal out there! Lock the door! Keep her out!

[*Monk closes and locks the bar entrance. There is a sudden quiet in the bar, except for the sobbing of Violet in the ladies' room, and a muted disturbance outside. Monk turns out the bar lights, all except the hurricane lamp on one table.*]

MONK: Doc, have a nightcap with me?

DOC: Yes, thanks I could use one. [*Monk sets a bottle and two shot-glasses at the one lighted table. They sit in profile on either side of the table. Doc speaks—as if answering a question.*] The birth of the baby was at least three months premature, so it was born dead, of course, and just beginning to look like a human baby. —The man living with the woman in the trailer said, "Don't let her see it, get it out of the trailer." I agreed with the man that she shouldn't see it, so I put this foetus in a shoe box. . . . [*He speaks with difficulty, as if compelled to.*] The trailer was right by the beach, the tide was coming in with heavy surf, so I put the shoe box—and contents—where the tide would take it.

MONK: —Are you sure that was legal?

DOC: Christ, no, it wasn't legal. —I'd barely set the box down when the man came out shouting for me. The woman had started to hemorrhage. When I went back in the trailer, she was bleeding to death. The man hollered at me, "Do something, can't you do something for her!"

MONK: —Could you?

DOC: —I could have told the man to call an ambulance for her, but I thought of the probable consequences to me, and

189

while I thought about that, the woman died. She was a small woman, but not small enough to fit in a shoe box, so I—I gave the man a fifty-dollar bill that I'd received today for performing an abortion. I gave it to him in return for his promise not to remember my name—[*He reaches for the bottle. His hand shakes so that he can't refill his shot-glass: Monk fills it for him.*] —You see, I can't make out certificates of death, since I have no legal right any more to practice medicine, Monk.

MONK: —In the light of what happened, there's something I'd better tell you, Doc. Soon as you left here to deliver that baby, Leona ran out of the bar to make a phone call to the office at Treasure Island, warning them that you were on your way out there to deliver a baby. So, Doc, you may be in trouble. —If you stay here. . . .

DOC: —I'll take a benzedrine tablet and pack up tonight and be on the road before morning.

[*The sound of a squad-car siren is heard. Leona appears at the door, shouting and pounding.*]

LEONA: MONK! THE PADDY WAGON IS SINGING MY SONG!

[*Monk lets her in and locks the door.*]

MONK: Go upstairs. Can you make it?

[*She clambers up the steps, slips, nearly falls. The squad car screams to a stop outside the bar. An Officer knocks at the door. Monk admits him.*]

Hi, Tony.

OFFICER: Hi, Monk. What's this about a fight going on here, Monk?

MONK: Fight? Not here. It's been very peaceful tonight. The bar is closed. I'm sitting here having a nightcap with—[*He indicates the Doc, slumped over the table.*]

190

OFFICER: Who's that bawling back there?

MONK [*pouring a drink for the Officer*]: Some dame disappointed in love, the usual thing. Try this and if it suits you, take the bottle.

OFFICER [*He drinks.*]: —OK. Good.

MONK: Take the bottle. Drop in more often. I miss you.

OFFICER: Thanks, g'night. [*He goes out. As Monk puts another bottle on the table, Leona comes awkwardly back down the stairs.*]

LEONA: Monk? Thanks, Monk. [*She and Monk sit at the table. Violet comes out of the ladies' room. She sees Leona at the table and starts to retreat.*] Aw, hell, Violet. Come over and sit down with us, we're having a nightcap, all of us, my brother's death-day is over.

VIOLET: Why does everyone hate me? [*She sits at the table: drinks are poured from the bottle. Violet hitches her chair close to Monk's. In a few moments she will deliberately drop a matchbook under the table, bend to retrieve it and the hand on Monk's side will not return to the table surface.*]

LEONA: Nobody hates you, Violet. It would be a compliment to you if they did.

VIOLET: I'd hate to think that I'd come between you and Bill.

LEONA: Don't torture yourself with an awful thought like that. Two people living together is something you don't understand and since you don't understand it you don't respect it, but, Violet, this being our last conversation, I want to advise something to you. I think you need medical help in the mental department and I think this because you remind me of a—of a—of a plant of some kind. . . .

VIOLET: Because my name is Violet?

191

LEONA: No, I wasn't thinking of violets, I was thinking of water plants, yeah, plants that don't grow in the ground but float on water. With you everything is such a—such a—well, you know what I mean: don't you?

VIOLET: Temporary arrangement?

LEONA: Yes, you could put it that way. Do you know how you got into that place upstairs from the amusement arcade?

VIOLET: —How?

LEONA: Yes, *how* or *why* or *when?*

VIOLET: —Why, I—[*She obviously is uncertain on all three points.*]

LEONA: Take your time: and *think*. How, why, when?

VIOLET: Why, I was—in L.A., and—

LEONA: Are you sure you were in L.A.? Are you sure about even that? Or is everything foggy to you, is your mind in a cloud?

VIOLET: Yes, I was—

LEONA: I said take your time, don't push it. Can you come out of the fog?

MONK: Leona, take it easy, we all know Violet's got problems.

LEONA: Her problems are mental problems and I want her to face them, now, in our last conversation. Violet? Can you come out of the fog and tell us how, when and why you're living out of a suitcase upstairs from the amusement arcade, can you just—

MONK [*cutting in*]: She's left the amusement arcade, she left it tonight, she came here with her suitcase.

192

LEONA: Yeah, she's a water plant, with roots in water, drifting the way it takes her.

[*Violet weeps.*]

LEONA: And she cries too easy, the water works are back on. I'll give her some music to cry to before I go back to my home on wheels and get it cracking up the Old Spanish Trail. [*She rises from the table.*]

MONK: Not tonight, Leona. You have to sleep off your liquor before you get on the highway in this fog.

LEONA: That's what you think, not what I think, Monk. My time's run out in this place. [*She has walked to the multi-selector and started the violin piece.*] —How, when, and why, and her only answer is tears. Couldn't say how, couldn't say when, couldn't say why. And I don't think she's sure where she was before she come here, any more sure than she is where she'll go when she leaves here. She don't dare remember and she don't dare look forward, neither. Her mind floats on a cloud and her body floats on water. And her dirty fingernail hands reach out to hold on to something she hopes can hold her together. [*She starts back toward the table, stops; the bar dims and light is focused on her.*] —Oh, my God, she's at it again, she's got a hand under the table. [*Leona laughs sadly.*] Well, I guess she can't help it. It's sad, though. It's a pitiful thing to have to reach under a table to find some reason to live. You can always tell when she's about to do it. She gets a look that's almost unconscious in those big, wet eyes that're too big for her face and her mouth hangs open a little. Then she does it. She hitches her chair up closer to the man next to her: then she lets something drop on the floor, bends over to pick it up, and one of her hands comes up but the other stays down. The man slouches down in his chair and takes little sips of his drink with a far away look like hers. Then you know she's worshipping her idea of God Almighty in her personal church.

It's her kick, and like they say, don't knock another man's kick. Why the hell should I care she done it to a nowhere person that I put up in my trailer for a few months? Well, to be honest about it, I know I got some lonely weeks ahead of me before I find myself another companion in wherever I'm going. I wish that kid from I-oh-a with eyes like my lost brother had been willing to travel with me but I guess I scared him. What I think I'll do is turn back to a faggot's moll when I haul up to Sausalito or San Francisco. You always find one in the gay bars that needs a big sister with him, to camp with and laugh and cry with, and I hope I'll find one soon—it scares me to be alone in my home on wheels built for two. . . . [*She turns as the bar is lighted and goes back to the table.*]

DOC: Have a drink with us, Leona.

LEONA: Thank you, no. I've had my quota, and I've got to haul ass up state in foggy weather. Well, I'll toss another shot down, then go to my home on wheels and get it moving up the Old Spanish Trail. Fog don't bother me unless it's fog in my head, and my head's completely clear now. —MONK, HEY, MONK! What's my tab here t'night?

MONK: Forget it, don't think about it, go home and sleep, Leona. [*He and Violet appear to be in a state of trance together.*]

LEONA: I'm not going to sleep and I never leave debts behind me. This twenty ought to do it. [*She places a bill on the table.*]

MONK: Uh-huh, sure, keep in touch. . . .

LEONA: Tell Bill he'll find his effects in the trailer-court office, and when he's hustled himself a new meal ticket, he'd better try and respect her, at least in public. —Well—

[*She extends her hand slightly: Monk and Violet are sitting with closed eyes. The Doc is looking down at the table.*]

194

—I guess I've already gone.

VIOLET [*dreamily*]: G'bye, Leona.

MONK: G'bye. . . .

DOC: G'bye, Leona. [*Leona lets herself out of the bar. The Doc rises unsteadily from the table.*] —G'bye, Monk.

MONK: G'bye, Doc. Keep in touch.

VIOLET: G'bye, Doc.

MONK: Take care.

[*The Doc departs.*]

VIOLET: —Monk? Let's go upstairs. Huh, Monk?

MONK: Hmm? Oh. Upstairs—Yeah, go on up and make yourself at home. Take a shower up there while I lock up the bar.

[*Violet crosses to the stairs and climbs a few steps.*]

VIOLET: Monk! —I'm scared of these stairs, they're almost steep as a ladder. I better take off my slippers. Take my slippers off for me. [*She holds out one leg from the steps, then the other. Monk removes her slippers. She goes on up, calling down to him.*] Bring up some beer with you, sweetheart.

MONK: Yeh, I'll bring some beer up. Don't forget your shower.

[*Alone in the bar, Monk opens the door on the boom of the ocean, then crosses to the confessional, pulling a chair with him.*]

—I always leave the door open for a few minutes to clear the smoke and liquor smell out of the place, and to hear the ocean. It sounds different this late than it does when people are on the beach-front. It has a private sound to it, a sound that's just for itself. Just for itself and for me. I'm going to stay down here till I hear the shower running. I don't hear it running. She

195

probably thinks she'd dissolve in a shower. I shouldn't have let her stay here. The Doc says she gave Steve the clap. I better not touch her up there, have no contact with her, maybe not even go up. —Till she's asleep. [*He lets one of the slippers fall by the chair, turns the other slowly in his hands.*] —A dirty, worn-out slipper that's still being worn, sour-smelling from sweat from being worn too long, but still set down by the bed to be worn again the next day, walked on here and there on— pointless—errands, till finally the sole of it's worn through. —But even then you can't be sure that it will be thrown away, no, it might be re-soled or just padded with cardboard, and still be put on to walk on, till it's past all repair—all repair. . . .

[*He goes on turning the slipper in his hands as the stage is dimmed out.*]

CURTAIN

THE FROSTED GLASS COFFIN

CHARACTERS

ONE

TWO

THREE

MRS. ONE (BETSY)

MRS. TWO

MR. KELSEY

THE FROSTED GLASS COFFIN

The setting is the street facade of one of those low-priced hotels in the Dallas Park section of downtown Miami. This one, called the Ponce de Leon, is patronized almost exclusively by retired old people, hardly one under seventy. Directly across the street is a very popular cafeteria where everything is priced one or two cents cheaper than at other restaurants. It is only open from 7:30 to 9:30 for breakfast, from 12 noon to 2:30 for lunch, and from 5:30 to 8:00 P.M. for dinner. The food suits the old people and so do the prices, but the capacity of the cafeteria is not large enough for all of its patrons, and so for at least half an hour, and sometimes for more than an hour, before the doors open for one of these three daily feeding-periods, there is a line-up along the walk to the cafeteria entrances. This line-up is regarded snobbishly by the old folks at the Ponce de Leon. They won't demean themselves to wait to be let in, even though this snobbery obliges them to accept undesirable tables when they finally enter. The Ponce de Leon entrance is directly onto the sidewalk; a bench and a wicker chair stand on one side and just a wicker chair on the other. It is about 7:10 A.M. in the month of March: the morning light is zinc white, and very intense: it washes out the colors of almost everything on the stage. It suggests frosted glass. The five characters in the play will be specified only by number except when their names are mentioned in the script. Two and Three, old men, come out of the hotel together and sit on the bench. Two is nearly eighty, and Three has passed that milestone. They are followed out by One, another old man. He feels a cut superior to his cronies, having once been mayor of a small town in the Carolinas. He is in his early seventies. His manner could be described as amiably condescending.

ONE: Mawnin', boys.

TWO: Yep, we know it's morning.

ONE: My wife was lookin' out of our living room window just now. [*He pauses to light a cigar.*]

TWO: What did she see out of your livin' room window?

ONE: She noticed that Dixie Mammy was not over there this mawnin', ringing the bell for breakfast. She says to me, Claude, do you suppose Dixie Mammy's a victim of their new penny-pinching program?

TWO: I know all about that and I got my information from Dixie Mammy herself. You know I always slip her a nickel or a dime when we come out after supper because she's a good ole-fashion blue-gum darky from Georgia, so she said to me last night when I slipped her a dime, "Mr. Sykes, I won't be out in the mawnin' till just before the door opens for breakfast." I said, "Why's that, Mammy?" —and she explained to me that a bunch of crankly old shut-ins here at the Ponce de Leon had set up a terrible howl against her ringin' that breakfast bell half'n hour before the cafeteria opens, she says they complained that the breakfast bell woke 'em up too early.

ONE: Aw, so that's why she's makin' a late appearance this mawnin'.

TWO: That's the explanation which I got straight out of the hawse's mouth last night.

ONE: Those ole bedridden complainers ought to be thankful for anything that wakes them up in the mawnin', early or late. They ought to feel damn lucky it isn't Gabriel's trumpet.

TWO: Well, now, let's be fair. Some of these shut-in old-timers don't get a sound night's sleep till the night's gone, nearly.

ONE: I know, I appreciate that, but Betsy and me were discussing last night whether we wouldn't do better, psychologically, to move to some hotel that ain't quite so full of geriatric

200

cases. Betsy's depressed by all the deaths that take place here. She feels that it would pick up our spirits to take a two-room suite in a hotel that's not so much like the last retreat of the old and dying, the terminal cases, and shut-ins.

TWO: How young does she think she is?

ONE: Betsy's a mighty lively old girl in her sixties.

TWO: Oh, she's lively if being lively is loud, and if being loud is lively, that applies to you too.

ONE: You talk like you got up on the wrong side of the bed.

TWO: Yeah, well where's the petition against the price-hike at the Dixie Mammy Kitchen?

ONE: Oh, that. I gave it to Betsy to canvass the old ladies with it. I've got all the old men's names on that petition and Betsy is gonna get all the old women's names on it. And we're adding an appendix to the petition which is a comparison of the new prices at the Dixie Mammy Kitchen with the prices for the exact items which the *Consumer's Index* regards as fair ones, and there is several cents' difference in every item.

TWO [*grudgingly impressed*]: Well. —The Dixie Mammy's management won't give it much attention unless it's published in the newspapers or there's a sudden drop in their trade.

ONE: Well, now, let's see how many's in the breakfast line-up this mawnin'. [*He advances to the proscenium, squinting and peering through the zinc-white and still rather crepuscular light of the early March morning.*]

THREE: What, what?

TWO: There's the usual number in the line-up.

THREE [*who is hard of hearing*]: What, what?

ONE: I'll bet you my bottom dollar you'll see a sizable decrease in the breakfast line-up tomorrow when the price-raise goes

201

into effect. That's why I'm int'rested in just how many are in it at [*consulting a pocket watch*] at seven-ten this mawnin'. Because at seven-ten t'morrow, I'm comin' out here to see how many's dropped out, and I am willing to bet you, the line-up, the senile brigade, will've shrunk to a fraction of what it is now. Um-hmmm. Thirty-five in it this mawnin', and as usual little Miss Walker from the Hotel Seminole is first in line to enter when they unlock the doors. Miss Walker is really Miss Creeper, that's the right name for her, but she creeps fast enough to just about always be the first one in the line-up, the senile brigade, for that great seven-cent cup of coffee. However tomorrow when it turns to a nine-cent cup of coffee and a nickel for each extra cup which used to be *free, complimentary,* I doubt that little Miss Walker, heh, heh, I mean Miss Creeper, will be in such haste to git there; in fact I bet she'll go on instant coffee in her hotel bedroom tomorrow.

TWO: Naw, she won't. The price of instant coffee has jumped up too and ole Miss Walker don't have a kitchenette at the Seminole.

ONE: She's got hot water in the bathroom, ain't she?

TWO: Ole Miss Walker don't have a private bathroom.

ONE: Well, then I reckon she'll just have to live with the price-hike at Dixie Mammy's. How much're they going up on French toast tomorrow?

TWO: That I don't know, but I *do* know a bowl of cream-of-wheat cereal with milk is going to cost you eleven cents tomorrow, and thirteen cents if you take it with half-and-half cream, and that even the cinnamon bun I take with my coffee and cereal will be two pennies higher. I'm through with Dixie Mammy's, you won't catch me in there again if I live to be a hundred.

ONE: Y'mean if next year you're still in the land of the living?

TWO: I'll be living next year and I'll still be short of a hundred by a long shot, mister.

ONE: Don't git mad: I was kiddin' you, boy.

TWO: Kid you'self, not me: you're not much younger, kiddo.

ONE: Boy, don't take this personal, but the first sign of senility in a man is losing his sense of humor, and senility don't have as close a connection with actual age as people imagine; it has more to do with the condition of the arteries in the brain, the amount of cerebral arterio-sclerosis that has set in and how far advanced it is.

TWO: You watch your own Goddam arteries.

ONE: In some folks less'n sixty, senility has already set in because the cerebral bloodstream is clogged and the brain cells are undernourished. That's when they turn to crotchety old eccentrics, not at a certain age but at a certain level of calcification or of fatty deposits in the cerebral arteries, boy.

TWO: Senility starts with bullshit, if you ask me, and I wish to hell you'd quit reading every Goddam morbid article on disease you can find in *Time* magazine and the *Reader's Digest*.

ONE: Aw, now boy.

TWO: I mean it, it's disgusting and it's depressing. When I come out here each morning, I ask myself, Now what, I wonder will that old windbag spoil my breakfast appetite with this morning, a discussion of prostate trouble, a lecture on cancer, or some crazy misinterpretation of something he read in some medical journal in the waiting room of that quack doctor he goes to.

ONE: I subscribe to the *Journal of Geriatrics*.

TWO: I don't care what you subscribe to: just remember my wife, God rest her soul, taught physical hygiene at the best high school in Atlanta.

[*Excited outcries across the street catch their attention.*]

ONE: What's that commotion over?

TWO: Looks like one of 'em's collapsed right before the locked door.

[*They rise and shuffle out to the proscenium, leaning forward, peering, commenting.*]

THREE: Man or woman?

TWO: Woman.

ONE: Then it ain't coronary, women don't git coronaries.

TWO: I've known 'em to get heart failure.

ONE: Unusual.

THREE: Too damn unusual.

VOICE [*offstage*]: Will somebody call an ambulance for this lady?

TWO: Can you see who collapsed, is it anybody we know?

ONE: Yep, it's little old Miss Walker. I thought it was but I wanted to be sure before I said so because in this company, it's absolutely imperative to be absolutely certain before you commit yourself to an opinion of something.

TWO: Little Miss First-One-In, well, how about that.

ONE: Yep, Little Miss First-One-In is now Miss First-One-Out before she even got in.

[*They chuckle together. Three loses his balance and almost falls into the orchestra pit.*]

VOICE [*shrieking*]: You men over there, will one of you run to the taxi stand on Flagler and git a taxi for this unconscious woman?

204

[*They turn about and shuffle back to their seats, not desiring involvement.*]

ONE [*sitting down*]: "Run," she said. [*He chuckles sadly.*] She must be practickly blind. In our age bracket you're living in a glass coffin, a frosted coffin, you just barely see light through it.

TWO: Yep: that's about it.

THREE: What?

ONE: Light, through it.

THREE: Who? What?

ONE [*turning away from Three who is cupping his ear*]: In some cases the conversation consists of almost nothing but one-syllable questions like who, who, what, what, where? The silent question is WHEN. The silent meaning of it is: when do I go? There's no one to answer that question, if it was asked out loud, and mighty damn few would have the guts to ask it if there was. Now take what happened last night to Mr. and Mrs. Kelsey. . . .

THREE: What, what? Who?

ONE: See what I mean about living in a frosted glass coffin unburied? He don't even know what happened last night to the Kelseys.

THREE: What about the Kelseys?

ONE: Frosted glass coffin, unburied! [*He raises his voice to Three.*] You mean to sit here and tell me you're the only resident of this twelve-story hotel that don't yet know what happened to the Kelseys last night at Mercy?

THREE: Not a word of it: what happened?

ONE [*oratorically and unctuously*]: At nine P.M. last night little Mrs. Kelsey was struck by what they thought was a little

205

gall-bladder trouble. She had put Kelsey to bed: you know he has to be cared for like an infant. Then this sharp pain hits her in her abdomin, in the gall-bladder region, so she got dressed and came down to the lobby so she wouldn't disturb ole Kelsey. I was down there, jawing with the night clerk. She don't come up to the desk. She sits down on a sofa. After a while I notice she's clutching the right side of her abdomin and that she had sweat on her forehead which she kept patting off with those sheets of toilet tissue she carries instid of Kleenex. I whispers to the night clerk, I said, "Sam, will you look at Mrs. Kelsey? That woman's in pain, and she's sitting down here at this hour so Kelsey won't know about it." Sam, he looked over at her and said, "Goddam it, you're right, she's got the death-sweat on her," and without another word he picked up the phone and called up Mercy Hospital to send an ambulance for her.

THREE: Holy Moses. Great Scott.

ONE: They picked her up and removed her to Mercy Hospital just before eleven P.M. An hour later I was about to go up to our room, when the telephone rang. It was Mercy. They said, "We'd like to speak to Mr. Kelsey about his wife." Sam said, "I don't think I better disturb Mr. Kelsey unless it's absolutely critical." Well, they said it was so critical that unless Kelsey got out there inside of an hour, they couldn't promise he'd see her alive again.

THREE: Lawdamighty!

ONE: Well, I woke up Betsy and between the two of us, we got Kelsey up. Of course we didn't inform him how critical it was, we just said Mrs. Kelsey had had a little stomach upset and had gone to Mercy.

TWO: Sam got a taxi for him and I give him the fare. Well, he got there too late.

206

ONE: Betsy went with him to Mercy. She says that Mrs. Kelsey had the sheet over her head and was already cold. You know what Kelsey said? He said, "She seems sort of weak," and Betsy said he wouldn't believe she was gone even when they rolled her down to the morgue at Mercy.

THREE: I never thought Mrs. Kelsey would go before Kelsey.

ONE: Vital statistics show that two or three times as many men go as wimmen.

TWO: That's a ridiculous statement: if that was true, the world population would of been nothing but female for a thousand years now.

ONE: I'm talking about OLD COUPLES! There must be—

TWO: Hold on a minute, Mr. *Reader's Digest!*

TWO: Excuse me: Mr. *Geriatrics Journal:* I'd like to point out that the men fight the wars and that the wars have hit every single generation of men in this country, and if, in addition to that—

ONE: You're off on some tangent.

TWO: Wait: if in addition to that, what you say is true about men dying two or three times the rate of wimmen—

ONE: Will you shut up for a second so I can say what I was actually saying?

[*There is a pause: One glares at Two in real fury.*]

TWO: —What was you actually saying?

ONE: —Nothing. My time and my breath are too valuable, too important to me, to—

THREE [*cutting in*]: Who would of thought that Kelsey would outlive his Mrs.? Why, Kelsey was in and out of Mercy like a jack rabbit.

TWO: Yep. Ev'ry whipstitch little ole Mrs. Kelsey would come down without him. I'd say, "Where's your ole man this mawnin'?" —The answer was: "Back in Mercy."

THREE: In, out, out, in, in, out like a jack rabbit. So now she's gone. Explains why they haven't come down yet. Did they keep him at Mercy?

ONE: Nope, he's back. Betsy had him hauled out of Mercy in a wheelchair and all the way out to the taxi he kept calling for Winnie. In the taxi she held onto his hand: and he thought her hand was his Missus'.

THREE: Don't he realize she's gone yet?

ONE: Betsy says he started to realize it when she'd got him back into bed and hollered to him, "Now go to sleep, Mr. Kelsey. Everything is going to be taken care of, don't you worry." Then he seemed to realize a little that Winnie was gone, not till then. —You know, it's not so surprising that Winnie went first after all, because old Kelsey has crossed that age limit where the human body, all its functions and its processes, are so slowed down that they live a sort of crocodile existence that seems to go on forever. The question is what to do with him.

TWO: He ought to have a practical nurse but can't afford one, I reckon.

ONE: The answer's a nursing home, huh?

TWO: I reckon that's the only possible answer unless they chloroform him like an old dog.

ONE: What time is it? They still haven't opened those doors, and the line-up is down to the corner. Well, tomorrow, at seven-thirty tomorrow, when they offer that nine-cent coffee and eleven-cent cream-of-wheat, they just might open those doors and find nobody outside 'em, not a soul.

208

TWO: *Hey! Look at this!*

[*He is peering in the entrance. Kelsey appears in the door and seems to be stopped as if stunned by the intensity of the zinc-white glare of the street.*]

ONE: Mawnin', Mr. Kelsey.

[*Kelsey gives no response except to start moving again, tapping each step before him with a cane, his advance onto the walk like that of an old turtle. When he has arrived on the walk he seems uncertain which way to turn.*]

ONE: Mawnin', Mr. Kelsey.

TWO: He don't have his hearing aid on.

ONE [*louder, into Kelsey's ear*]: KELSEY!

[*Kelsey raises his hand in a shaky restraining gesture, seems to find his direction and walks to the isolated chair on the other side of the entrance. He feels his way carefully down into the chair, and blinks out at the zinc-white glare: motionless, expressionless. There is another hush: when the men start talking again, their voices are different, subdued.*]

ONE: I count fifty-two old folks in the line-up now.

TWO: Miss Walker has come back strong. She's started knocking at the door with her umbrella handle.

ONE: It's time for the doors to be opened.

TWO: You'd think those doors were the pearly gates to heaven the way they line up at them.

ONE: It ain't so bad at breakfast and in the spring, but at noon in summer, it's a terrible thing. The management could put an awning up for them. Do they? Nope, they don't. Too cheap to protect their customers from heat prostration in summer. [*There is a pause.*] The hotel stationery has a line at the bottom of the page that gives out the information, totally false, that heat prostration is unknown in Miami, despite the fact that directly across the street from them they can observe every noon that senile brigade, that line-up, of two or three hundred geriatric cases, exposed to prostration and sunstroke. I've seen them drop in summer, I've seen them drop to the pavement like a silent revolver had shot them through their hearts. . . . I hope I die before I git so far in years that I would shuffle across this street and stand in that line for them to let me in for their nine-cent cup of coffee and the extra nickel for the lukewarm second cup of it.

[*His wife appears in the doorway behind him, drawing on a pair of white cotton gloves.*]

—Cheapness is worse than crime, there's very few crimes more disgusting to me than cheapness: I think it ranks with murder. Now what's holding up Madame Betsy? That's a mighty brisk little woman when she wants to be quick at something, but when I'm waitin' for her, she revels in taking her time.

[*His wife overhears these comments and draws on her gloves like the rubber gloves of a surgeon enraged at the patient.*]

Women can take more time cause they've got more of it to take: like I told you, vital statistics don't lie and they have established the fact that the average woman outlives the average man by a good ten years. At least! That explains their total disregard of time coming and going, when a man's waiting for them.

[*His voice has taken on an elegiac tone.*]

They secretly, in their subconscious, enjoy! revel! —in their extra ten years on earth, and secretly enjoy and revel in the man's rapid decline. Just observe their attitude when they go along with their husband to his doctor's. They sit in that waiting room while he is being examined like they were looking at

210

a comedy on TV. No shoot. They do. When he comes out, he sometimes catches their secret, subconscious, pleased look. But oh, what a long face they pull when the doctor comes out, then. "Doctor? Can I speak to you in private?" —"Yes, of course, Mrs. Whozit." —In they go but sometimes you hear their voices. "Now Doctor, I'm a brave woman, I want the truth and can bear it. It *is* malignant, ain't it? Tell me, I have to know." And even if he says it's just a minor affliction, natural to his age, a tiny touch of incipient diabetes, they raise their voice and say, "Oh, God, I know what you mean, he's going!" —When they come out of this consultation, they give you a brave little smile and call you sweetheart. "We better go home now, sweetheart"—and ask the receptionist, "Will you please call a taxi, my husband's not well enough to walk back to the hotel," which is two blocks away. "He has to conserve his strength for what he has to go through. . . ."

TWO: Have you finished? Can I say something to you?

ONE: Say it, you don't have lockjaw.

TWO: Unless you're the nambiest-pambiest man on earth, there's no believable reason why you stay with this Betsy. You say she wants to outlive you. Well, if you don't die soon, you're going to try her patience, you might even try it so far that she'll go to the corner drugstore for a large box of "Death on Rats."

ONE: That's not how they operate. They have the time advantage, and so they just outwait you.

THREE: What, what?

[*Mrs. One now steps into their view.*]

MRS. ONE [*with a disparaging inflection*]: Good mawnin', gentlemen.

TWO: The same to you, Ma'am, many of them.

211

MRS. ONE: Why, thank you Mr. Sikes, and oh! Mr. Sikes, your wife just asked me to tell you she didn't sleep well after the tragedy last night, so would you please fetch her a carton of orange juice and a carton of double black coffee and some Danish pastry from the White Castle on Flagler.

[*One chuckles.*]

THREE: What, what?

TWO: All right, return her this message: when I move from this bench it'll be just to cross the street to Dixie Mammy's Kitchen for my own breakfast and that if she's decided to live on room service, she can move over to the Fountain-Blow on the Beach, if she figures she can afford it.

MRS. ONE: Now, now Mr. Sikes, you don't mean that, not a word, and oh, she wants you to bring her the *Morning Herald* back, too.

THREE: What's that, what?

MRS. ONE: Well, I've delivered her message and that's all I can do.

ONE: All of you ladies have suffered a terrible shock because old Kelsey's happened to outlive his wife.

MRS. ONE: That's a very unfortunate thing for Mr. Kelsey since he was so completely dependent on her. I don't suppose any of you have bothered to speak a word of condolence to him?

TWO: He couldn't hear it, he don't have his hearing aid on.

MRS. ONE: If you take the trouble to speak slowly, loudly and distinctly, close to his ear, he can hear.

[*A bell clangs across the street.*]

ONE [*rising*]: They've opened: let's go over.

212

MRS. ONE: You boys go over and hold a couple of chairs for me and Mr. Kelsey; I'm going to take him across: old and blind as he is, he always takes his hat off in the elevator and tips it to me when I meet him outside, and ladies appreciate little courtesies like that.

[*She crosses briskly to Kelsey.*]

Mr. Kelsey? Can you hear me? This is Betsy Fletcher!

[*For the first time he seems to emerge from his stupefaction: he reaches out toward the little woman shouting into his ear and starts to rise on his cane.*]

KELSEY: Winnie! Winnie!

[*The three old men pause near the right exit and look back.*]

BETSY [*slowly, loudly, distinctly, into his ear*]: No, no. Mr. Kelsey, you don't have your hearing aid on; this isn't Winnie, this is Betsy Fletcher. I want to help you across the street to the cafeteria for breakfast because it's been arranged for you to go to a little nursing home near Fort Lauderdale; the ambulance is coming to pick you up here this morning, and since it's a tiring trip, you have to be fortified by a bit of hot breakfast. Now come on, take my arm, get up now, Mr. Kelsey!

[*The quality of her voice makes it evident to him that she is not Winnie: he lets himself back down in the wicker chair.*]

Mr. Kelsey, come on now. The doors are open; I will help you across.

[*Mr. Kelsey raises a hand and makes a sign of negation, holding the hand palm outward and waving it back and forth between himself and this strange, loud little woman.*]

ONE: Betsy, leave him alone.

TWO: We'll bring him back a paper cup of coffee.

213

MRS. ONE: Yes, well, I've done all I can. Last night I thought I'd finally convinced him that Winnie was gone but I'm afraid, now, his mind's clouded over again. He's sitting here waiting for Winnie to take him over to Dixie Mammy's Kitchen.

ONE: Come on over before every table is taken.

[*She joins their cluster, as the iron bell rings.*]

Dixie Mammy's ringing the bell for breakfast!

TWO: Come on, let's go over, the line-up is all in, now.

MRS. TWO: Yes, Dixie Mammy is still going to ring for breakfast, but not before the doors open.

TWO: She's not ringing loud this morning.

ONE: Nope, she's not ringing loud enough to wake up the dead this mawnin'.

[*Their voices fade as they straggle toward the pedestrian-crossing zone off right. Then the bell stops and there's stillness; the zinc white brightens, eclipsing the faded colors of everything on the street facade on the Ponce de Leon Hotel. Kelsey raises his cane and brings it down hard on the pavement: the light begins to dim out to a crepuscular pallor. Kelsey closes his cataract-blinded eyes and opens his jaws like a fish out of water. After a few moments, a sound comes from his mouth which takes the full measure of grief.*]

CURTAIN

THE GNADIGES FRAULEIN

The Gnädiges Fräulein was first presented, as part of a double bill entitled *Slapstick Tragedy*, by Charles Bowden and Lester Persky in association with Sidney Lanier, at the Longacre Theatre, in New York City, on February 22, 1966. It was directed by Alan Schneider. The sets were designed by Ming Cho Lee; the costumes, by Noel Taylor. Music was composed and selected by Lee Hoiby, and the lighting was by Martin Aronstein. Production was in association with Frenman Productions, Ltd. The cast, in order of appearance, was as follows:

POLLY	ZOE CALDWELL
MOLLY	KATE REID
PERMANENT TRANSIENT	DAN BLY
THE GNADIGES FRAULEIN	MARGARET LEIGHTON
COCALOONY	ART OSTRIN
INDIAN JOE	JAMES OLSON

PRODUCTION NOTES

The setting is Cocaloony Key, in the present time. The exterior of a frame cottage on the Key is visible, with a totally unrealistic arrangement of porch assorted props, steps, yard, and picket fence. The main playing area, the porch, should be to the front, with maybe the yard displaced to upstage left—as if Picasso had designed it. It's windy gray weather: sky, frame building, picket fence, porch, wicker rockers—everything is in the subtle variety of grays and grayish whites that you see in pelican feathers and clouds. Even the sun is a grayish-white disk over the lusterless gray zinc roof that sits at the angle of Charlie Chaplin's derby on the house which is apparently a rooming house since there's a "vacancy" sign in the outsize window that faces the audience. Most of the time all we see in this big window are the "vacancy" sign and the dirty net curtains, but once or twice in the play a bloom of light behind the window reveals a poetically incongruous Victorian parlor, like the parlor of a genteel bordello in the eighties or nineties, and this alone violates the chromatic scale of the pelican: it is a riotous garden of colors, provided by crimson damask, gilt frames and gilded tassels, a gaudy blackamoor pedestal for a light fixture, etc.—the designer will think of many more items or better items than I can. It's like the recollections of the Gnädiges Fräulein, her scrapbook of a past that had splendors: perhaps it's less like the parlor of a Victorian bordello than it is like the parlor of a suite in the Hotel Bristol in Vienna, at least as it was a few years ago.

The costumes of the women, Molly and Polly, are also in pelican colors. But the costume and make-up of the Gnädiges Fräulein (which will be described in detail when she appears) are as vivid a contrast as the slow-blooming interior through the big window. So is Indian Joe. He is a blond Indian, tawny gold as a palomino horse but with Caribbean-blue eyes. He has

217

practically no lines, so he doesn't have to be anything but an erotic fantasy in appearance, but with a dancer's sense of presence and motion onstage.

The Gnädiges Fräulein should be played by a singer, and I think of Lotte Lenya for this part as I think of Maureen Stapleton for the part of Molly, Lucille Benson for the part of Polly. It's a play with music, like *The Mutilated*. (The two plays should be performed together, I think.)

A bird called a cocaloony appears very briefly in the play: I think of it as a sort of giant pelican; in fact, all through the first draft of the play I have typed the word "pelican," scratched it out and written over it "cocaloony." There is a Bird-Girl in *The Mutilated* who could also appear as the cocaloony in this one.

Polly, the Society Editor of the Cocaloony Gazette, *comes on forestage as if driven by the moaning wind, clutching her pelican-gray shawl with one hand and, still more tightly, a Pan-Am zipper bag. There is a loud swoosh above her. She crouches. Then she straightens as the swoosh fades out. But it suddenly recurs and she crouches again. And she speaks to herself and the audience about the incident.*

POLLY: Was that two cocaloony birds that flew over or was it just one cocaloony bird that made a U-turn and flew back over again? OOPS! Bird-watchers, watch those birds! They're very dangerous birds if agitated and they sure do seem to be agitated today. OOPS! [*She crouches under another swoosh.*] —I might as well remain in this position if it wasn't so inelegant for a lady in my position. What is my position? Why, I'm the southernmost gossip columnist *and* Society Editor of the southernmost news organ in the Disunited Mistakes. OOPS! [*The same sound and action are repeated.*] —Everything's southernmost here because of a geographical accident making this island, this little bit of heaven dropped from the sky one day, the southernmost bit of terra firma of the—OOPS! I've lost concentration! [*She stares blankly for a couple of moments.*] —My mother said that the way you tell a lady is that a lady never steps out of her house, unless her house is on fire, without a pair of gloves on, and that's how you tell a lady if you want to tell one and you got something to tell one. Have I got my gloves on? No! And I didn't hear the fire engine, all I heard was that swoosh and flap sound in the air of a cocaloony, so I must get back concentration! [*She raps herself on the head.*] Oh, I got it back now, yais, perfect! What I was saying was that everything's southernmost here, I mean like this morning I did the southernmost write-up on the southernmost gang-bang and called it "Multiple Nuptials" which is the southernmost gilding of the southernmost lily that any cock-eyed sob sister and society editor, even if not southernmost, ever dreamed of, let alone—OOPS!— perpetrated. . . . [*The same sound and action are repeated.*] Yais, everything's southernmost here, like southern fried chicken is southern*most* fried chicken. But who's got a chicken? None of us southernmost white Anglo-Saxon Protestants are living on fish and fish only because of thyroid deficiency in our southernmost systems: we live on fish because regardless of faith or lack of it, every day is Friday, gastronomically speaking, because of the readjustment of the economy which is southernmost too. OOPS! [*The same sound and action are repeated.*] —Did I lose concentration? No. . . it's nice not to lose concentration, especially when you've got to deliver an address to the Southernmost Branch of the Audubon Society on the vicious, overgrown sea birds which are called cocaloonies, and are responsible for the name and notoriety of this—OOPS! [*The same sound and action are repeated.*] particular Key. OK, I'll deliver the address without notes, since the atmospheric turbulence made me drop them. Cocaloonies! They never fly off the fish-docks except in hurricane weather. Except in hurricane weather they just hang around and goof off on the fish-docks, mentally drifting and dreaming till animated by the— [*She whistles between two fingers as if calling a cab.*] —of a fish-boat coming in with a good haul of fish. Oh, then they're animated, they waddle and flap, flap and waddle out toward where the boat's docked to catch the fish thrown away, the ones not fit for the markets, but delectable or at least cordially acceptable to the cocaloonies, they flap and waddle out to the boat with their beaks wide open on their elastic gullets to catch the throwaway fish, the discards, the re-jecks, because, y'see,—tell it not in Gath!—the once self-reliant-and-self-sufficient character of this southernmost sea bird has degenerated to where it could be justly described as a parasitical creature, yes, gone are the days when it would condescend to fish for itself, oh, no, no, *no*, it— [*The porch of Molly's house is lighted and Molly comes out with a mop and a bucket: she ignores Polly. Molly plunges the* *mop in the bucket and starts mopping the steps to the porch. Polly makes a slight turn and glares over her shoulder.*] —Oh, it's her, a vulgar, slovenly bitch with social pretensions, pretending not to see me, because, y'see, she fancies herself very highly as the social leader of Cocaloony Key, and there she is on her front veranda, with mop and bucket like a common domestic. I'll bring her down. HEY! MOLLY!

MOLLY [*without turning*]: Who's that shouting my name out like they know me?

POLLY: *It's Polly,* Molly.

MOLLY: *Aw. You.*

POLLY: Yes, me! [*A cocaloony flies over; both ladies crouch. The light flickers, ending the prologue.*]

POLLY [*crossing to the porch steps*]: *Whatcha moppin' up, Molly?* [*They shout at each other above the wind.*]

MOLLY: *Blood.*

POLLY: The best time to mop up blood is before daybreak.

MOLLY: It wasn't shed before daybreak.

POLLY: Well, the next best time to mop it up's after dark.

MOLLY: That's not the policy of a good housekeeper.

POLLY: There's been some violence here?

MOLLY: Yep. I chopped the head off a chicken.

POLLY: On the front porch, Molly?

MOLLY: Nope. In the back yard, Polly. [*The wind subsides.*]

POLLY: It sure did make a long run, all the way 'round the house and up the front steps and right on into the parlor, yep. I know a chicken can run with its head cut off, but I never known it to make such a long run as that with such a good sense of direction. Molly, this explanation that you are mopping up chicken blood don't hold water. There's been some violence here and the victim wasn't a chicken, that I know, as well as I happen to know that you ain't had a live or dead piece of poultry on these premises since that old Rhode Island Red hen that you was fattenin' up for Thanksgivin' died of malnutrition before Hallowe'en.

MOLLY: Yeah, well, why don't you go over to your desk at the *Cocaloony Gazette* and work on your gossip column, Polly, and let me finish this mopping up operation without the nasal monotone of your voice to distract me and annoy me to distraction! Huh, Polly?

POLLY: How long is it been since you got a favorable mention in my society column?

MOLLY: Never read it. When a lady's sure of her social position as I am, she don't concern herself with gossip columns.

POLLY: You're asking for a bad write-up.

MOLLY: Couldn't care less, pooh, for you.

POLLY: You don't mean that.

MOLLY: Yes, I do.

POLLY: I see you got a "vacancy" sign in your window.

MOLLY: What about it?

POLLY: You got a "vacancy" sign in your window and you're mopping up blood on your porch.

MOLLY: No connection, none at all whatsoever.

POLLY: *Aw?* [*She laughs skeptically.*]

MOLLY: They's always a "vacancy" sign in that window since I knocked out the walls of the private bedrooms to make the big dormitory. Because in a big dormitory they's always room for one more. I do a quantity business. Also a quality business but the emphasis is on quantity in the big dormitory because it's furnished with two- and three-decker bunks. It offers accommodation for always one more.

POLLY: Yeah, well, this type of material is OK for the classified ads but not for the gossip column and the society page, so I reckon I'll toddle on. Toodle-oo! [*She has opened her Pan-Am zipper bag and removed a suspiciously thin cigarette.*]

MOLLY [*with covetous interest*]: Whatcha took outa your Dorothy bag, Polly, a Mary Jane?

POLLY: Ta-ta, toodle-oo, see you someday. . . maybe.

223

MOLLY: Polly, sit down in this rocker and rock. I guarantee you material for your column.

POLLY: That's mighty nice of you, Molly— [*She lights the cigarette.*] —but I really do have to be going, I have to cover —well, *something—somewhere.* . . .

MOLLY: Polly, I promise you, sweetheart, that in the course of this late afternoon no matter how the sky changes through light and shadow, I'll give you material for the Goddamnest human and inhuman interest story you ever imagined, Polly. Besides, your ankles look swollen, set down in a comfortable rocker and let's rock together while we turn on together. Huh, honey? [*She pushes her into the rocker.*] Wait! Let's synchronize rockers! Hold yours still till I count to three. OK?

POLLY: Count away!

MOLLY: ONE! TWO! THREE! *ROCK!* [*They rock with pelvic thrusts as if having sex.*]

POLLY: WHEEE!

MOLLY: Now we're rocking in beautiful unison, Polly!

POLLY: In tune with the infinite, Molly!

MOLLY: In absolute harmony with it!

TOGETHER: HUFF, HUFF, HUFF, WHEE!

MOLLY: I love to rock. It reminds me of my girlhood romances, Polly!

POLLY: One of your girlhood romances is still in traction, ain't he?

MOLLY: That's a lie, he gets around fine! —On crutches. [*They cackle together.*] Now, Polly about the big dormitory, Polly!

POLLY [*throwing up her legs gaily*]: Huff, huff, huff, WHEEE!

224

MOLLY: I said about THE BIG DORMITORY, Polly!

POLLY: WHEEE!

MOLLY [*through the megaphone*]: THREE, TWO, ONE! STOP ROCKERS! [*She stops Polly's rocker so abruptly that Polly is nearly thrown to the floor.*] Let's have a little propriety and some decorum on the front porch, Polly, you're not out back of the woodshed! I was saying: about the big dormitory. The overhead, the operating expenses such as free limousine service, are astronomical, Polly.

POLLY: Oh?

MOLLY: So! —I can't afford to buy advertising space in the *Cocaloony Gazette*, and in the light of this situation which is a mighty dark situation, I could use and would surely appreciate the use of a knockout feature story in your next Sunday supplement, Polly, a two-page spread with photos of personages and captions without a word of profanity in them. How does that strike you, Polly?

POLLY: It don't strike me, Molly, it whistles over my head like a cocaloony.

MOLLY: I'm dead serious, Polly.

POLLY: It's natural to be serious when you're dead, WHEEE! [*She resumes rocking. Molly stops the rocker so forcibly that Polly slides on the porch floor.*] OW!

MOLLY: COW! —Get back in your rocker and listen to what I tell you. You'd go a long way out of your way to find a richer gold mine of material in the class category than I got here in the big dormitory, under the rooftree of God, I've got REAL PERSONAGES here! [*A fantastically tattered old wino, the "permanent transient," with fishing tackle, comes around the side of the building, tipping his topless bowler with a clown's grin and staggering in several directions.*]

225

POLLY: Including that one?

MOLLY: That's, uh, that's an old family domestic I keep on the premises for sentimental, uh—reasons. [*She picks up a megaphone and calls through it*]: WILLIAM? I want the Rolls to roll me to vespers at sunset. [*She snaps her fan open. The wino takes two steps backward, with a hiccough, and then staggers off.*] I was saying? Oh, personages, yaiss! Take the Gnädiges Fräulein, one instant for an instance, there's a personage for you, internationally celebrated for yea many years on this earth if not on other planets, yes, I've got the Fräulein to mention only a few of the more or less permanent guests of the big dormitory under the rooftree of God.

POLLY: How about Indian Joe?

MOLLY: Yes, how about Indian Joe, that's a personage, Polly, a blond Indian with Caribbean-blue eyes, moving in beauty like the night of cloudless climes, and so forth. [*The parlor blooms into light. We see Indian Joe spraying his armpits with an atomizer and patting his pompadour.*]

POLLY [*in a religious voice*]: I catch his inimitable and ineffable aroma somewhere in the near distance: is it outside or in? If I turn around, I'm afraid it would make me giddy, I might lose concentration.

MOLLY: Sit back down in your rocker but don't rock. —What was I saying? —Oh, the big dormitory. Don't be misguided by the "vacancy" sign. On weekends, Polly, as God's my judge, I hang out the SRO sign for standing room only in the big dormitory!

POLLY: You sell standing room in the big dormitory, Molly?

MOLLY: You bet your sweet ass I do. You take a permanent transient that's ever in his existence had a run-in with the law and show me a permanent transient that hasn't. It's four A.M.

No intelligent permanent transient prefers to stay on the street at that desperate hour when even the Conch Gardens closes. Not in a state of the Union where they's eighteen different kinds of vagrancy charges that a lone man on the streets at night can be charged with. All right. That SRO sign looks mighty good to a permanent transient, it shines to him like the star of Bethlehem shone to the kings that came from the East.

POLLY: And do they sleep standing up?

MOLLY: Unless they can find a voluntary bed-partner.

POLLY: Flamingoes can sleep standin' up on one leg, even.

MOLLY: Anything havin' a leg to stand on can sleep standin' up if it has to.

POLLY: Don't they fall down, Molly?

MOLLY: They fall down and get back up.

POLLY: Well, Molly, when one of your standing-up sleepers falls down, don't it disturb the sleep of the horizontal sleepers?

MOLLY: Polly, a permanent transient is a wonderful sleeper. He sleeps heavy and late in the calm and security of the big dormitory, as God is my witness in heaven.

POLLY: When is the check-out time?

MOLLY: They wake up to music which is provided by the Gnädiges Fräulein. [*On this cue, the Fräulein sings: "Open wide the windows, open wide the doors, and let the merry sunshine in!"*] There, that's reveille for them. Hear them rising? [*Noise is heard inside: groans, howls, etc.*]

WINO [*sticking his head out the window*]: Bathroom privilege?

MOLLY: Granted. [*She tosses a key in the window.*]

POLLY: It'll be fun to watch 'em coming out, Molly.

227

MOLLY: They have to go out the back way because it's daylight and they make a better public appearance by starlight on a starless night because of embarrassing subtractions from their wardrobe, like some of them can't find their shoes when they go to get up in the morning and some of them can't find their shirts or their pants when they go to get up in the morning and some of them can't find a Goddam bit of their wardrobe when they go to get up in the morning, including their lingeree, Polly. And some of them can't find their equilibrium or concentration or will to continue the struggle for survival when they go to get up in the morning and some of them don't get up in the morning, not even when the Gnädiges Fräulein sings the reveille song.

POLLY: Obstinate?

MOLLY: Nope, dead, Polly. [*Polly breathes out a sound like the wind in the pines, rolling her eyes above a wicked grin.*] Yep, the Dark Angel has a duplicate key to the big dormitory and faithfully every night he drops by to inspect the sleepers and check their dog-tags. He wanders among the two- and three-decker bunks and never leaves without company, nope, never leaves unattended and no one grieves when he leaves.

POLLY [*lisping*]: Between the dark and the daylight—

MOLLY: When the gloom of doom is in flower—

TOGETHER:
Comes a pause in the night's occupation
Which is known as The Angel's Dark Hour
[*The Gnädiges Fräulein appears indistinctly behind the screen door.*]

FRAULEIN [*at screen door*]: May I come out? [*Molly ignores the request. Polly puts on her glasses to peer at the Gnädiges Fräulein. She calls out louder.*]: May I come out?

228

POLLY: Molly, a lady in there wants to come out; she's asking permission to come outside the house.

MOLLY: I know. I heard her. She can't.

POLLY: Why can't she come out, Molly?

MOLLY: She's lost porch privilege.

POLLY: Aw. Then let her go in the yard.

MOLLY: She's lost yard privilege, too.

POLLY: What privilege has she still got?

MOLLY: Lavatory and kitchen. Her kitchen privilege depends on her bringing in something to cook, which don't seem likely today.

FRAULEIN: May I come out?

POLLY: Mah-wah-com-ahh.

MOLLY: Don't mock her. In spite of her present condition she's still a personage, Polly.

POLLY: Well, let her out, lemme have some fun with her.

MOLLY: How could you have fun with her?

POLLY: I could interview her, I could ask her opinions.

MOLLY: She's long past having opinions.

POLLY: Aw, now, let her out, Molly.

MOLLY: What's the deal if I do?

POLLY: A real classy write-up.

MOLLY: Pooh. Don't need one.

POLLY: A Mary Jane? All to yourself?

MOLLY [handing her the megaphone]: Tell her to come out. Address her as Gnädiges Fräulein, she comes from Middle

229

Europe and circumstances of genteel circumstances. You got to holler at her, she's got calcified eardrums.

POLLY [*opening the door*]: Come out, Ganniker Frowline. [*There is a pause.*] —Not coming out.

MOLLY: Give her time, she's preparing.

POLLY: Now she's comin' out now. I better think what to ask her.

MOLLY: Ask her how's fishing today, or which she prefers, a mackerel or a red snapper. 'Cause if she wants to maintain a residence in the big dormitory, after sundown, the subject of fish has got to be kept active in her thought waves.

POLLY: She's not outfitted for fishing.

MOLLY: She's got on the remnants of her theatrical wardrobe.

POLLY: I think I'll ask her some fashion questions and some questions about makeup and hairstyles.

MOLLY: Let's have some protocol here. The Gnädiges Fräulein is a personage, yeah, but she's still a social derelict, and a social leader like me takes precedence over a social derelict like her, so give her a couple of short sentences, then concentrate the rest of the write-up on ME. [*She turns her rocker crossly away from Polly. The Gnädiges Fräulein is now out on the porch. She wears a curious costume which would not be out of place at the Moulin Rouge in the time of Toulouse-Lautrec. One eye is covered by a large blood-stained bandage. Her hair is an aureole of bright orange curls, very fuzzy. She sits on the steps and opens a big scrapbook.*]

POLLY: She sat in a pool of blood, Molly.

MOLLY: 'Sall right, it's her own blood.

POLLY: *Aw!* Not a chicken's blood, huh?

MOLLY: OOPS, I made a boo-boo, did I ever make a boo-boo!

POLLY: So the Ganniker Frowline was the victim of violence here.

MOLLY: Well, I'd be a fool to deny it and you'd be a bigger fool to believe the denial. Yep, her scroll has been charged with a good deal of punishment lately.

POLLY: Lately as today. Hmm. Ask her if she would like to make a short statement.

MOLLY: Ask her yourself, you're interviewing the Fräulein: I'm not even speaking to her until she reestablishes her credit here with a good catch of fish.

FRAULEIN: Number, please. [*She is holding out a faded sheet of paper.*]

POLLY: Does she think she's a telephone operator?

MOLLY: She wants you to pick out a number for her to sing on that program she's holding out to you.

POLLY: How does she sing?

MOLLY: She *sings*.

POLLY: I don't think I'll take a chance on it. However, she might do for a human interest story. Don't you think so?

MOLLY: She's human.

POLLY: Is she?

MOLLY: Take that program from her; she's holding it right in my face so I got to lean over if I want to look out. [*Polly takes the program.*]

FRAULEIN: Number, please.

POLLY: Give me time to pick one out that I like.

MOLLY: She didn't hear that. Not a word.

POLLY: Ask her to rotate, Molly.

MOLLY: Why d'ya want her to rotate?

POLLY: I'm describing her outfit in the write-up. [*She is making notes.*] I want a look at the other side of her costume.

MOLLY: Walk around her.

POLLY: I don't feel like getting up.

MOLLY: Read me the part of the write-up where you mention the big dormitory.

POLLY: I haven't got to that yet.

MOLLY: That ought to be in the first paragraph of the write-up. Why don't you begin the write-up like this, Polly. "One of our most prominent social leaders. . ." —No, begin it this way, this is the way to begin it—"The social season got off to a brilliant start when—"

POLLY: Hold it, she's startin' to rotate. Very gradually, though. She's pivoting majestically toward me. I never gild the lily in my write-ups. Hmmm. She's made a full turn now. I've seen all sides of her costume without getting up. I guess we ought to ask for a vocal selection, but I can't read this old program, it's too faded. See if she can recite it.

MOLLY: Remember, it's your idea. [*She shouts through the megaphone.*] GNADIGES FRAULEIN! BITTE! RECITE NUMBERS ON PROGRAM!

FRAULEIN: Number One: "Pale Hands I Loved Beside the Shalimar" by the celebrated tunesmith, Amy Woodforde-Finden. Number Two: "I Dream of Jeannie With the Light Brown Hair" by permission of ASCAP. Number Three: "All Alone" by the celebrated tunesmith, Irving Vienna. Excuse me, Berlin. Number Four: "Smiles" by some long-ago smiler, and—

232

POLLY: Tell her some number to sing, any number.

MOLLY [*shouting through the megaphone and striking her on the shoulder at each count*]: Ein, zwei, drei! [*Then the Fräulein assumes a romantically theatrical pose on the porch and begins to sing.*]

FRAULEIN:
Stars are the win-dows of Heaaa-ven
That an-gels peek throooogh!

[*She stops in mid-gesture, frozen.*]

POLLY: —Has she finished the number?

MOLLY: Naw, she lost concentration. [*She picks up a baseball bat.*]

POLLY: If you conk her with that she won't get back concentration or even consciousness till this time tomorrow, Molly, but do you care?

FRAULEIN [*resuming from the start*]:

Stars are the win-dows of Heaaa-ven
That an-gels peek throooough!

[*She freezes again in mid-gesture, opens and closes her mouth like a goldfish.*]

POLLY: Now what's she up to?

MOLLY: She's demonstrating.

POLLY: What's she demonstrating?

MOLLY: Either a goldfish in a goldfish bowl or a society reporter in a soundproof telephone booth.

FRAULEIN [*audible again*]:
That an-gels peek throoough!
When we are happy they're hap-*peeee*,
When we are blue they turn b*luuuue!*

233

POLLY: Enough, enough of that, stop her!

MOLLY: You started her, you stop her.

POLLY: How do I do that?

MOLLY: Put her back in the house.

POLLY: And how do I do *that?*

MOLLY: Turn her, she can be turned, then shove her, she can be shoved.

POLLY: I can't shove her through the screen door.

MOLLY: You open the screen door for her.

POLLY: I don't want to get up.

MOLLY: Well, stay on your fat ass, you slob.

POLLY: Shut your fat mouth, you fink. [*The swoosh and whistle of cocaloonies is heard.*] Oops!

MOLLY: Cocaloonies! [*Both cover their eyes with their hands, the Gnädiges Fräulein hits an unexpected high note and dashes back into the house. The parlor lights up and she can be seen through the window, ineffectually hiding among the feathery foliage of a great potted fern.*]

POLLY: HORRIBLE!

MOLLY: HIDEOUS! SCAT! [*A Cocaloony has entered the yard and is stalking jerkily about, poking its gruesome head this way and that with spastic motions, as if looking about the premises for something.*]

POLLY: Make conversation, say something casual, Molly.

MOLLY: You say something casual and I'll answer.

POLLY: I'll say something reminiscent.

MOLLY: No, casual.

234

POLLY: *Reminiscent!*

MOLLY: Have it your way, a casual reminiscence. [POLLY *loses concentration: Molly observes her condition.*] Oh, God, she's lost concentration. [*Molly shouts at her through the megaphone.*] POLLY! [*Polly regains concentration abruptly and starts for the door. Molly catches the back of her skirt, which rips off. Polly finds the screen door has been latched by the Fräulein. The Cocaloony struts up onto the porch and sits down in Molly's rocker. The ladies freeze by the door.*] Don't move: keep on talking.

POLLY: I wasn't talking. I'm going to throw something at it.

MOLLY: What?

COCALOONY [*ominously*]: AWK.

MOLLY: I think it heard you plotting to throw something at it.

POLLY: Pooh. I have behind me the power of the press.

MOLLY: It would be more useful in *front* of you, right now, ducks.

COCALOONY: AWK.

POLLY [*politely*]: Awk.

COCALOONY [*severely*]: *AWK!*

POLLY: The power of the Fourth Estate is behind me and in front of me, too, it's like the air that surrounds me, it surrounds me completely as the grace of God, you know that.

MOLLY: Your voice has got a funny vibrato sound to it, a sort of a shrill vibration like you had a tin larynx with the wind whistling through it. [*The Cocaloony rises, knocking over the rocker, and flaps off the porch, but remains in the yard.*]

235

POLLY: Well. Let's go back to the rockers before I collapse.

MOLLY: You take this rocker.

POLLY: No, no, I wouldn't dream of it, that's your rocker, and I know how important it is to feel the familiar beneath you.

MOLLY: Shall we rock or just sit? With our teeth in our mouth saying nothing?

POLLY: I'm going to say something.

MOLLY: Well, SAY it, don't just *say* you're going to say it!

POLLY: PHEW! I never knew a cocaloony bird had such a powerful odor. It smells like that mysterious old sea monster that washed up and rotted on Dizzy Bitch Key after Hurricane Lulu.

TOGETHER: Ugh! Oof! Phew!

POLLY: It's stalking and strutting around like Napoleon on the ramparts. It's certainly a hell of a three-sheet to have in front of the big dormitory. It's not a status symbol by any manner of means.

MOLLY: Mention this in the write-up and you will find yourself featured in the obituaries next issue.

POLLY: Pooh.

MOLLY: No pooh about it, I got connections with the Mafia and with the syndicate, too, so roll that up in your Mary Jane and smoke it.

COCALOONY: AWK. AWK.

POLLY: Awk.

MOLLY: Will you quit talkin' back to it?

POLLY: I wanted to pacify it.

236

MOLLY: Wrong policy, Polly. Take your hands off your eyes and stare straight at it, return its furious stare, and go it one better.

POLLY: How?

MOLLY: By stamping your foot.

POLLY: A vulgar, petulant action? Also provocative action? Not me, I'm not about to, you stamp your foot at it.

MOLLY: Okay, scaredy-cat.

POLLY: Well, go on, stamp it. [*Molly raises her foot and sets it down soundlessly.*] You call that stamping your foot? You raised your delicate slipper and set it back down like you were outside of all gravity, Molly, in weightless ozone.

COCALOONY: Awk.

POLLY: Awkward, an awkward creature, as awkward a creature as—

MOLLY: Shh.

COCALOONY: AWK. AWK. AWK.

POLLY: What a limited vocabularly it's got! It's strutting up closer, Molly.

MOLLY: Don't report the obvious to me, Polly.

POLLY: What's obvious to me is it's looking for someone or something.

MOLLY: Who in hell isn't, Polly?

POLLY: If I should hazard a guess as to what or whom, and I guessed correctly, would you admit and confirm it?

MOLLY: —Well. . . .

POLLY: —What?

MOLLY: Under God's rooftree there's no room for successful prevarication. Yep. He's looking for something that's someone and this something-someone is the Gnädiges Fräulein, I shamelessly, blamelessly admit it. —Continue interrogation: you can't hide a cat when the cat's out of the bag, as way out of it as the Gnädiges Fräulein is out of the bag and into the lacy fronds of that fern potted in the parlor. So, all right, take it from there. I'm too straightened out, now, to care about any outcome except my income.

POLLY: Well, I'm not a star in the mathematics department, but I do know that two plus two makes one less than five and one more than three: —the Frowline has provoked the vengeful enmity of the cocaloonies, Molly. And what provokes enmity under the rooftree of God is *competition*, huh, Molly?

MOLLY: I shamelessly, blamelessly admit that the Gnädiges Fräulein has gone into competition with the cocaloonies for the thrown-away fish at the fish-docks.

POLLY: Why and wherefore, Molly?

MOLLY: Well, having passed and long passed the zenith of her career in show-biz and as a B-girl at the Square Roof and Conch Gardens, the Gnädiges Fräulein has turned her attentions and transferred her battleground for survival to the fish-docks, Polly. She's shamelessly, blamelessly, gone into competition with the cocaloonies for the throw-away fish. When a fish-boat whistles and the cocaloonies waddle rapidly forward, out she charges to compete for the catch. Well, they got a closed shop, the cocaloonies, they seem to be unionized, Polly, and naturally regard the Gnädiges Fräulein as a wildcat operator and take a not-so-bright view of her dock activities, Polly. Nothing is more intolerant, Polly, than one parasite of another. So dimmer and dimmer became the view they took of her, till, finally, today, there was a well-organized resistance movement against her. Yep, they turned on her today and she returned from the fish-docks in a damaged condition, no fish in her bucket and no eye in one eye socket. [*During this the Cocaloony stands still cocking his head with a wing to his ear—occasionally stomping.*]

POLLY: *Gouged?*

MOLLY: Yes, *out!*

POLLY: Oh-oh, oh-*HO!* [*She scribbles notes.*]

MOLLY: I'm not at all happy about this situation because the Gnädiges Fräulein is required to deliver three fish a day to keep eviction away and one fish more to keep the wolf from the door, and now that the cocaloonies have turned against her, will she have guts enough to fight the good fight or will she retire from the fish-docks like she did from show business, under pressure!?

[*Indian Joe enters the yard with a tomahawk and a bloody scalp. His hair is bright yellow and his skin is deep red and glistening. He is dressed like a Hollywood Indian, that is, he wears a breech-clout of deerskin and some strings of wampum, perhaps.*]

POLLY [*excitedly*]: Indian Joe! [*Indian Joe and the giant Cocaloony square off at each other.*]

COCALOONY [*stamping and flapping*]: Awk, awk, awk, awk, awk, awk, awk, awk, AWKKK!

INDIAN JOE: *Ugh!*

COCALOONY: AWK!

INDIAN JOE: UGH!

POLLY: Reminds me of the Lincoln-Douglas debates. Don't it remind you of the Lincoln-Douglas debates?

MOLLY: No.

POLLY: What's it remind you of then?

239

MOLLY: Nothing reminds me of nothing.

POLLY: You mean you're stoned on one stick?

MOLLY: Concentrate on the action.

POLLY: What action, it's just a standoff. They squared off to a standoff. [*During this incongruously desultory dialogue on the porch, Indian Joe and the Cocaloony have continued to menace each other, Indian Joe waving his tomahawk over his head with steady, pendulum motions and the Cocaloony bird poking its gruesome head backward and forward in spastic rhythm.*] I guess this is what they say happens when the unmovable object meets the irresistible force: that's a standoff, ain't it?

MOLLY: Nope, that's a collision.

POLLY: Let's call it a standoff collision and quit the argument, Molly.

MOLLY: Look. Action. [*The Cocaloony bird has begun to retreat from Indian Joe's resolute, slow advance. It suddenly flaps off, racing for a takeoff, great swoosh over the scene as it hits the empyrean. Indian Joe shrugs and stalks onto the porch.*]

POLLY: HOW.

INDIAN JOE: POW.

MOLLY: WOW. [*He jerks the screen door open and enters the interior.*]

POLLY: Strong character!

MOLLY: Devastating. —But lazy. —Indolence is the privilege of great beauty, yep, great beauty wears indolence like the stripes on a four-star general at a state banquet. Look at him in there, now. [*The inner stage of the parlor brightens: Indian Joe is seated in a ballroom chair, holding a mirror as the Gnädiges Fräulein makes him up for his next appearance: she is fluttering with enchantment.*]

240

POLLY: The Frowline has eyes for Indian Joe?

MOLLY: Eyes is plural and she's just got one eye. [*She snaps her fingers: the parlor dims out.*] —Have you got eyes for him, Polly?

POLLY: Let's just say I got eyes.

MOLLY: Well, then, don't compete with the cocaloonies for the throw-away fish and don't compete with the Gnädiges Fräulein for the Viennese dandy.

POLLY: Did you say Viennese dandy?

MOLLY: If I did, I must have lost concentration for a moment. Didn't we synchronize rockers?

POLLY: I'm standing, not rocking but rocked. [*The sound of a fish-boat whistle is heard.*]

MOLLY: Crocked! *Oh! A fish-boat whistle!*

POLLY: Why do you mention it like a thing unheard and unheard-of before?

MOLLY: I'm anxious to see if the Gnädiges Fräulein will sally forth to meet it or if she's reconciled to eviction from the big dormitory.

POLLY: I never would have dreamed—

MOLLY: What?

POLLY: —*Dreamed.* . . .

MOLLY: WATCH OUT, I HEAR HER COMING, SHE COMES OUT FAST! DON'T BLOCK HER, MAKE WAY FOR HER, POLLY! [*The Gnädiges Fräulein charges out of the house with a tin bucket.*] Bravo, she's back in action! That's the Spirit of the big dormitory for you! Encourage her, applaud her, don't sit on your hands! [*The fish-boat whistles twice more. The Gnädiges Fräulein disappears rapidly, flapping her skinny arms like the wings of a sea bird and making harsh cries.*] —My God, her scroll has been charged with so much punishment lately I thought her spirit was vanquished!

POLLY: This is material for a human interest story. Should I phone it in for general release or wait till I know the outcome?

MOLLY: Outcomes don't always come out quickly, Polly. Let's just sit here and rock on the spacious veranda of the big dormitory. And synchronize rockers. Hold your rocker still till I say rock and then rock. ONE. TWO. THREE! ROCK ROCKERS! [*They rock together on the porch.*] You can occupy this quiet interlude by working on the write-up. Describe me in it. Me, me, me, me, *mee!*

POLLY: I've already described you.

MOLLY: How?

POLLY: I mentioned your existence.

MOLLY: How about my position?

POLLY: Position in what?

MOLLY: Society. My preeminence in it.

POLLY: You can gild the lily without a lily to gild.

MOLLY: Balls! —Synchronize rockers again: you're rocking too fast. I have to over-exert to keep up with you. [*An outcry is heard far off.*]

POLLY: A human outcry?

MOLLY: Distant, still, too distant. [*Another outcry and other sounds of commotion are heard.*]

POLLY: Closer.

MOLLY: Still fairly far. [*The commotion increases in volume.*] Honey, get up and practice your profession. Report on whatever is visible from the walk.

242

POLLY: Not me, old rocking-chair's got me. [*There is another outcry.*]

MOLLY: Another outcry, still human. The Gnädiges Fräulein is on her way back from the fish-docks. [*She rises and peers through the telescope.*] It buggers description, Polly. Oh, God. I think I better go in and check on the check-outs in the big dormitory.

POLLY: Let me help you.

MOLLY: Help yourself, God help you! [*At this moment as they start for the door, the Gnädiges Fräulein comes stumbling rapidly back along the picket fence, feeling for the gate. An oversize fish is protruding tail-first from her bucket. She is hard pressed by the cocaloonies. We hear them flapping violently above her, the stage lights flicker from their wing-shadows. Molly covers her eyes with both hands, peeking between her fingers ever so slightly. Not locating the gate successfully, the Gnädiges Fräulein crashes through the picket fence and makes a wild dash around the side of the cottage, holding the lid on the big fish in the bucket. Terrific flapping and whistling noises are heard.*] In?

POLLY [*peering around the side of the cottage*]: Out!

MOLLY: In?

POLLY: Out!

MOLLY: Still out?

POLLY: In! [*Molly rushes in and rushes right back out.*]

MOLLY: A cocaloony bird has got in with her! [*Indian Joe rushes out on the porch, imitates cocaloony birds and points inside.*]

POLLY: What's he telling you, Molly?

MOLLY: He's complaining about the cocaloony, Polly!

243

POLLY: Phone the police.

MOLLY: Phone's in the house and I don't intend to go in till the cocaloony goes out. [*A Cocaloony bird sticks its gruesome head out an upper window.*]

COCALOONY BIRD: AWK. AWK. [*Indian Joe shakes his tomahawk at the window. The Cocaloony bird runs out the front door with a large fish in its beak. It runs flapping down the walk, building up speed for a takeoff.*]

INDIAN JOE: Ugh. [*He spits disgustedly and kicks a section of the fence down as he goes off.*]

FRAULEIN [*at the door*]: May I come out?

MOLLY: Take a look at her, Polly. Describe her condition to me.

POLLY: She's alive, still in the land of the living.

MOLLY: Please be more specific about her condition.

POLLY: Her vision is now zero-zero.

MOLLY [*shouting through the megaphone*]: COME ON OUT HERE AND REPAIR THIS FENCE, FRAULEIN!

POLLY: Aw, no, Molly, give her time to come out of shock and stop bleeding.

MOLLY: I don't tell you how to run your society page and I'll thank you not to interfere with the management of the big dormitory, Polly. [*The Fräulein begins to sing "All Alone." Molly lowers her voice.*] She thought I requested a number.

POLLY: If you open the door for her she'll come out.

MOLLY: What would you call her voice? A lyric soprano?

POLLY: She flats a little in the top register, Molly.

MOLLY: I think her recent experience has upset her a little.

244

POLLY: I think she's coming out, now. Yes, she is. Coming out.

MOLLY: —She's out, now?

POLLY: Almost. [*The Gnädiges Fräulein is appearing gradually on the front porch. She sings as she appears, hands clasped spiritually together, a bloody bandage covering the whole upper half of her face and an aureole of pink-orange curls, very fluffy, framing the bandage which is tied in back with a large butterfly bow. Her costume is the same except that her tulle skirt, or tou-tou, is spangled with fresh drops of blood that glitter like rubies and her legs, bare from mid-thigh to ankle, are likewise streaked with blood. However, her voice is clear and sweet as a bird's: I mean songbird's. Her motions are slow, very slow. Now and then she extends a thin arm, to feel her way forward as she is still moving forward. She is transfigured as a saint under torture.*]

MOLLY: Is she or isn't she OUT, now?

POLLY: Why don't you see for yourself?

MOLLY: You're a reporter, ain't you, Miss Society Reporter? Then report! Report, for Chrissakes, is she or isn't she out on the front porch, now!

POLLY: SHUT UP! SHE'S SINGING, GOD DAMN IT!

MOLLY: I know she's singing! I didn't ask if she's singing. I asked is she out or in! [*Polly sings with her. The Fräulein stops singing.*]

POLLY: —I think you scared her. She's quit.

MOLLY: She always quits when somebody else chimes in, she will only sing solo.

POLLY: Can't stand the competish?

MOLLY: Yep. She's out again, now. I didn't want to look at her till my nerves was prepared for the shock of her appearance.

POLLY: I think she's remarkable. I'm going to call her remarkable in the write-up.

MOLLY: Don't overdo it.

POLLY: Watch her: she's about to walk off the steps.

MOLLY: She's gonna walk off the steps. She's gonna *nearly* walk off 'em: then stop short. —Intuition takes over when the faculties fail. I'm willing to make book on it.

POLLY: She's shuffling along with caution.

MOLLY: Yep. That's what I told you.

POLLY: Look. She's stopped and set down. Let's shout bravo, applaud her, intuition or caution, she stopped at the edge of the steps.

MOLLY: Don't turn her head. I don't want self-satisfaction to become the cornerstone of her nature.

POLLY: *Oh, God, look, do you see what I see?!*

MOLLY: I don't know what you see so I can't be expected to say if I do or I don't.

POLLY: She's picked up a book and—

MOLLY: She has picked up her scrapbook, her album of press clippings. What about it? She put it down and now she's picked it back up. People do things like that. What's peculiar about it?

POLLY: It just occurred to me, Molly, that unless her scrapbook is printed in Braille, the Frowline is not going to make much out of her old press clippings —is she?

MOLLY: She's reading them out loud, now.

FRAULEIN [*in a high, sing-song voice, like a priest saying Mass*]: "The talented young soubrette astonished her audience as well as her fellow performers when she cleverly intercepted a rather large mackeral thrown to the seal by catching this same rather large mackerel in her own lovely jaws!" — Ahhhhhh! Ahhhhhh . . . . . [*The final sounds are a blend of triumph and regret.*]

MOLLY: Polly? From *memory: perfect!* [*She turns to the Fräulein and gives her a little round of applause. The Fräulein tries to bow: totters slightly forwards and backwards. Then she resumes her incantation.*]

FRAULEIN: "Veritable—dressing-room—afterwards"—ahhhhh. . . . . [*The Fräulein places a hand to her forehead.*]

POLLY: She's stuck! Her memory's failed her!

MOLLY: Temporary amnesia resulting from shock . . .

POLLY: Take a look at her now.

MOLLY: What for?

POLLY: I want you to see what she's doing, it buggers description, Molly.

MOLLY: All I see is she's holding up her lorgnon.

POLLY: That don't seem peculiar to you?

MOLLY: Not in the least. She always holds up her lorgnon when she reads her press clippings.

POLLY: But she can't read her old press clippings.

MOLLY: That's not the point.

POLLY: Then what is the point in your opinion, Molly?

MOLLY: Habit! Habit! Now do you get the point?

POLLY: You mean it's a habit with her to hold up her lorgnon when she is reading her scrapbook?

MOLLY: Absolutely. It's a custom, a habit, a—now, look! Now, look. And listen! She is expressing the inexpressible regret of all her regrets.

FRAULEIN [*regretfully*]: AHHHHHHHHHH! HHHHHHHHHH

POLLY: —Saddest soliloquy on the stage since Hamlet's. . . .

FRAULEIN: —AHHHHHHHHHHH. . . . HHHHHHHHHH

MOLLY: I hope she don't repeat it.

FRAULEIN: AHHHHHHHHHHH. . . . HHHHHHHHHH HHHHHHHHHH

MOLLY: Tell her not to repeat it.

POLLY [*to Gnädiges Fräulein*]: Don't repeat it.

MOLLY: Aw, shoot. You think she overheard that little whisper? [*She shouts through the megaphone.*] FRAULEIN! DON'T REPEAT IT! —I do believe she heard me.

POLLY: —She's putting her lorgnon away.

MOLLY: She put it in her bosom.

POLLY: She's taking it out again, now.

MOLLY: She's rubbing the lenses on her white tulle skirt.

POLLY: She's holding it up again, now.

MOLLY: She's still dissatisfied with it. She's putting it down again now.

POLLY: She's raising it up again, now.

TOGETHER: SHE'S THROWN IT AWAY, NOW! AHHH-HHHH!

FRAULEIN: Ahhhhhh. . . .

POLLY: She's holding her scrapbook out.

MOLLY: I'm looking at her. I'm observing her actions.

POLLY: I think she wants you to put her scrapbook away.

MOLLY: It will be interesting to see what she finally does with it when she discovers that no one is going to accept it from her hand, Polly. [*The Fräulein suddenly tosses the scrapbook into the yard, raising her arms and crouching: a dramatic gesture accompanied by another dismal soliloquy of one vowel, prolonged. . . .*]

POLLY: Sudden. —Action.

MOLLY: Yes. —Sudden. [*The whistle of a fish-boat is heard. Polly faces Molly with an air of wild surmise. There is dumb play between them as the Gnädiges Fräulein cups an ear with a trembling hand and crouches toward the direction of the fish-docks. Molly whispers shrilly.*] Polly! *Give her this bucket!*

POLLY: Don't be silly! Don't be absurd! She ain't going back to the fish-docks!

MOLLY: Oh, yes, but she is! I assure you! Look! She's in starting position.

POLLY: Yeah, but she ain't started, Molly. [*The second whistle of a fish-boat is heard.*]

MOLLY: She never takes off till the fish-boat has whistled three times.

POLLY: How many times has it whistled?

MOLLY: Twice!

249

POLLY: Only twice?

MOLLY: Just twice! [*At this moment the fish-boat whistles a third time and the Fräulein is off, flapping her long, thin arms and waddling very rapidly like a cocaloony. Unable to locate the gate, she crashes through the picket fence. She stops short and screams.*]

FRAULEIN: BUCKET, BUCKET, FISH BUCKET!

POLLY: I think she wants her *fish*-bucket.

MOLLY: Here, take it out to her, Society Reporter.

POLLY: Take it out to her yourself, Society Leader! [*Molly snatches the wine-bottle or "stick" from Polly's hand. With her other hand raised as if to threaten a blow. Polly glares back at her for a moment, then complies with Molly's order and rushes to the Fräulein with the bucket. The Fräulein is stationary but flapping on the front walk. Polly thrusts the bucket with some difficulty into one of the Fräulein's flapping hands. The Fräulein immediately takes off, disappearing while flapping. Polly returns to the porch.*] Pooh to you, Social Leader.

MOLLY: Pooh to you, too, Society Editor.

POLLY: A bad write-up in a society column has been known to wreck a brilliant social career.

MOLLY: My social position is unassailable, ducks.

POLLY: A social position is unassailable only when the holder of the position has retired without violence or disorder to a plot of expensive ground beneath a dignified monument in the Protestant cemetery. Not until— [*Indian Joe kicks the door open and appears on the porch. His long straight hair is blond as a palomino's mane and his eyes are sky-blue. As he appears on the porch, he drums his massive bare chest and exclaims—*]

INDIAN JOE: I feel like a bull!

250

POLLY: MOOOO! MOOOOO! [*Molly cuffs her warningly with the back of her hand. Indian Joe returns to the big dormitory, immediately followed by Polly who repeats her lovelorn "Moooo" several times inside as Molly struggles to open the latched screen door. As the scene dims. . . .*]

DIM OUT OR CURTAIN

*Stars have appeared in the sky (and tender is the night, etc.)
when Polly staggers out of the big dormitory in a fantastic state
of disarray and disequilibrium. Her skirt removed, draped over
an arm, exposing polka-dot calico knickers and butterfly garters,
her feathered hat on backwards. Giggling and gasping, she
moves two steps forward, then two steps back, as if she were
on the promenade deck of a ship in heavy seas. Molly regards
her with a coldly objective eye.*

MOLLY: She's lost concentration and equilibrium, both, and
her taste in lingerie is influenced by Ringling Brothers Circus.
It wouldn't hurt to preserve a pictorial memento of the occasion in case she gets a bug in her bonnet about an exposé of the
moral conditions in the big dormitory reflecting corruption in
the administration. [*She snatches up a camera and takes a flash-
photo of Polly.*] A glossy print of that informal photo, dis-
patched in plain cover to the Society Department of the *Cocaloony Gazette*, will insure a better tone to the write-up. [*She
puts the camera under the rocker.*]

POLLY: Molly?

MOLLY: Yes, Polly?

POLLY: Is my hat on crooked?

MOLLY: No, just backwards, ducks, and I do have to admire
the elegant, negligent grace in the way you carry your skirt.

POLLY: The zipper broke. Have y'got a safety pin?

MOLLY [*removing large safety pins from her blouse*]: Naw,
but I have this solid platinum brooch which'll do just as good,
so step back into your sweet little checkerboard skirt and I'll
pin it on you. [*Polly staggers about trying to step into her
skirt.*] Ready, ready, now! Steady! [*Molly jabs Polly with the
pin.*]

252

POLLY: *OWWW!* [*Indian Joe charges out of the big dormitory.*]

INDIAN JOE: *POWWW!*

MOLLY AND POLLY [*together*]: *WOWWW!* [*Indian Joe goes off rapidly whistling "Indian Love Call." They sink together into rockers.*] *Now. . . .*

POLLY: Angels are peeking through the windows of heaven, as the Frowline would put it. I wonder if she made it back from the municipal fish-docks or if she decided to set up residence there, till something better opens up for her, career-wise?

MOLLY [*sympathetically*]: All of us, Polly, sally forth once too often. It's an inexorable law to which the Gnädiges Fräulein seems not to be an exception.

POLLY: Shall we have a silent moment of prayer or just synchronize rockers?

MOLLY: *One, two, three, rock rockers!*

POLLY: *Three, two, one, stop rockers!*

MOLLY: Now what bug have you got in your bonnet?

POLLY: I just thought, to look on the bright side of things, the fact that the Frowline never came back from the fish-docks gives a little more topicality to the write-up, Molly. You must've heard of the newspaper file-case which is known as "the morgue." It's where the historical data, the biographical matter on a mortal celebrity is filed away for sudden reference, Molly. I mean the hot-line between the mortuary and the *Gazette* sounds off, and instantly you leaf through the yellowing, mellowing files and jerk out the copy on the lately no longer so lively.

MOLLY: OK. Now open your notebook and spit on the point of your pen. I'm gonna give you the historical data on the

253

Gnädiges Fräulein. [*She rises from rocker, slings drum over her shoulders and advances onto the forestage.*] I'm going to belt it out with my back to you and the face of me uplifted to the constellation of Hercules toward which the sun drifts with the whole solar system tagging along on that slow, glorious joyride toward extinction. [*She beats the drum.*] —"The Gnädiges Fräulein!" —Past history leading to present, which seems to be now discontinued! [*She beats the drum.*] —Upon a time, once, the Gnädiges Fräulein performed before crowned heads of Europe, being the feminine member of a famous artistic trio! [*She beats drum.*]

POLLY: Other two members of the artistic trio?

MOLLY: Consisted of a trained seal and of the trained seal's trainer. [*Drum.*]

POLLY: This don't sound right, it don't add class to the write-up.

MOLLY: The trained seal trainer was a Viennese dandy. [*Drum.*] Imagine, if you can, a Viennese dandy —can you?

POLLY: Continue!

MOLLY: This was in the golden age of Vienna, the days of the Emperor Franz Josef and the trained seal trainer, the Viennese dandy, was connected collaterally with the House of Hapsburg—a nobleman, a young one, with a waxed blond mustache and on his pinkie a signet ring with the Hapsburg crest engraved on it. Now! [*Drum.*] Imagine, if you can, the Viennese dandy. . . .

POLLY: Figure?

MOLLY: Superb.

POLLY: Uniform?

MOLLY: Glove-silk: immaculate: gold epaulettes, and, oh, oh, oh, many ribbons, all the hues of the rainbow. Eyes? Moisture-proof, but brilliant. Teeth? Perfect. So perfect you'd think they were false, as false as the smile that he threw at his admirers. Now can you imagine the Viennese dandy?

POLLY: Sure I can, I *know* him.

MOLLY: Everybody's known him somewhere and sometime in their lives —if they've *lived!* —in their lives. [*Drum.*] Now hear this! [*Drum.*] Scene: a matinee at the Royal Haymarket in London? Benefit performance? Before crowned heads of Europe?

POLLY: The Gnädiges Fräulein?

MOLLY:The Gnädiges Fräulein! —The splendor, the glory of the occasion, turned her head just a bit. She overextended herself, she wasn't content that day just to do a toe dance to music while bearing the paraphernalia back and forth between the seal and the trainer, the various props, the silver batons and medicine ball that the seal balanced on the tip of his schnozzola. Oh, no, that didn't content her. She had to build up her bit. She suddenly felt a need to compete for attention with the trained seal and the trained seal's trainer.

POLLY: How beautiful was the beautiful Viennese dandy?

MOLLY: I described him.

POLLY: I lost concentration during the description.

MOLLY: Imagine the Viennese dandy like Indian Joe. [*Polly gasps and scribbles frantically for a few mome*nts.] Now then. . . the climax of the performance. [*Drum.*] The seal has just performed his most famous trick, and is balancing two silver batons and two gilded medicine balls on the tip of his whiskery schnozzle while applauding himself with his flippers. [*Drum.*] The audience bursts into applause along with the seal. [*Drum.*] Now, then. The big switcheroo, the surprising gimmick. The trained seal trainer throws the trained seal a fish.

255

What happens? It's intercepted. Who by? The Gnädiges Fräulein. NO HANDS. [*She imitates the seal.*] She catches the fish in her choppers! [*Drum.*] Polly, it brought down the house! [*Drum.*] This switcheroo took the roof off the old Royal Haymarket, and she's got clippings to prove it! I seen them in her scrapbook!

POLLY: Why'd she do it?

MOLLY: Do what?

POLLY: Intercept the fish that was thrown to the seal.

MOLLY: Why does a social leader like me, in my position, have to defend her social supremacy against the parvenu crowd, the climbers and Johnny-Come-Latelies? [*She shouts through the megaphone.*] HANH? HANH?! ANSWER ME THAT!

POLLY: I figured that maybe she had a Polynesian upbringing and dug raw fish.

MOLLY: You're way off, Polly. Y'see here's how it was, Polly. Always before when he threw a fish to the seal, he would throw to the Gnädiges Fräulein an insincere smile, just that, a sort of a *grimace*, exposing white teeth and pink gums, while clicking his heels and bending ever so slightly in an insincere bow.

POLLY: Why?

MOLLY: WHY! —He regarded her as a social inferior, Polly. A Viennese dandy? Elegant? Youthful? Ravishingly attractive? Hapsburg crest on the signet ring on his pinkie? What could he throw to the Gnädiges Fräulein but an insincere smile with a very slight insincere bow that broke her heart every time she received it from him. He couldn't stand her because she adored him, Polly. Well, now. A gimmick like that, a switcheroo, a new twist as they say in show biz, well, it can't be discarded, Polly. If the public buys it, it's got to be kept in the act, regardless of jealous reactions among the rival performers. Well— [*Drum.*] There was, of course, a hell of a hassle between the trained seal's agents and the Gnädiges Fräulein's. There was complaints to Equity and arbitrations and so forth. But it was kept in the act because it was such a sensation. The trained seal's agent threatened to break the contract. But popular demand was overpowering, Polly: the new twist, the switcheroo, had to be kept in the act. The trained seal's agent said: Sit tight! [*Drum.*] Bide your time! [*Drum.*] And it appeared for a time, for a couple of seasons, that the trained seal and the trained seal trainer would accept, acquiesce to *force majeure*, as it were! However—Now hear this! [*Drum.*] At a gala performance before crowned heads in Brussels, no, no, I beg your pardon, before the crowned heads at the Royal in Copenhagen! [*Drum.*] —Tables were turned on the Gnädiges Fräulein! [*Drum.*] — When she made her sudden advance, her kangaroo leap, to intercept the fish that was thrown to the seal, the seal turned on her and fetched her such a terrific CLOUT!! [*Drum.*] —Left flipper, right flipper! [*Drum.*] —To her delicate jawbone that her pearly whites flew from her mouth like popcorn out of a popper. [*Drum.*] Honest to Gosh, sprayed out of her choppers like foam from a wild wave, breaking! [*Drum.*] — They rang down the curtain. —The act was quickly disbanded. . . . After that? She drifted. The Gnädiges Fräulein just drifted *and* drifted and *drifted*. . . . —She lost her sense of reality and she drifted. . . . —Eventually she showed on the Southernmost Key. Hustled B-drinks for a while at the old Square Roof. Celebrated Admiral Dewey's great naval victory in the Spanish-American War, by mounting a flag-pole on the courthouse lawn in the costume of Lady Godiva but with a GI haircut. All this while she was running up a big tab at the big dormitory. However!— [*Drum.*] —In business matters, sentiment isn't the cornerstone of my nature. I wasn't about to carry her on the cuff when her cash gave out. Having read her press clippings, I said, OK! Hit the fish-docks, baby! Three fish a day keeps

257

eviction away. One fish more keeps the wolf from your door! —All in excess of four fish do as you please with! —POLLY! TELESCOPE, PLEASE! [*She has turned her attention to a sudden increase of disturbance down at the fish-docks. Polly tosses a telescope to her as she crosses to the gate.*]

POLLY: —Any sign of her, Molly?

MOLLY: Yep, she's on her way back.

POLLY: Alone?

MOLLY: No. With a cocaloony escort.

POLLY: Is she making much progress?

MOLLY: Slow but sure. I admire her.

POLLY [*sentimentally*]: I admire her, too.

MOLLY: I hope you'll give her a sympathetic write-up.

POLLY: I'm gonna pay tribute to her fighting spirit.

MOLLY: Don't forget to mention the big dormitory.

POLLY: I'll call it The Spirit of The Big Dormitory.

MOLLY: *Hold the door open for me. I'm going in fast!* [*She starts back to the porch, but Polly enters the house before her and slams and latches the door. Molly crouches way over, peeking between her fingers, as the Gnädiges Fräulein appears on the sidewalk in terrible disarray but clinging tenaciously to her tin bucket containing a rather large fish. Great flapping noise of cocaloonies in pursuit. She crashes through the picket fence and scampers around the side of the house, disappears. Polly comes back out as the hubbub subsides again.*]

POLLY: Something came in the back way.

MOLLY: Yep. I think she made it.

POLLY: I don't hear a sound, do you?

MOLLY: I hear some kind of activity in the kitchen.

POLLY: Cocaloony or human?

MOLLY: I'm not positive, Polly, but I think the cocaloonies have gone back to the fish-docks.

POLLY: Wouldn't that be lovely.

MOLLY: I heard a boat-whistle blow: then swoosh! Flap, flap, then swoosh! —Then silence, and a light turned on in the kitchen.

POLLY: What's this? [*She has picked up some bright orange fuzz.*]

MOLLY: Oh, my God, they scalped her!

POLLY: This is human hair, Molly?

MOLLY: It's hair from the head of the Gnädiges Fräulein.

POLLY: She must be a blond Hottentot.

MOLLY: Results from staying too long and too often under electric dryers in second-rate beauty parlors. OH! GOD BLESS HER SOUL! —I hear the sizzle of deep fat in the kitchen!

POLLY: She must be frying a fish.

MOLLY: Yais, I would make book on it.

POLLY: Is this fish number four? For her personal consumption?

MOLLY: Fish number one. She ain't even paid for kitchen privileges yet.

POLLY: You gonna carry her on the cuff?

MOLLY: I don't have a cuff. She's got to pick up where she left off in show biz.

POLLY: Or else?

MOLLY: Go on drifting, drifting, away from the big dormitory, away from everywhere maybe.

POLLY: Losing a sense of reality as she drifts?

MOLLY: Losing or finding, all according to how you interpret it, Polly. [*The Fräulein appears at the screen door.*]

FRAULEIN: May I come out? [*The ladies are awed by her present appearance. All of her costume has now been torn away: she appears in flesh-colored tights, streaked and dabbled with blood. Patches of her fuzzy light orange hair have been torn away. She carries, before her, a skillet containing a fish with a big kitchen fork sticking in it. She repeats her request for permission to come outside. After a slight pause she says, "Thank you" and comes out on the porch. Polly seizes the handle of the fork and removes the fish from the skillet: the Gnädiges Fräulein is unaware of this action. She calls out:*] TOIVO! TOIVO!

MOLLY: She's calling him to supper.

POLLY: Who?

MOLLY: Indian Joe.

POLLY: Why does she call him Toivo?

MOLLY: Toivo was the name of the Viennese dandy.

POLLY: That threw her the fish before the crowned heads of Europe?

MOLLY: He threw the fish to the seal. To the Gnädiges Fräulein he threw an insincere smile. She bored him because she adored him!

FRAULEIN [*advancing to the porch steps and continuing to call during the following speeches*]: TOIVO, TOIVO!

260

POLLY: But she intercepted the fish to the surprise of the seal and the Viennese dandy, you told me.

MOLLY: Yes. I think she imagined, fondly, that it would alter the smile, that it would give a touch of sincerity to it, but emotional limitations cannot be coped with, Polly. You got to accept them or give up the ghost in this world. However, under the flattering shadow of memory, smiles are sometimes transfigured. Possibly now she remembers the smile as sincere. WELL! I see that *you* have intercepted a fish! [*Polly is touching the fish to see if it's cooled off. It keeps scorching her fingers. She whistles sharply and sticks her fingers in her mouth and then shakes them in the cool twilight air.*]

POLLY: Am I invited to supper? [*Molly snatches the fish-fork.*]

MOLLY: I'll mail you the invitation in the morning. [*Polly picks up wine bottle from the Pan Am bag.*]

POLLY: Evening, duckie. [*She starts off.*] Ta ta! Toodle-ooo!

MOLLY: A chilled white wine is *de rigeur* with a fish course. —Chow time, Polly.

POLLY: Oh, I've already gotten the invitation! Hold the door open for me, my hands are full! [*Molly opens the screen door. The Society Editor enters grandly.*]

FRAULEIN: Toivo, Toivo! —Toivo? Toivo? [*She twists her head about nervously as if looking for him in various directions, including the sky, as Indian Joe ambles up to the gate. She draws a long, loud breath, inhaling the aroma of his close presence. He looks in the skillet: as he removes it from her grasp she makes a sort of obeisance, at the same time lifting a hand in a warning gesture.*] Is it all right? I can't imagine how I happened to catch it, it was so dark at the fish-docks. It just landed in my jaws like God had thrown it to me. It's better to receive than

261

to give if you are receiving to give: isn't it, Toivo, *mein liebchen?*

INDIAN JOE [*shouting*]: NO FISH IN SKILLET!

FRAULEIN [*with a warning gesture*]: Watch out for the bones in it, darling! [*Indian Joe repeats his shout, louder. The Gnädiges Fräulein interprets this shout as a request for a vocal selection: she bursts into song—"Whispering Hope"—and Indian Joe enters the house. The formal parlor is lighted as he joins Molly and Polly at a small, festive table. A fish-boat whistle is heard. The Gnädiges Fräulein stops singing, abruptly, and cups a hand to an ear. The boat whistles again. She assumes the starting position of a competitive runner and waits for the third whistle. It's delayed a bit for the interior pantomime. Indian Joe pushes one lady to the left and one to the right and seats himself at the table picking up the fish. Polly holds out the wine bottle to him. The parlor dims out as the third whistle sounds—the Gnädiges Fräulein starts a wild, blind dash for the fish-docks.*]

THE STAGE IS DIMMED OUT

A PERFECT ANALYSIS GIVEN BY A PARROT

CHARACTERS

BESSIE

FLORA

WAITER

TWO SONS OF MARS

A PERFECT ANALYSIS
GIVEN BY A PARROT

The Set: The interior of a St. Louis tavern, which may be represented by a backdrop painted in the style of the colored comics. There should be two doorframes, one exterior and the other to the ladies' room. The other essential properties are a small round table and a juke box. The light is focused on the table. Into this lighted area enter two girls in the late afternoon of their youth, which is close to forty. They are Flora and Bessie. Flora is thin to the point of emaciation and Bessie is correspondingly stout. They are dressed much alike. Both have on big cartwheel hats and black dresses and long black gloves, but the cartwheel hats are in vividly contrasting colors, Bessie's being magenta and Flora's chartreuse. When and if they want to look at each other, it is necessary to tilt their heads far back. They are both loaded with ornaments, brass hoops and bangles, so that every movement is accompanied by a small percussion. A grotesque and garish effect should prevail in everything.

BESSIE [as they enter]: Wild horses couldn't hold you in that cab!

FLORA: Two more blocks and we couldn't of paid the fare!

BESSIE: "Driver, driver, stop here, this place looks lively!"

FLORA: It did, outside!

BESSIE: Yes, it looked like a tacky funeral parlor! A snare and a delusion if I've ever seen one!

FLORA: Am I responsible?

BESSIE: Yes!

FLORA: We passed five places I would of been willing to stop at, including Dante's Inferno! But you kept telling the driver, "Go on, go on," like it was a chariot race in a Roman forum!

BESSIE: He sure in hell took us out of the lively district!

FLORA: At your insistence, honey—a child shall lead them! But now that we're here we might as well make the best of it.

BESSIE: And how are we going to go about doing that?

FLORA: By setting down here and getting organized, honey. The waiter is cute.

BESSIE: I ask one favor of you, and only one!

FLORA: What is that, Bessie?

BESSIE: Don't get us involved with th' waiter.

FLORA [*sweetly and clearly*]: Waiter?

BESSIE: I think we'd better take account of finances before he comes. How much've you got left?

FLORA: Six bits and a bunch of these little round paper things.

BESSIE: Mills!

FLORA: How much're they worth?

BESSIE: One tenth of one cent!

FLORA: Heigh-ho! [*She tosses them into the air.*]

BESSIE [*bitterly*]: Somebody seems to be in awfully good spirits! [*Flora has rushed to the juke box and started it playing "Funiculi Funicula." The Waiter comes to the table, a plump little Italian in a green apron.*] Waiter, this place is just a tissue of lies!

WAITER: Why do you call it that, lady?

BESSIE: Outside is a sign that says: "Dancing and Floor Show Every Saturday Night!" But where is the dancing and where is any floor show?

WAITER: The band is quit, ladies.

BESSIE: Oh, I see! How ducky! That solves all our problems!

FLORA: When does the joint liven up?

WAITER: Ladies, at one o'clock the joint is jumping!

BESSIE: Five of nine, and the joint is paralyzed.

FLORA: We're members of the Women's Auxiliary of the Jackson Haggerty Post of the Sons of Mars in Memphis!

BESSIE: Come up here for the National Convention!

FLORA: However, we've got separated from Charlie and Ralph, the boys who came up in our party!

BESSIE: So now we're just out "on the town"!

FLORA: But haven't located a single boy that we know!

BESSIE: Never have seen a convention in such confusion!

FLORA: Nobody knows where anybody's located!

BESSIE: We've wo'n ou'selves out jus' tryin' t' get hold of people!

FLORA: The earth has swallowed up ev'ry boy that we came with!

BESSIE: We always go to the annual convention, but this one has been a terrible—

FLORA: Disappointment! But two girls by themselves can have a good deal of fun as long as they know how to be good sports about it.

BESSIE: As long as they can agree on major isues. We'll have two beers.

WAITER: Nickel glasses or twenty-six ounces for a dime? [*Flora throws up her hands and Bessie clasps her bosom.*]

BESSIE: Bring us two fish bowls!

FLORA: Of liquid amber, please! [*The Waiter withdraws.*]

FLORA [*looking after him*]: Kind of cute, huh?

BESSIE: Honey, no man that broad in the beam is cute.

FLORA: Chacun à son gout. [*She calls.*] Waiter, don't any Sons of Mars come here?

WAITER [*returning with fish bowls*]: Two of 'em come in just before you ladies.

BESSIE: Honest t'God?

WAITER: One of the two was drippin' wet with water!

FLORA: What!

BESSIE: How come?

WAITER: He said they had dropped paper sacks full of water out of the hotel windows and one of these paper sacks had landed on his head and busted open and spilt all the water on him. [*Bessie and Flora scream with amusement but the Waiter continues to look horrified at the incident.*]

FLORA: Aren't they cards?

BESSIE: Don't they think of the craziest things to do?

FLORA: That's what I like about them!

BESSIE: That's what I love!

FLORA [*chuckling appreciatively*]: You know what they are? Just great—big—overgrown—Boys!

BESSIE: My girl friend and I have took in ev'ry convention since—

FLORA: Time immemorial—yes! I wonder which hotel they dropped the paper sacks out of?

BESSIE: I bet you it was the Statler.

FLORA: Why the Statler?

BESSIE: The Statler's always so lively!

FLORA: It might just as well have been the Coronado, or the Jefferson.

BESSIE: Not the Jefferson.

FLORA: Why not the Jefferson?

BESSIE: The Jefferson's such a dignified hotel.

FLORA: There is no such thing!

BESSIE: Well, there is only one hotel in America that I am right down sentimental about.

FLORA: Which one is that?

BESSIE: The Sherman Hotel in Chicago! [*She rolls her eyes and shakes her bangles.*] Shades of the 1926 Convention! Best of 'em all without a single exception!

FLORA: It all depends on the crowd you get thrown with!

BESSIE: Sociability's all that really counts! Although the Sons are a serious organization. In many respects.

FLORA: The country would be in a terrible fix without them.

BESSIE: You're not whistling Dixie! But I tell you, the boys are terrible cutups!

WAITER: You heard what they done on Washington Avenue?

FLORA: No!

BESSIE: What?

WAITER: They stripped the clothes off a girl an' sent her home in a Yellow Taxicab! [*He moves, comically, out of the spotlight. The girls throw their heads way back and split their sides.*]

FLORA [*finally catching her breath*]: I double-dog-dare ennybody to try that on me! [*She sweeps the deserted cafe with a challenging glance.*]

BESSIE: A Son of Mars wouldn't blow his nose on this place.

FLORA: Well, you was all for stoppin' at th' Statler.

BESSIE: And what's wrong with the Statler?

FLORA: When did we ever have any luck at the Statler?

BESSIE: Twice.

FLORA: In whose recollection?

BESSIE: Mine! You wasn't along.

FLORA: Nope, I guess I wasn't.

BESSIE: But you've heard me speak of that restaurant man from Chicago?

FLORA: Heard you speak of him? Continually—yes. . . .

BESSIE: The Statler was where I made that man's acquaintance.

FLORA: And well do I remember how that turned out.

BESSIE: I don't regret it; I have no regret whatsoever.

FLORA: Bessie, you've got no pride where men are concerned.

BESSIE [*slowly and sententiously*]: No, I've got no pride where men are concerned, and you haven't got any pride where men are concerned and nobody's got any pride where men are

270

concerned. That's how it is, so let's face it! I'm not coldhearted and when I get out with a boy I am just as anxious as he is to have a good time.

FLORA: More.

BESSIE: Yes, that's right, often more. That is to say, I always go halfway with him.

FLORA: More than halfway, honey.

BESSIE: Yes, I sometimes even go more than halfway and I see no reason why I should be criticized for it.

FLORA: Nobody's spoken a word of criticism.

BESSIE: I do my part to create some happiness in the world, even if it's just for one night only. It isn't a crime to give a good time and a pleasant memory, even to a stranger.

FLORA: Whoever said that it was?

BESSIE: Some people seem to take that attitude.

FLORA: I certainly never.

BESSIE: You talked about pride as if I didn't have any. [*She leans way back with considerable effort in order to stare at Flora from under the brim of the cartwheel.*]

FLORA [*quickly*]: I said false pride, not pride. There's a difference, Bessie.

BESSIE: That's exactly what I was pointing out.

FLORA: All I mean is a girl mustn't compromise with her self-respect.

BESSIE: She don't need to—and I don't see why she should.

FLORA: That's exactly the point I was making.

BESSIE: Except you sometimes go to the other extreme.

271

FLORA: I do?

BESSIE: Uh-huh.

FLORA: Extreme of what, may I ask?

BESSIE: Self—respect.

FLORA: You mean I'm not a good sport?

BESSIE: That is just the opposite of my meaning.

FLORA: Your meaning is private as far as I am concerned.

BESSIE: The trouble with you is your mind wanders off a subject but you go right on chopping your gums together as if you weighed every single word that was spoken. [*She is powdering furiously.*] That's what makes it so difficult to talk with you!

FLORA: Oh—foot! [*She looks slowly and wearily away from her girlfriend, but Bessie's look remains on Flora. Flora's head begins to droop like a heavy flower on a thin stem.*]

BESSIE [*suspiciously*]: A penny for your thoughts, Miss Merriweather.

FLORA: I had my character read this afternoon.

BESSIE: Who by? A gypsy?

FLORA: No, it was read by a parrot.

BESSIE: Are you kidding?

FLORA: No. I gave a man a dime and he opened the parrot's cage and the parrot hopped out and stuck his head in a box and picked up a piece of paper in his beak. I took the piece of paper, and guess what it said?

BESSIE: How would I guess what it said on that piece of paper?

FLORA: I'll tell you, Bessie. "You have a sensitive nature, and are frequently misunderstood by your close companions!"

BESSIE: Huh!

FLORA: Imagine it, Bessie. A perfect analysis given by a parrot!

BESSIE: I don't have very much faith in that sort of thing. [*Flora tilts her head way back to give her girlfriend a long and critical look.*]

BESSIE: [*nervously*]: Well?

FLORA: Wipe your chin off, Bessie. You've got foam on it.

BESSIE: Thank you, Miss Merriweather. [*There is a pause.*] May I ask you a question?

FLORA [*suspiciously*]: What, Miss Higginbotham?

BESSIE: Are you still keeping up those Youthful Beauty treatments?

FLORA: I had a Youthful Beauty treatment this afternoon.

BESSIE: How are you satisfied with what they're doing?

FLORA: I have noticed one-hundred-percent improvement in my skin since I started taking those Youthful Beauty treatments, Bessie.

BESSIE: I'm glad you've noticed it, honey.

FLORA: Why, haven't you?

BESSIE [*lighting a cigarette*]: Flora, your main beauty problem is not blackheads. It's large pores, honey.

FLORA [*with fierce conviction*]: I haven't a single blackhead left in my face, just a few little whiteheads, and this little do-hickey here which is just a spot where I squeezed out one with a hairpin!

273

BESSIE: Well, Flora, your problem is skin and you might as well face it.

FLORA: Everyone's problem is skin, including yours, Bessie. But of course your primary problem is keeping down weight.

BESSIE: I am a type that can carry a good deal of weight because I have large bone structure. However, it's always been well-distributed on me.

FLORA: As long as you won't face facts, it's no use talking. Complacency's one thing and—optimism's another!

BESSIE: What does a man look at with greater int'rest, a straight-back chair or a rocker?

FLORA: Depends on the man an' the relative size of the rocker. [*Bessie tilts her head way back to study Flora's face, but gravity brings it back down with a jolting motion.*]

FLORA [*continuing sweetly*]: You know what would do you an awful lot of good, Bessie?

BESSIE: No. What?

FLORA: Bending exercise!

BESSIE: I thought you was going to say "Yogi"—but who wants to bend?

FLORA: Everyone does who wants to keep youthful contours! You've got to resign yourself to making some effort, unless you prefer to let things take their course. [*There is a reflective pause. Then she continues slowly, gravely.*] Nature is not on the side of a girl over thirty.

BESSIE: For once in your life you are not just whistling Dixie! [*There is another brief meditation.*]

FLORA [*brightly*]: Honey, why don't you and I play golf on Sundays?

274

BESSIE: Have you struck oil on your property?

FLORA: What's that got t' do with it?

BESSIE: Expense! It's a millionaire's sport!

FLORA: It's not so expensive except you pay caddies and all.

BESSIE: And all is correct. Buying the balls and losing them and buying more. You can't take up golf without an initial outlay of something like thirty-five dollars. And that's the beginning—only!

FLORA [*plaintively*]: You don't have to lose balls, do you?

BESSIE [*vaguely*]: Maybe you don't have to, but you do.

FLORA: Well, outdoor sports are a wonderful basis for friendship.

BESSIE [*gravely*]: You mean with men?

FLORA: *Uh*-huh.

BESSIE: Eunice McPheeters, to mention a case in point, has been playing golf for going on fifteen years. Has she ever made such brilliant contacts with men?

FLORA: Probably has; don't see enny reason t' doubt it! Consider the number and types of men that play golf!

BESSIE: Consider—Eunice! Her face is frozen in a perpetual sneer. A girl like her could be marooned on an island and, though outnumbered fifty to one by males, escape without even so much as a mild flirtation!

FLORA: You don't appreciate Eunice. Eunice has got common sense and it shows in her face.

BESSIE: Is that what shows in her face?

FLORA: Any girl's been through what Eunice McPheeter's been through with her home situation and all can't be expected to look upon life as one continual joy ride.

275

BESSIE: But why talk of golf as the be-all and end-all of living?

FLORA: Who did, and who ever does?

BESSIE [*vaguely*]: Eunice and you—although she does and you don't.

FLORA: I'm just attempting to think of something to help you.

BESSIE: Accept my thanks, my heartfelt appreciation—but please don't strain your thinking apparatus!

FLORA: Sarcasm, Bessie?

BESSIE: No, honey, but I came out for the purpose of seeking diversion. That's my whole purpose in leaving my hotel bedroom. If you're in accord with that purpose—good! If otherwise—good-bye! Separation is simple. You go to the Statler and I to the Coronado, or whichever way you prefer it, but don't try to pull me into a state of depression! I've had rotten luck with men. Not once but always! You've had your share of disappointments also. So far, so good. But when you start harping on Yogi—on Eunice's home situation—girlie, good-bye! We have come to the sad, sweet parting! I mean of the ways. . . . [*She takes a long drink of beer, gags and spews it up. Both girls scramble back from the table in time to avoid a deluge. The incident is immediately forgotten.*]

FLORA [*dreamily*]: Bessie—

BESSIE: Huh?

FLORA: After Howard, you know you let yourself go.

BESSIE: Just like you after Vernon. I went through an awful period for a while. . . .

FLORA: You took a negative attitude toward things. Acted as if all hope had gone out of life. But instead of wasting away, you put on flesh. Honestly, Bessie, you blew up like a balloon!

276

BESSIE: I used to wear a sixteen.

FLORA: Bessie, that must've been long before I knew you.

BESSIE: In 1930.

FLORA: That recently, honey?

BESSIE: I had no figure problem until the winter of 1932. But you were always bedeviled by your complexion. Isn't that so?

FLORA: Only because I have such a fine-grained skin.

BESSIE [*doubtfully*]: Possibly, but also—

FLORA: What?

BESSIE: You never have hit on a really becoming hairdo!

FLORA: What's wrong with the one I got last week at Antoinette's?

BESSIE: Honey, the upswept style is not for your face. Every type of face requires a different style of hairdo, just in the way diff'rent figures can't put on the same type of clothes. Now what you call for is horizontal lines because of the distance between your chin and your forehead.

FLORA [*slowly*]: I haven't forgotten the time you called me "Horse-Face."

BESSIE: All I meant is you have the long type of face the same as I have the broad one. Now what you need is bushing out at the temples, the aureole type.

FLORA: Oriole? like a bird?

BESSIE: No, honey. The spelling is diff'rent. But never mind that. What I mean is Antoinette's is not a good friend of yours —not from the grotesque things which they do to your face! [*There is a pause. Flora stares at her friend and her lips begin to tremble. Slowly her face droops downward on the delicate stem of her throat and the cartwheel hides her tears.*]

BESSIE [*gently and sorrowfully*]: You harp on Yogi and Eunice McPheeter's golf, and claim that your sensitive nature is misunderstood by everyone but a parrot! But let me give you some well-intended advice—and tears, tears, tears! A regular fountain of them! [*She opens her purse and produces assorted cosmetics.*] Repair the ravages and we'll go to the Statler. [*Bessie has picked up a lipstick and Flora a sheet of Kleenex, when all at once the front door of the tavern erupts on a pair of male figures in the blue-and-white summer parade uniforms of the Sons of Mars. One crouches by the door and the other leaps over his back, which action is repeated until they arrive at the girls' table where they abruptly halt, blow shrill blasts on toy bugles and extend their elbow. Electrified with joy, the girls have sprung to their feet. Bessie seizes one's arm, Flora the other's, and they strut gaily around the table, singing "Mademoiselle from Armentieres."*]

CURTAIN

New Directions Paperbooks—A Partial Listing

For complete listing request free catalog from
New Directions, 80 Eighth Avenue, New York 10011

†Bilingual

Frédéric Mistral, *The Memoirs*. NDP632.
Eugenio Montale, *It Depends*.† NDP507.
  Selected Poems.† NDP193.
Paul Morand, *Fancy Goods / Open All Night*.
  NDP567.
Vladimir Nabokov, *Nikolai Gogol*. NDP78.
  Laughter in the Dark. NDP729.
  The Real Life of Sebastian Knight. NDP432.
P. Neruda, *The Captain's Verses*.† NDP345.
  Residence on Earth.† NDP340.
New Directions in Prose & Poetry (Anthology).
  Available from #17 forward to #55.
Robert Nichols, *Arrival*. NDP437.
  Exile. NDP485.
J. F. Nims, *The Six-Cornered Snowflake*. NDP700.
Charles Olson, *Selected Writings*. NDP231.
Toby Olson, *The Life of Jesus*. NDP417.
  Seaview. NDP532.
George Oppen, *Collected Poems*. NDP418.
István Örkeny, *The Flower Show /
  The Toth Family*. NDP536.
Wilfred Owen, *Collected Poems*. NDP210.
José Emilio Pacheco, *Battles in the Desert*. NDP637.
  Selected Poems.† NDP638.
Nicanor Parra, *Antipoems: New & Selected*. NDP603.
Boris Pasternak, *Safe Conduct*. NDP77.
Kenneth Patchen, *Aflame and Afun*. NDP292.
  Because It Is. NDP83.
  Collected Poems. NDP284.
  Hallelujah Anyway. NDP219.
  Selected Poems. NDP160.
Ota Pavel, *How I Came to Know Fish*. NDP713.
Octavio Paz, *Collected Poems*. NDP719.
  Configurations.† NDP303.
  A Draft of Shadows.† NDP489.
  Selected Poems. NDP574.
  Sunstone.† NDP735.
  A Tree Within.† NDP661.
St. John Perse, *Selected Poems*.† NDP545.
J. A. Porter, *Eelgrass*. NDP438.
Ezra Pound, *ABC of Reading*. NDP89.
  Confucius. NDP285.
  Confucius to Cummings. (Anth.) NDP126.
  A Draft of XXX Cantos. NDP690.
  Elektra. NDP683.
  Guide to Kulchur. NDP257.
  Literary Essays. NDP250.
  Personae. NDP697.
  Selected Cantos. NDP304.
  Selected Poems. NDP66.
  The Spirit of Romance. NDP266.
  Translations.† (Enlarged Edition) NDP145.
Raymond Queneau, *The Blue Flowers*. NDP595.
  Exercises in Style. NDP513.
Mary de Rachewiltz, *Ezra Pound*. NDP405.
Raja Rao, *Kanthapura*. NDP224.
Herbert Read, *The Green Child*. NDP208.
P. Reverdy, *Selected Poems*.† NDP346.
Kenneth Rexroth, *An Autobiographical Novel*. NDP725.
  Classics Revisited. NDP621.
  More Classics Revisited. NDP668.
  Flower Wreath Hill. NDP724.
  100 Poems from the Chinese. NDP192.
  100 Poems from the Japanese.† NDP147.
  Selected Poems. NDP581.
  Women Poets of China. NDP528.
  Women Poets of Japan. NDP527.
Rainer Maria Rilke, *Poems from
  The Book of Hours*. NDP408.
  Possibility of Being. (Poems). NDP436.
  Where Silence Reigns. (Prose). NDP464.
Arthur Rimbaud, *Illuminations*.† NDP56.
  Season in Hell & Drunken Boat.† NDP97.
Edouard Roditi, *Delights of Turkey*. NDP445.
Jerome Rothenberg, *Khurbn*. NDP679.
  New Selected Poems. NDP625.
Nayantara Sahgal, *Rich Like Us*. NDP665.
Saigyo, *Mirror for the Moon*.† NDP465.

Ihara Saikaku, *The Life of an Amorous
  Woman*. NDP270.
St. John of the Cross, *Poems*.† NDP341.
W. Saroyan, *Madness in the Family*. NDP691.
Jean-Paul Sartre, *Nausea*. NDP82.
  The Wall (Intimacy). NDP272.
P. D. Scott, *Coming to Jakarta*. NDP672.
Delmore Schwartz, *Selected Poems*. NDP241.
  Last & Lost Poems. NDP673.
  In Dreams Begin Responsibilities. NDP454.
Shattan, *Manimekhalaï*. NDP674.
K. Shiraishi. *Seasons of Sacred Lust*. NDP453.
Stevie Smith, *Collected Poems*. NDP562.
  New Selected Poems. NDP659.
Gary Snyder, *The Back Country*. NDP249.
  The Real Work. NDP499.
  Regarding Wave. NDP306.
  Turtle Island. NDP381.
Enid Starkie, *Rimbaud*. NDP254.
Stendhal. *Three Italian Chronicles*. NDP704.
Antonio Tabucchi, *Indian Nocturne*. NDP666.
Nathaniel Tarn, *Lyrics . . . Bride of God*. NDP391.
Dylan Thomas, *Adventures in the Skin Trade*.
  NDP183.
  A Child's Christmas in Wales. NDP181.
  Collected Poems 1934-1952. NDP316.
  Collected Stories. NDP626.
  Portrait of the Artist as a Young Dog. NDP51.
  Quite Early One Morning. NDP90.
  Under Milk Wood. NDP73.
Tian Wen: *A Chinese Book of Origins*. NDP624.
Uwe Timm, *The Snake Tree*. NDP686.
Lionel Trilling, *E. M. Forster*. NDP189.
Tu Fu, *Selected Poems*. NDP675.
N. Tucci, *The Rain Came Last*. NDP688.
Martin Turnell, *Baudelaire*. NDP336.
Paul Valéry, *Selected Writings*.† NDP184.
Elio Vittorini, *A Vittorini Omnibus*. NDP366.
Rosmarie Waldrop, *The Reproduction of Profiles*.
  NDP649.
Robert Penn Warren, *At Heaven's Gate*. NDP588.
Vernon Watkins, *Selected Poems*. NDP221.
Eliot Weinberger, *Works on Paper*. NDP627.
Nathanael West, *Miss Lonelyhearts &
  Day of the Locust*. NDP125.
J. Wheelwright, *Collected Poems*. NDP544.
Tennessee Williams, *Baby Doll*. NDP714.
  Camino Real. NDP301.
  Cat on a Hot Tin Roof. NDP398.
  Clothes for a Summer Hotel. NDP556.
  The Glass Menagerie. NDP218.
  Hard Candy. NDP225.
  In the Winter of Cities. NDP154.
  A Lovely Sunday for Creve Coeur. NDP497.
  One Arm & Other Stories. NDP237.
  Red Devil Battery Sign. NDP650.
  A Streetcar Named Desire. NDP501.
  Sweet Bird of Youth. NDP409.
  Twenty-Seven Wagons Full of Cotton. NDP217.
  Vieux Carre. NDP482.
William Carlos Williams,
  The Autobiography. NDP223.
  The Buildup. NDP259.
  Collected Poems: Vol. I. NDP730.
  Collected Poems: Vol. II. NDP731
  The Doctor Stories. NDP585.
  Imaginations. NDP329.
  In the American Grain. NDP53.
  In the Money. NDP240.
  Paterson. Complete. NDP152.
  Pictures from Brueghel. NDP118.
  Selected Poems (new ed.). NDP602.
  White Mule. NDP226.
Wisdom Books: *Early Buddhists*. NDP444;
  Spanish Mystics. NDP442; *St. Francis*. NDP477;
  Taoists. NDP509; *Wisdom of the Desert*. NDP295;
  Zen Masters. NDP415.

For complete listing request free catalog from
New Directions, 80 Eighth Avenue, New York 10011

†Bilingual